THE KINGDOM OF MYCENAE

To my parents and my brother

The Kingdom of Mycenae

A Great Kingdom
in the Late Bronze Age Aegean

by
Jorrit M. Kelder

CDL Press
Bethesda, Maryland
2010

LIBRARY OF CONGRESS CATALOGING-IN-PUBLICATION DATA

Kelder, Jorrit M.

The kingdom of Mycenae : a great kingdom in the late Bronze Age Aegean / by Jorrit M. Kelder.

p. cm.

Includes bibliographical references and index.

ISBN 978-1-934309-27-8

1. Mycenae (Extinct city) 2. Aegean Sea Region—Antiquities. 3. Bronze age—Aegean Sea Region. 4. Historic sites—Aegean Sea Region. 5. Excavations (Archaeology)—Aegean Sea Region. 6. Aegean Sea Region —History, Local. 7. Aegean Sea Region—History. I. Title.

DF221.M9K45 2010

938'.01--dc22 2010000179

ISBN 978-1934309-278

— CONTENTS —

— LIST OF MAPS —

— ACKNOWLEDGMENTS —

This author owes a great debt to several persons and institutions. Financial support for research in Egypt and Greece was provided by the Netherlands Organisation for Scientific Research and the Alexander S. Onassis Foundation.

This work could not have been written without the continual encouragement of Bert van der Spek and Frans Wiggermann, my teachers at the Vrije Universiteit, Amsterdam. And I would like to thank Calie Sharman, Matthew Haysom, and Frans Wiggermann for their proofreading of the original manuscript of this work.

Much of this study was written in Athens, in the library of the Netherlands Institute at Athens, and in the library of the British School at Athens. I am indebted to the librarians and staff of those institutions, particularly to Mrs. Janta van Lienden (NIA) and Amalia Kakissis (BSA).

Many friends and colleagues have encouraged me and improved this work with their frank comments. I am indebted to Diederik Burgersdijk, Jan Paul Crielaard, Floris van den Eijnde, Petra Goedegebuure, Willem van Haarlem, Matthew Haysom, Myrte Jansen, Jacke Phillips, Willemijn Waal, Fred Woudhuizen, and Gert Jan van Wijngaarden.

Amsterdam 2010

— PROLOGUE —

The study at hand presents a new evaluation of the data and our understanding of the political landscape in Greece during the Late Bronze Age, especially during the fourteenth and thirteenth centuries BC. Over the last several years there has been a flood of new publications on this topic, in popular magazines, monographs, and scholarly publications. It seemed time to bring together the various different views and to evaluate them. During this effort, I increasingly came to see the Mycenaean world as a unified state, a concept that, as a result of my research, has become the main argument of this work. My thesis is the existence of a large territorial entity covering most of the Greek mainland, the isles in the Aegean, and the center on the Anatolian west coast that was later known as Miletus. This entity was known as Ahhiyawa to the Hittites and as Tanaju to the Egyptians, and Mycenae, its capital, was its focus of economic, political, and ritual life.

In the pages below, I will deal with contemporary scholarship, but before that I should perhaps provide an overview of earlier scholarship. As seems to be customary in this field, I begin with the very man that is generally considered to have been the "father" of the study of Aegean prehistory, Heinrich Schliemann.

Schliemann's excavations at Hissarlık brought him fame with the general public and, certainly at the end of his life, recognition by most of his fellow colleagues in the field of archaeology and philology. Notwithstanding the many objections to the man, his methods and his interpretations, Schliemann brought to life a society that was far older than the known Classical Greek world.

Before Schliemann, the Mycenaean world could be studied only by reading the Classical texts (mainly Homer), which had, essentially since antiquity, been considered to be a more or less accurate reflection of the Greek world in the Late Bronze Age. It was not until the late eighteenth century that it was felt necessary to check the reality of the Homeric epic and question whether *The Iliad* was largely, or even wholly, fictional. From these questions sprang two "groups" of scholarship, which Joachim Latacz calls the "Positivisten" (those who believed that at least the essence, *Grundtatbestände*, of the Homeric stories reflected Bronze Age reality) and the "Fiktionalisten" (those who believed that even the essence of the stories was fictional). I use the word "believed" deliberately, as both opinions at that time were based on nothing but conviction. It is worthwhile to quote here a protagonist from each conviction: first, the fictionalist Rückert, who argued that the Homeric tales were composed as a justification for the seizure of the Troad by Aeolic settlers in the eighth century BC:

> Die Sage, die sich später an den ungeheuren kyklopischen Trümmern Ilions und den hohen Grabhügeln am Gestade des Hellesponts emporrankte, schiebt ihn [the Aeolic seizure of the Troad] weit in die mythische Zeit zurück und lässt die Mythischen Ahnherren der Achäer, die Aeakiden und Pelopiden, ihren Nachkommen die Ansprüche auf jenes schöne Land erkämpfen...

Second, the positivist Welcker, who argued that a story as grand as *The Iliad* could not possibly have been the product of imagination or the need to justify the seizure of new lands:

> Die Sänger der Aeolischen Kolonisten mussten Taten von diesen, etwa die Eroberung einer Stadt, im Zusammenhang der Zeitverhältnisse sowohl in Griechenland als in Troas, darstellen und konnten dabei [durchaus] eine frühere Besitznahme durch Achilleus und unter Agamemnon erdichten, um durch diesen Vorgang das Recht der Enkel noch mehr hervorzugeben, der erworbenen Heimat ein höheres Alter zu geben. Aber etwas Gedichtetes und Früheres von solchem Umfang und Zusammenhang an die Stelle von etwas Wirklichem und Späterem das doch selbst gross und denkwürdig war, zu setzen, alle Helden und deren Taten und Geschicke gänzlich fallen zu lassen und völlig verschiedene zu erfinden, [das] konnte Niemanden einfallen...

The excavations of Schliemann changed this discussion. Schliemann's uncovering of a powerful Bronze Age settlement at the site of what, at least in later Classical times, was known as Ilion (even if his initial identification of the second stratigraphic layer at that site as the "Homeric Troy" was utterly wrong), as well as his discoveries at Mycenae, Tiryns, and Orchomenos, showed that the world described in the Homeric epics was remarkably reminiscent of Bronze Age reality. Many scholars took this as evidence that the Homeric songs were "real," that

Agamemnon and his companions once lived and fought for Troy, and that they had lived in splendid palaces such as those that had now been found at Mycenae and Tiryns. This was most true of Schliemann himself, who had always been a believer, a "positivist."

In general, it seems that after Schliemann's excavations the popular consensus was that the Homeric stories contained at least some core of Bronze Age reality, a belief that grew with the slightly later discoveries in Crete, where several large "palatial" structures were excavated. Most notable among these was the palace at Knossos, which was being unearthed by Sir Arthur Evans. Evans' excavations at Knossos put Schliemann's finds in a better perspective, showing not only that a much older culture had preceded the mainland civilization that had by now been coined "Mycenaean," but also that Mycenaean society owed much to its Cretan predecessors in virtually every field of religion, "art," and social organization.

Yet, Evans' excavations also cast a shadow that was to last for several decades over Bronze Age scholarship. Although not explicitly stated in his early work, Evans increasingly considered the Minoan civilization not only as a major influence on the mainland society of the Mycenaean palaces, but saw those palaces as Minoan dependencies, subject to the rule of Knossos. This view was to dominate scholarship for decades. Indeed, such was his influence on contemporary scholarship that those who did not agree with his views (but rather thought of Mycenaean society as an independent phenomenon) were stripped of their academic positions. The most famous example in this respect was the director of the British School at Athens during those years, Alan Wace. Wace and his American colleague Carl Blegen were among the few archaeologists that openly questioned Evans' views of Minoan hegemony over Greece and argued that, in fact, it was the Mycenaeans that had eventually overrun Minoan Crete.

Time would redeem Wace. With the decipherment of Linear B by Michael Ventris, it became clear that there was no evidence whatsoever that the palaces of the mainland had been Minoan dependencies. Rather, it was now beyond doubt that the Mycenaeans spoke Greek, albeit an archaic variant of it, but Greek nonetheless. The texts also indicated that it was the Mycenaeans who eventually had overrun Knossos, and not vice versa, for the texts in the Knossian archives were written in Linear B Greek, not in Linear A.

The shock brought about by the realization that Evans' Minoan paradigm had stalled academics for decades and that Linear B now offered a wealth of information coming, so to say, directly from the Mycenaeans themselves was no doubt enormous and we may suspect that it was this shock that resulted, at least occasionally, in an overestimation of the value of Linear B texts. Ventris himself was already painfully aware of the limitations of the texts, pleading for caution as to how far the texts could bring scholarship to a realistic reconstruction of the Mycenaean world. Indeed, over the years it has become increasingly clear that the Linear B texts refer only to (an unspecified) part of the palatial economies, often dealing with the last months, or even less, of the existence of the respective palaces. However, although these limitations are acknowledged, the tendency still is to model most of the Mycenaean palatial societies and states on the information derived from Linear B texts. The most striking example, I think, is the reconstruction of the territorial extent of the Theban kingdom. Some academics argue that parts of Euboea fell under the Theban sway simply on the basis of the Linear B texts, which specify occasional shipments of cattle to the center on the Kadmeion hill. Examples of this type of over-reliance on the Linear B evidence abound and I should perhaps simply quote Galaty and Parkinson in stating that:

> Unfortunately, the majority of these theoretical models [of Mycenaean palatial society] are vestiges of the era in which Linear B was first deciphered.

Another result of the decipherment of Linear B texts was the total loss in the academic world of the belief in the "historicity" of the Greek legends. Oliver Dickinson in his handbook "The Aegean Bronze Age" made the following comment:

> The belief in the warlike propensities of Mycenaean society in this period seems in fact to derive largely from the belief that this society is accurately mirrored in the Homeric epics and other legendary material. But the world of Homer's heroes, in which wealth is essentially represented by livestock and movable treasures, and to acquire these by raiding is not thought at all reprehensible, seems completely at odds with the world of orderly taxation of territories' produce reflected in the Linear B texts.

With the belief in Homeric truth gone, there was no more reason to suppose a larger political entity. The result was that the administrative units, i.e. the palatial realms, were considered to be independent political entities themselves. As will be discussed below, there is little in the Linear B texts against this notion, nor does archaeology necessarily indicate a different situation. The fact that the Hittite and Egyptian texts spoke against a model of regional states was, of course, problematic. However, this was reasoned away by arguing that those texts only reflected the perception of the Hittites and Egyptians on the Aegean and, therefore, did not necessarily reflect Late Bronze Age political reality. In many cases, this discrepancy with the Hittite and Egyptian texts was not even mentioned.

Over the years the number of Hittite texts dealing with the Aegean has increased and the contents and contexts of these texts are increasingly better understood. In addition, archaeology indicates that the Aegean was, in the fourteenth and thirteenth centuries at least, fully incorporated into a system of gift exchange of prestige goods, often items specifically manufactured for the purpose of enhancing the social status of their recipient (and therewith the status of the one who had sent it). These items were made specifically for the purpose of "tying together" the various elites throughout the Late Bronze Age Eastern Mediterranean, using a range of hybrid symbols of power and prestige that were widely understood throughout the region. As a result, it is increasingly untenable to argue that the Mycenaean world was a remote *terra incognita* for the royal houses of the Near East and that neither the Egyptians nor the Hittites had any notion of the political structures and relations in a region that they so evidently had contact with.

We are thus faced with the dilemma that our current understanding of the political structure of the Mycenaean world, with its various smaller political entities, does not seem to fit the picture conjured by the contemporary Near Eastern texts. This, then, is the problem that stood at the beginning of the present research, a problem I hope to solve in the pages below.

— INTRODUCTION —

Traditionally, Greece during the Late Bronze Age is seen as a patchwork of small states, states that were culturally similar, but politically independent from each other.[1] This view was mainly informed by the Linear B texts, which suggest that each of these states was ruled from a palatial center, to which the revenues from the realm were brought to be stored, administered, and redistributed.[2] To control the flow of goods and men within their respective realms, the palace administrations kept records on unbaked clay tablets, examples of which have survived at various centers, mainly because of their accidental burning in the fiery destructions that brought about the end of most of the palaces around 1200 BC. The records kept track of the distribution of goods and manpower throughout the region. So far, no Linear B tablets have been found dealing with anything else. In contrast with neighboring lands, such as Egypt or Hittite Anatolia, Greece has not yielded historical or judicial texts and no such things as treaties or diplomatic letters have been found.

On the other side of the Aegean, just two hundred kilometers to the east, Hittite texts dating from the period between 1400 and 1220 BC, refer to a kingdom of Ahhiyawa, which, according to recent developments in our understanding of Hittite geography, should be sought beyond the Anatolian coast, i.e. on the isles in the Aegean or on the

---

1. Galaty / Parkinson 1999a; Dickinson 1994, 77 ff.; Chadwick 1976a, 12 ff. See Map 2.
2. Shelmerdine 1999a; Dickinson 1994, 81 ff.; Chadwick 1976a, 102 ff., esp.139–56.

Greek mainland.[3] Around 1250 BC, the Hittite king Hattušili III wrote a letter full of complaint about Ahhiyawan activity on the Anatolian west coast, but respectfully called his Ahhiyawan colleague "Great King." This title has been the topic of much debate and its exact connotation seems to have differed through time and per region, but it is clear that it was, more or less, the equivalent of what one nowadays calls a "Great Power": an independent state, with significant military power and of sizable territory.[4] As such, the title was attributed only to those monarchs who, in effect, ruled the urban, civilized world. Most notable amongst these were the kings of Egypt, Hatti (the Hittites), and Babylon. Over time, the king of Mittani and, after his demise, the king of Assyria would become part of this "Great Powers' Club." Not recognized as such by the Hittites, but accepted as equals by the kings of Amarna Age Egypt, were the rulers of Alashiya (now safely identified as

---

3. Hawkins 1998, 2. As a result of a new reading of the Karabel Pass Relief proposed by Hawkins, it has become clear that this area represented the border between the kingdom of Mira and the kingdom of Seha. As a consequence, references in Hittite texts to the position of the previously unidentified lands Arzawa / Mira can now be set against the "fixed point" that is Mira. The picture thus evolving in western Anatolia does not leave room for Ahhiyawa on the Anatolian mainland. With references such as "across the sea" and with the apparent proximity of Ahhiyawan territory to Arzawa and Assuwa, there can be no doubt that Ahhiyawa should be situated west of the Anatolian coast, i.e. on the isles and/or in the Greek mainland. See also Hope Simpson 2003; Niemeier 1998; Bryce 1989a. The localization of Ahhiyawa in the Aegeis has recently been criticized by Gerd Steiner (2007, 596 ff.), but his arguments for an Anatolian-based Ahhiyawa are not convincing: the reference to chariot transport to Ahhiyawa cannot be used as evidence against an Aegean Ahhiyawa, since chariots could go to Millawanda, from where one proceeded by ship, nor is there any reason to suppose (*contra* Steiner 2007, 293) that the Hittite kings had only a vague understanding of western Anatolian geography (which would allow for the presence of a territorially very small Anatolian based Ahhiyawa, with the unexplained militarily/political power of a Great King). From a purely linguistic point of view, the identification of Hittite *Ahhiyawa* as the Greek 'Αχαιοί is generally considered to be difficult, although not impossible (but see Finkelberg 1988, 127–34, who proposes a linguistic correspondence between Ahhiyawa and Akhaioi via (the unattested) *Ahhiaw- > *Ahhyaw- > *Akhaw-.
4. Cf. Cohen / Westbrook 2000, esp. Liverani 2000, 15–27.

part of Cyprus) and Arzawa (a kingdom that rose to prominence in western Anatolia during a period of Hittite decline).[5]

Ahhiyawan membership in the Great Powers' Club appears to have been an exclusively Hittite perception on interstate politics. There is no certain reference to an Ahhiyawan kingdom in Levantine or Egyptian texts, although we know from a Hittite text dated to *ca.* 1220 (the so-called Šaušgamuwa treaty) that Ahhiyawan ships did frequent Levantine harbors.[6] Only during the reign of Merneptah is there mention of "Ekwesh" (what may be the Egyptian pronunciation of Hittite Ahhiyawa) as part of the Sea People movement.[7] On the other hand, Egyptian texts dating to the reign of Thutmoses III and Amenhotep III do refer to the kingdom *Tnj*, usually vocalized as Tanaju, comprising at least parts of the Greek mainland.[8] On at least one occasion, messengers from the king of Tanaju are reported to have brought greeting gifts to the Egyptian court.[9] A textual reference to Tanaju dating after the reign of Amenhotep III is not yet attested.

In both Egypt and the Levant, the Mycenaean world is omnipresent in the archaeological record. The Levant, especially, has yielded an abundance of Mycenaean pottery, mainly in harbor cities such as Ugarit.[10] The Mycenaean pottery seems to have had a limited diffusion to inland centers. In Egypt, Mycenaean pottery is found less frequently, although several major centers have yielded considerable amounts of Mycenaean vessels. Chief amongst these is the site of El Amarna, known in antiquity as Akhetaten, the "Horizon of the Solar Disk," and the capital of Egypt under its heretic king Akhenaten. Other important sites include Deir el Medina near present-day Karnak and Luxor, and Qantir, the site of ancient Pi-ramesse, in the eastern delta.

---

5. Cf. Ragonieri 2000, esp. 45–53 for discussion on status in Great King diplomacy. For the identification of Alashiya as part of Cyprus, see Goren / Bunimovitz / Finkelstein / N'aman 2003, 233–55.

6. Cf. Latacz 2001a. But see Singer 2006, 252. See for extensive discussion below.

7. Cf. Woudhuizen 2006, 56, table 1.

8. Cf. Latacz 2001b, 166; Cline 1998; Helck 1995, 24; Edel 1988; Goedicke 1969; Edel 1966. For an extensive discussion, see below.

9. Cf. Haider 1988a, 10; Latacz 2001b, 164. See extensive discussion below.

10. Cf. van Wijngaarden 2003, with references, for an exhaustive discussion of the distribution of Mycenaean pottery in the Levant.

Map 1: The Major States in the Late Bronze Age Eastern Mediterranean

The abundance of Mycenaean pottery in the Levant and Egypt is not paralleled in western Anatolia. Finds of Mycenaean pottery and, for that matter, other artefacts in western Anatolia have been remarkably few and are concentrated among a few major centers, including the sites of Miletus and Hissarlik. The scarcity of Mycenaean artefacts in Anatolia is matched by the dearth of Anatolian objects found on the Greek mainland. Egyptian objects are, on the other hand, more common, especially at Mycenae.

The observations above present us with a problem. How do the various Mycenaean principalities, argued for on the grounds of Linear B texts, relate to Hittite Ahhiyawa? How does Ahhiyawa relate to the Aegean kingdom that the Egyptians called Tanaju? Is it compatible with the admittedly scrappy archaeological record in Greece, western Anatolia, and Egypt? It is the aim of this research to present some new thoughts and to offer a new synthesis of the various historical and archaeological datasets.

To do so, the various datasets will be presented separately and will be compared to each other. The major issues in doing so concern the extent to which these datasets overlap and the explanation for any discrepancies. The datasets are presented in roughly the same order as they are introduced above: Linear B texts first, followed by the Hittite texts, the Egyptian texts, and the archaeological data.

Map 2: Mycenaean Palatial States

Dots represent areas where Mycenaean culture is dominant; densely packed dots represent areas where a Mycenaean palatial state is suspected; black represents area with attested Mycenaean palatial states or territories.

1. Iolkos (Dimini)
2. Orchomenos
3. Thebes
4. Athens
5. Salamis
6. Mycenae
7. Lacedaemon (Pellana)
8. Pylos
9. Miletus
10. Lazpa (Lesbos)
11. Elis
12. Kythera
13. Knossos

— THE TEXTUAL EVIDENCE —

THE LINEAR B TABLETS

The Palatial Realms

The period known as the Late Bronze Age spans the years between 1600 and *ca.* 1100 BC. In Greece, this period was characterized by the rise of several palatial centers, of which Pylos, Tiryns, Midea, Orchomenos, Thebes, and Athens are notable. Most famous of all is the site of Mycenae, situated in the northeast of the Argive plain, to which the material culture of Late Bronze Age Greece owes its name. Although many of these centers appear to have been sizable settlements during the Middle Bronze Age and the first two centuries of the Late Bronze Age, it is from *ca.*1400 BC onward that these centers can be characterized as "palatial," with large, imposing megaron structures as the focus of economic, and presumably social and religious, life.[11]

A salient feature of palatial Greece is the use of script for the administration of each palace's realm. The script, Linear B, which was inscribed on clay tablets, was used for the day-to-day administration of each palace economy. Lists of produce, men, women, livestock, and other goods that were at the palace's disposal are preserved, as well as lists concerning the movement of people and goods, and such things as offerings to specific gods. Linear B tablets have been found at various centers, including Mycenae, Tiryns, Thebes, Knossos, and Pylos. As has

11. Cf. Dickinson 1994, 291; Shelmerdine 1999a; Chadwick 1976a, 102 ff. esp. 139–56; but see Sherratt 2001.

been noted, the texts concern only administrative issues and, while they do offer some insight into the administrative reach of the various palatial centers, are of limited value for the reconstruction of ancient Greece's political landscape. Also, since most "archives" represent the day-to-day administration of the palaces' final year(s),[12] i.e. shortly before the destruction of the palaces around 1200 BC, the Linear B texts *à priori* are of limited value when dealing with earlier periods. Yet despite these limitations, the Linear B texts are the only preserved written records from the Mycenaean world.

Although most of the palatial archives have only partly been preserved, the impression from the tablets is that the palatial administration throughout Greece was highly uniform, using the same language (Mycenaean Greek), the same terminology, and the same systems of taxation and distribution.[13] Indeed, and we shall come to that below, even the shapes and sizes of the clay tablets used for the various palatial administrations appear to have been uniform throughout Greece.[14] Considering this sense of uniformity, the evidence coming from the most fully preserved and most completely published archive, that of the palace of Pylos, is usually taken as representative of all the palatial centers.

As noted above, the Linear B texts mainly concern administrative issues: the flow of goods and people throughout the realm of the respective palace. The lists of revenues from subsidiary centers are generally used to reconstruct the approximate territorial extent of the various Mycenaean palatial states.[15] In the case of Pylos, it appears that the palace ruled an area roughly comparable to the modern "nome" of Messenia, with prominent hills and ridges serving as boundaries. This seems to have been the case with most palaces: they exercised a regional

12. See Chadwick 1976a, 18 ff.; Hooker 1982, 209. Bennett 1956, 109 notes that in some cases the tablets (esp. the E-series) cannot have ante-dated the fire by more than a few weeks.

13. See for the uniformity of language (and hints of underlying dialects) Chadwick 1976a; for terminology and systems of taxation, Vermeule 1957, 200; Shelmerdine 1999b (who argues for very minor regional differences in the Linear B administration); Olivier 1984. See also Ventris / Chadwick 1956, 199; Palmer 1955.

14. Postgate in Killen / Voutsaki 2001, 160.

15. Cf. Bennet 1988, 19–41; 1999, 9–24; Chadwick 1977.

rule, which seldom extended beyond the natural borders of their realm. Only at Mycenae can a case be made for a larger territory, including the Argolid, Korinthia, and Achaea, as shall be argued below. For Thebes, it has been proposed that its territory covered the eastern part of Boeotia.[16] While some even argue that parts of Euboea should be included on the basis of an occasional delivery of animals from the towns of Karystos and Amarynthos to Thebes,[17] I fail to see why the occasional exchange should indicate Theban dominance over that center in Euboea.

Whatever the case, each Mycenaean kingdom was in principle governed from the palace. Palaces exercised control over most, if not all, the industries within their realm.[18] This included not only those in or near the palace, but also those at large provincial centers.

It appears that palatial territory was divided into several provinces, each headed by its own administrative center. Pylian territory was divided into two provinces, generally called the "hither" and the "further" province, of which the latter was probably administered by the secondary capital of Leuktron, *re-u-ko-to-ro* in Linear B.[19] The Aigaleon ridge in all likelihood served as a natural boundary between the two,[20] although some have argued for an east-west division of the Pylian realm.[21] The provinces themselves were divided into several smaller districts, known as *damoi*. Some of these may have been headed by a *g^{u}asileus*, the ancestral form of the later Greek *basileus*. To the Mycenaeans this title seems to have had a less exalted meaning than to the later Greeks, as it is also used to designate, for example, the chief of a group of smiths.[22]

16. Aravantinos / Godart / Sacconi 2001, 356; Sergent 1994, 730.
17. Eder 2003, 303.
18. Killen 1999, 88–89.
19. Chadwick 1973, 139; 1998–99, 19. See Map 3 for a reconstruction of the kingdom of Pylos.
20. Eder 2003, 298; Shelmerdine 1981, 319–25.
21. Bintliff 1977, 39–40, 51–54.
22. Ventris / Chadwick 1976a, 70. This rather ordinary connotation may be compared to Homer, as we read in the *Odyssey* of many *basilees* in Ithaka (*Od.* I.394–95).

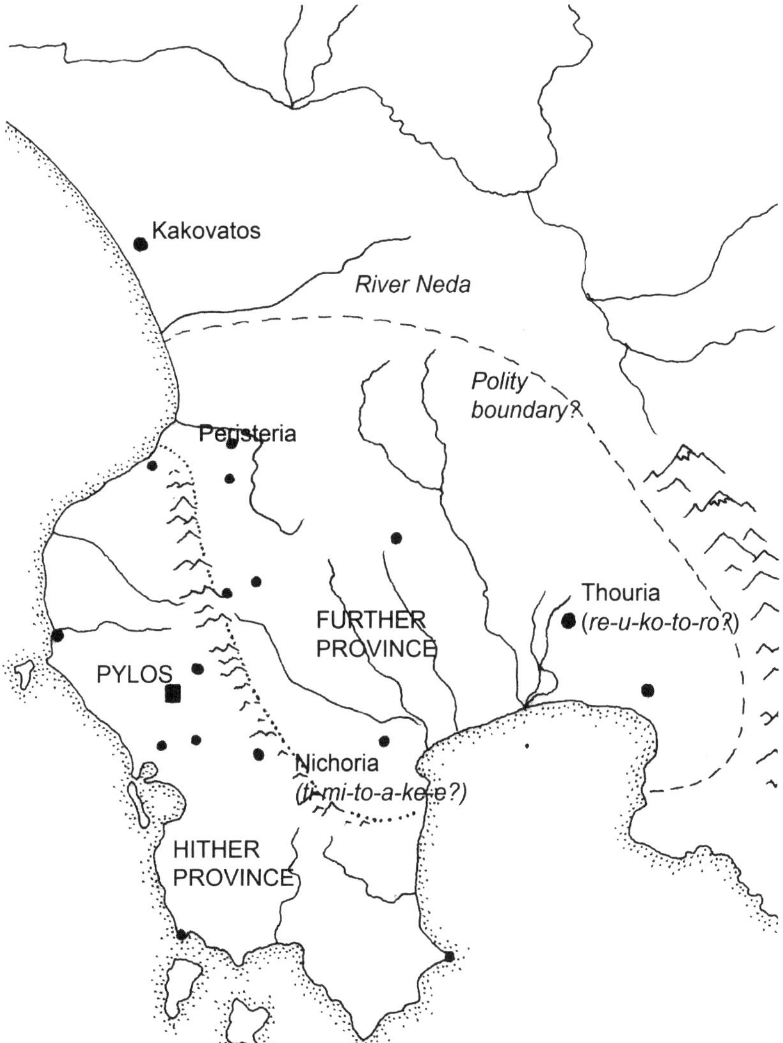

Map 3: A Reconstruction of the Pylian Kingdom according to the Linear B Texts

The "Wanax" and the "Lawagetas"

There is little doubt in the scholarly discourse about the head of state of the typical Mycenaean state. The activities of the *wanax* cover virtually all aspects of palatial life, as the Linear B texts show the *wanax* partaking in religious feasting and offerings, as well as being involved in the distribution of goods and craftsmen or troops. On the basis of his widespread involvement in Mycenaean society, the *wanax* is generally understood as the "king" of the typical Mycenaean state, whereas the *lawagetas*, an official whose activities seem to roughly overlap with the *wanax*'s, is usually seen as each kingdom's second-in-command (though the specific function of the *lawagetas* remains debated; I will come to this below). Both appear to have had an exalted status, as only the *wanax* and the *lawagetas* are reported to have been the holders of a *temenos* (an officially designated plot of land, possibly with some religious connotation). The texts, moreover, indicate that both were the major (though not the only) landholders within the Pylian realm, although the *wanax*, whose lands appear to have been three times the size of those of the *lawagetas*, seems to have been most important in that respect.

With the *wanax* widely considered as each kingdom's head of state, the absence of an overlord in the palatial archives flies in the face of any argument in favor of any degree of overarching authority, as various Hittite texts seem to indicate. But how firm are our data on the political structure of the Mycenaean world? Is there indeed no trace of an overlord in the Linear B texts? Any attempt to address these questions must naturally start with the evaluation of our evidence regarding the position of those officials who appear to have been most prominent in Mycenaean society: the *wanax* and the *lawagetas*. We will focus first on the position of the *wanax* and then on the position of the *lawagetas*.

Linear B texts found at Pylos, Knossos, and Thebes (while at Tiryns and Chania the *wanax* is attested in inscriptions on pottery)[23] indicate that the *wanax* was engaged in religious, economic, and military life. A number of these texts, which we review below, have been interpreted as indicative of the *wanax*'s exalted status in the Mycenaean kingdoms.

23. Hooker 1979, 100 lists the occurrences of "wanax" at Pylos; see Hallager 1987, 117 for Ghania; Catling / Millett 1965, esp. 48 for Thebes (but note that most of the inscribed stirrup jars at Thebes were of Cretan manufacture); Catling *et al.* 1980, 88 ff., Godart / Olivier 1975, 38, and Sacconi 1974, 41 (with Fehlzitat) for attestations at Tiryns.

However, as will be argued in the lines below, there is no further specification of his function within the Pylian state; there is no indication of the *wanax*'s duties, rights, and powers in the Linear B texts. As a result, our understanding of the political composition of the various Mycenaean kingdoms remains very limited, to the extent that their respective political independence must be considered unproven. Let us now turn to the various relevant Linear B texts.

From a text from Pylos, Er 312, we can infer that the *wanax* is the owner of a *temenos* three times the size of that of the *lawagetas*:

Er 312. 1. wa-na-ka-te-ro te-me-no
2. to-so-jo pe-ma GRA 30
3. ra-wa-ke-si-jo te-me-no GRA 10
4. *vacat*
5. te-re-ta-o to-so pe-ma GRA 30
6. to-so-de te-re-ta VIR 3
7. wo-ro-ki-jo-ne-jo e-re-mo
8. to-so-jo pe-ma GRA 6 [

1. The preserve of the king,
2. seed at so much: 3600 l. wheat
3. The preserve of the *lawagetas*, seed at so much: 1200 l. wheat
5. (The lands) of the fief-holders (*te-re-ta-o*), so much seed: 3600 l. wheat;
6. and (there are) so many fief-holders: 3
7. The unencumbered (land) of the cult association,
8. seed at s much: 720 l. wheat

translation adapted from Ventris / Chadwick 1956, 266

This text has been interpreted as evidence of the *wanax*'s superior position over the *lawagetas*. However, although the text clearly indicates the prominence of the *wanax* as a (perhaps *the*) major landholder and that *temenos*, with its close analogy in Homer's *temenos basileion* (Σ 550), seems to indicate an exalted status of the *wanax* within the Pylian kingdom, these inferences about Er 312 cannot

> serve to establish this as proof of the proposition that the *wa-na-ka* stood at the head of state....It does indeed, go some way towards establishing the status of the *wa-na-ka*, but it enables nothing to be said for certain about his functions; and a knowledge of his functions would be of far greater significance, since it is quite possible for an office-

holder to continue to enjoy high status long after his functions have become purely honorific.[24]

That craftsmen, designated as "wanaktero" in various other texts, are of a similar ambiguity, as this does not say anything about their precise status (they may work permanently for the *wanax*; they may occasionally be called into service). It is, of course, of interest to note that the *wanax* had an interest in the production of pottery (Eo 371) or in a fuller (En 74.3), but so too, one might presume, did the average farmer in the Pylian kingdom. There is, moreover, often no clarity about the nature of the *wanax* involved: he may have been divine, he may have been human.[25]

Whatever the details, there can be no doubt that the Pylian kingdom knew at least one human *wanax*, considering text Ta 711: *o-wi-de pu$_2$-ke-qi-ri o-te wa-na-ka te-ke au-ke-wa da-mo-ko-ro*, which is usually understood as "when the *wanax* appointed *au-ke-wa (as) da-mo-ko-ro* (a title rather than a personal name)."[26] Here, the *wanax* is clearly regarded as human, performing an act of considerable importance (since otherwise it would not have been mentioned in the text). In the same text, the *wanax* is associated with the inspection of precious items that can only be considered to have been property of the palace, thereby placing the *wanax* in that same context. Despite the fact, however, that Ta 711 thus proves that the *wanax* was an official of significant stature, it does not prove that he was the only ruler of the Pylian kingdom.[27] Moreover, there is reason to question the notion of the *wanax* as the supreme ruler of the Pylian kingdom since, although he holds a *temenos*, the revenues of that *temenos* as listed in Er 312 are equalled by the revenues

---

24. Hooker 1979, 102.

25. "Anax" in Homer is also used to designate Zeus. Palmer considers the *wanax* (written *wa-na-ka-te*, i.e. dative) as the recipient of the olive oil listed in the Fr. Series (above), and therefore considers the *wanax* most likely to have been a divinity. Cf. Palmer 1963, 247–58. But see P. Carlier, 1987; Adrados 1969, esp. 149–50, for the argument that the *wanax* "*era un dios agrario innominado*" and that the *te-re-ta* were priests of his cult.

26. Cf. Olivier 1967. For the interpretation of *te-ke* in Ta 711 as "appointed," see Killen 1998, 421–22; Palaima 2000, 236–37.

27. I consider this text to be a clear indication that the kingdom of Pylos knew only one *wanax* (whatever his position in the Pylian state may have been), since had there been more, this *wanax* would have been specified (named). *Contra* Hooker 1979.

of the holdings of only three *te-re-ta* (a designation for common landholders; compare to Classical Greek *telestai* > *telos*, "service," "duty").[28]

At Knossos, too, the *wanax* must have been a person of distinction, since specific clothes were made for him and it is also clear that the *wanax* at Knossos was involved in economic (the production of olive oil and perfumes) and religious matters. However, there is no unequivocal evidence to consider the *wanax* as the supreme head of state, nor is his relation to other important figures, such as the *lawagetas*, clear in any way. The same holds for the texts and inscriptions from the other sites, especially since a number of texts inscribed on pottery may have been imported (e.g., a number of inscribed stirrup jars from Thebes seem to have come from Crete).[29]

These uncertainties apply, to an even greater extent, to the position of the *lawagetas*. The *lawagetas*, *ra-wa-ke-ta* in Linear B, is attested in texts from Pylos and Knossos. The most important text, usually seen as indicative of the lower status of the *lawagetas* in regard to the *wanax*, comes from Pylos:

Un 718. 1. sa-ra-pe-da po-se-da-o-ni do-so-mo
2. o-wi-de-ta-i do-so-mo to-so e-ke-ra_2-wo
3. do-se WHEAT 4 WINE 3 BULL 1
4. tu-ro2 *TU* + *RO_2* ko-wo SKIN + *KO* 1
5. me-ri-to CT 3
6. vacat
7. o-da-a_2 da-mo WHEAT 2 WINE 2
8. RAMS 2 *TU* + *RO_2* 5 a-re-ro *A* + *RE* + *PA* + CT 2 SKIN + *KO* 1
9. to-so-de ra-wa-ke-ta do-se
10. RAMS 2 me-re-u-ro *65 CAS 6
11. WINE CQ 2 o-da-a_2 wo-ro-ki-jo-ne-jo ka-'ma'
12. WHEAT CAS 6 WINE CQ 1 *TU* + *RO_2* 5 me-ri[
13. [ ] CQ 1 CT 1

1. The Sa-ra-pe-da to Poseidon, its contribution
2. As far as one can see, Ekhelawōn will give so much as a contribution:

28. Cf. Hooker 1979, 105. See also Hallager 1987, 182, for similar doubts on the status of *wanax* in post LM IIIA2 Crete (Knossos).

29. Cf. Catling / Millett 1965, 7; Catling *et al.* 1980; Palmer 1963.

3. 480 l. wheat, 108 l. wine, one bull,
4. ten cheeses, one sheepskin,
5. 6 l. of honey
6. *vacat*
7. And similarly the village (will give). 240 l. wheat, 72 l. wine,
8. two rams, five cheeses, 4 l. Fat, one sheepskin.
9. And the *lawagetas* will give so much.
10. two rams, 72 l. flour,
11. and 24 l. wine. And similarly the estate of the cult association (will give):
12. 72 l. wheat, 12 l. wine, five cheeses,
13. 14 l. of honey.

translation adapted from Ventris / Chadwick 1973, 282–83

Here, the *lawagetas* is listed as one of the contributors to a sacrifice in the otherwise unknown Pylian district *sa-ra-pe-da*. On the basis of analogies with other Linear B texts (for example, Er 312), it has been proposed that the contributor listed first (and who is contributing most to the sacrifice) may have been the *wanax*, in which case this text would provide us with the only name of a Mycenaean monarch, *E-ke-ra*$_2$*-wo* (Ekhelawōn), so far.[30] It is on the basis of this text and the aforementioned text Er 312 that the *lawagetas* is usually considered to have been second in power (after the *wanax*), as his entry in the tablets is second—after, normally, the *wanax*—and his landholdings seem smaller than those of the *wanax* (in Er 312 a third of the *wanax*'s property).

Other attestations of the *lawagetas* in Pylian tablets include An 724.7 and Un 219.10, as well as *ra-wa-ke-si-jo* in Ea 782, Ea 814, Ea 882, Eq 59.4, Er 312.3, and Na 245; and *ra-wa-ke-si-jo-jo* in Ea 421, Ea 809, and Ea 823. These texts indicate that, apart from being a landowner and having a number of skilled workmen attached to his office, the *lawagetas* was involved in the deployment of rowers (An 724).

Contrary to Palaima's claim that there is a clear distinction between the spheres of influence of the *wanax* and the *lawagetas* in the Linear B texts (this remark appears to be entirely based on the fact that the affairs of both officials are listed in separate series: Ea and Eb/En/Eo/Ep),[31]

30. The list is similar in structure to the aforementioned Er 312. See for extensive discussions Palaima 1998–99, 205–21; Heubeck 1966.

31. Palaima 1995, 129.

their actual state business, in effect, seems to have been much the same, if on a different scale: they both hold plots of land (the designation *temenos* seems to be exclusively used for the plots of land held by these two officials, and is not used to denote the landholdings of, for example, the *te-re-ta*); they both appear to have had specialized craftsmen in their service; they are both recorded as taking part (or providing offerings) in religious activities; and they both are involved (though not unequivocally proven) in military affairs, such as the deployment of troops.[32] The only clear distinction between the *wanax* and the *lawagetas* in the Linear B texts is the size of their property. The *wanax* seems to have outdone the *lawagetas* in this respect and, therefore, can plausibly be considered to have been of a higher social status. But that is about all we can reasonably deduce from the texts.

Similarly, attempts to deduce the function of the *lawagetas* in Mycenaean society on etymological grounds appear to be problematic. Of these attempts, the one most often heard is that the *lawagetas* was the military commander of the typical Mycenaean state, a concept based on the assumption that *laos* refers to the population able to carry weapons, i.e. the army. As noted, this is an assumption and there is, in fact, no direct evidence to support it.[33]

In sum, although we can grasp the nature of some of the activities of the *wanax* and the *lawagetas* in Mycenaean society, we have little idea of their exact position within the political organization of the Mycenaean states. Whether the *wanax* exercised regional authority only or was, in fact, an overlord of several palatial polities (each perhaps ruled by a

---

32. See for example PY Un 718 for their contributions to a ceremonial banquet to Poseidon, and PY An 724 for their involvement in the deployment of rowers in the Pylian fleet.

33. But see Wundsam 1968, 58; van Effenterre 1968, 559–73. See Lindgren 1973,134 ff. for full references on the etymology of *lawagetas*. See, for an alternative derivation (άγω), Aura Jorro 1993, 230, who also notes that the attestations of the *lawagetas* in various contexts in the Linear B texts "sin que sea possible limitar su esfera de acción a una función específicamente militar o cultural, como campo professional exclusive de este alto dignitario." Nikoloudis, in an as-yet-unpublished Ph.D. dissertation, proposed that the *lawagetas* served as a liaison between the palatial elite and the lower classes of the Pylian realm, as a "minister of multi-cultural affairs" (lecture in Melbourne, October 2007). For a full evaluation of the occurrence of the *wanax* and *lawagetas* in Linear B texts and their possible roles in Mycenaean society, see Kelder 2008.

lawagetas, a leader of the people, as his title implies?) cannot possibly be determined solely on the basis of the Linear B texts.

Supra-Regional Affairs

The dearth of conclusive evidence on the exact position of the *wanax* and the *lawagetas* in the Linear B texts is matched by the absence of evidence on the relations between the various palatial polities. Though there is the occasional reference to areas that appear to have been outside the administrative grasp of the respective palaces, the implications of these references appear to be rather ambiguous. Below, we will explore some examples.

Pylian troops are reported to have ventured far from home, with small numbers being dispatched to centers in Elis and Oikhalia, the latter on the Pylian-Arcadian border. Though that specific detachment of men may have consisted of "special forces," as Geschnitzer suggests,[34] more common troops, such as rowers, are known to have been sent to regions beyond the Pylian border. Tablet An 12 [1] from Pylos reports that 27 of these rowers were dispatched to *pe-re-u-ro-na-de*, which may plausibly be identified as Pleuron, on the northern shore of the Gulf of Corinth.[35] One may wonder why such small numbers of men were deployed in regions far beyond the borders of the Pylian state. Whatever the exact nature of this deployment, it demonstrates that at least occasionally the palace of Pylos was engaged in regions well beyond its borders. This is further illustrated in tablets that name slaves from several centers and regions in the Aegean, including Miletus and Lesbos.[36] The Pylians certainly had the naval capacity to travel to those areas, as is clear from the Linear B texts[37] and the Mycenaean harbor installations near Voidokoilia.[38]

Tablets from other centers indicate some supra-regional contacts as well: goods go from Mycenae to Thebes and at Knossos people from Nauplion and Cyprus are present, as well as an Egyptian.[39] The prob-

---

34. Geschnitzer 1999, 259–60.
35. Cf. Ventris/Chadwick 1956, 149.
36. Parker 1999, 499; Chadwick 1976a, 80.
37. Palaima 1991, 280–82.
38. Zangger 1998, 96 ff.; Shelmerdine 1997, 542 ff.
39. Palaima 1991, 280–82.

lem with the evidence as quoted above is that although supra-regional contacts are attested, the nature of these contacts remains difficult to establish. At Pylos, for example, women from Miletus (and various other western Anatolian regions) are recorded as slaves, yet Miletus was a Greek center, at least culturally speaking.[40] This then may indicate bellicose actions between Mycenaean centers. However, it is also possible that these slaves were acquired at Miletus and were not of Mycenaean origin.[41]

Interstate contact was, perhaps, not confined to trading encounters or even the deployment of small numbers of troops. The recurrence of the names of officials at several major centers is an indication of supra-regional engagement.[42] Indeed, it may point to more, as has been noted by Killen: "several names [...] appear in more than one archive, suggesting at least the possibility that all these persons were members of a single ruling dynasty."[43] The texts indicate that these people served as collectors, which may point to some centralized gathering of resources, although it is equally possible that these collectors served in the process of gift exchange between the different Mycenaean centers.[44] It is not

---

40. Niemeier 1998, 34; Mee 1978, 133; for Anatolian slaves in Linear B texts, see Ergan 2007 forthcoming.
41. Chadwick 1976a, 80.
42. Killen 1979, 179; Chadwick 1973, 102–3.
43. Killen 1999, 88.
44. Although at Knossos "collectors" may have been owners of land and livestock in regions at some distance from the palace, rather than palace officials. Cf. Bennet 1992, 65–101; 1988, 32–33. Deger-Jalkotzy argues that the "collectors" at Pylos and Thebes do not indicate supra-regional government, but are the result of the cultural koinè of Mycenaean Greece, with virtual identical bureaucracy, palatial architecture, and ideology. That some collectors have the same name can be ascribed to the widespread occurrence of Greek names in general on the Greek mainland during the thirteenth century BC. At the same time, she does however allow for dynastic and political ties between the various polities, including military cooperation. Cf. Deger-Jalkotzy 2006, 19–35. See also Parkinson 1999, 84; Olivier 2001, 129–59 and the comment of Postgate (p.160), noting that the recurrence of specific names as "collectors," "if we are indeed looking at 200 years and five or more generations" is surprisingly strongly motivated. See also Carlier 1992 for the differences in functions of the "collectors" at Knossos and Pylos.

clear, however, whether we are dealing with the same people in different centers or with different people bearing the same names.[45] But even if the latter, one could argue that the recurrence of names in elite families all over Greece points toward at least dynastic ties. In addition, the fact that the manner of administrating the palatial territories, including

45. The precise status and function of these "collectors" is a matter of debate. At Knossos, some of these "collectors" appear to have been owners of land and flocks of sheep in regions at some distance from the palace, and this has been taken as evidence that they cannot have been officials of the Knossian palace (Bennet 1992, 65–101). However, these persons appear also in the archives of Boeotian Thebes, again with the same function (as collectors or "owners" of flocks and workers in the sheep and cloth industry). This striking degree of coincidence had already been observed by John Killen in 1979 and is difficult to explain within the framework of independent Mycenaean palatial states (Killen 1979, 176). One explanation may be that the "collectors" were divinities, yet at least some of the collectors appear in the archives in contexts that make it clear that they were humans. Killen proposed that these collectors are most likely to have been members of a ruling dynasty, especially considering the close connection at Pylos among "collectors," the *e-qe-ta*, and the *lawagetas* (Cf. Killen 1979, 177–78; Killen, 1999, 88; Lindgren 1973, 143–44). If this is the case, the recurrence of names in these high social echelons might be the result of an "upper-class tradition" in which royal scions were given names only from a certain limited stock (Killen's argument that the collectors, with the same name, function, and activities may have been members of a single ruling family is supported with parallels from contemporary European royal houses: the high proportion of Danish kings named Christian and of English monarchs named Edward (Plantagenet, esp. Angevins), Henry (Plantagenet; esp. Lancaster), or George (House of Hanover). The important point here is that ruling families, regardless of intermarrying with other (foreign) nobility, tend to retain a number of specific names, names that could almost be called emblematic for a certain dynasty. This phenomenon is apparent also in Late Bronze Age states in the Near East, such as Egypt (18th-dynasty names: Amenhotep, Thutmoses; 19th-dynasty names: Ramesses and Seti) and the Hittite empire [Hattušili, Suppiluliuma, and Muršili]). This hypothesis has received only limited attention in the scholarly debate, and has not gained widespread acceptance. Deger-Jalkotzy argued that the recurrence of names may be ascribed to the widespread occurrence of Greek names in general in the Mycenaean world (Deger-Jalkotzy 2006, 19–35). At the same time, she did, however, allow for dynastic and political ties between the various polities, including military cooperation. Of course, the possibility that high-status persons holding identical titles in the various palatial administrations bore the same names as a result of a widespread cul-

several flaws, is more or less similar at all palatial centers is difficult to explain as a result of a cultural "koinè" only.[46]

Despite this, there is no indication of a supra-regional entity such as Ahhiyawa known in the Linear B texts. Ahhiyawa itself is mentioned only once: in a tablet from Knossos, as *a-ka-wi-ja-de*, but this may refer to a town just as well as to a state.[47] As a result, the Linear B texts offer only limited and ambivalent evidence with regard to supra-regional, interstate contacts among the different palatial states and, for that matter, their relation with regions beyond the Aegean. Although the existence of such a state as Ahhiyawa from the Hittite texts certainly is not contradicted in the Linear B texts, clear evidence for it is absent.

---

tural koinè cannot be excluded, but it seems unlikely that the combination "name + title" reappears in the archives of various sites in a similar setting (cloth industry) only as a result of cultural uniformity. Moreover, as has been observed by Nicholas Postgate, the recurrence of specific names as "collectors," if we are indeed looking at 200 years and five or more generations, is surprisingly strongly motivated. I am aware of the discussion surrounding the date of the Linear B archives at Knossos. For convenience's sake, I will follow the "traditional" date, holding that Knossos was destroyed about 200 years before the end of the Mycenaean centers on the mainland. Considering the early date of the archive of Knossos, this dynastic tie between the Theban and Knossian collectors may have originated in the late fifteenth century, around the end of LM II. If the re-dating of the Knossian tablets to *ca.* 1200 BC is proven correct, however, the collectors at Knossos and Thebes should then be considered not only name-sakes and peers, but also contemporaries, a combination of facts that to my mind would easiest and, therefore, best be explained if the collectors at Thebes and Knossos were the same persons. Although there is the risk of a circular argument here, one might even consider the recurrence of the collectors at Thebes and Knossos as an additional argument in favor of re-dating the Knossos archive to the late-thirteenth century BC. For an extensive discussion of the position of the *wanax* and *lawagetas*, in which I propose to identify the *wanax* as a peripatetic Great King (and the *lawagetas* as a local vassal ruler), see Kelder 2008.

46. Nicholas Postgate noted that, to a Near Eastern archaeologist, the uniformity of shape and size of the Linear B tablets throughout Greece appears to indicate political unification, since in the Near East every polity was characterized not only by its own specific way of administration, but also by the shapes and sizes of the tablets. See Killen / Voutsaki 2001, 160.

47. Chadwick 1973, 138.

AHHIYAWA AND WESTERN ANATOLIA

As has been noted in the introduction, Hittite texts referring to Ahhiyawa date to the period 1400 to 1220 BC. For almost two centuries, there evidently was diplomatic contact between the Hittite court and the Ahhiyawan court, sometimes of an apparently peaceful nature, but more often involving Ahhiyawan aggression in areas subject to the Hittite crown. Sommer listed a total of 16 Hittite texts referring to Ahhiyawa in his 1932 *Ahhijava Urkunden*. Today the number of texts referring to Ahhiyawa has grown to about 25, with an additional number of fragments that may bear the name Ahhiyawa.[48]

The scene for Hittite-Ahhiyawan relations was the west coast of Anatolia (see Map 4 for an overview). There are several Hittite texts dealing with this region. Six Hittite texts deal with the Aššuwa League,[49] which dominated western Anatolia until its fall to the Hittites in the late fifteenth century BC. Arzawa, a kingdom that rose to power after the collapse of Aššuwa, is mentioned several times as well, most notably in the Annals of Muršili II[50] and several treaties.[51] Apart from Hittite texts, a letter from Egyptian El-Amarna is apparently written to the king of Arzawa, while another was sent from Arzawa to the pharaoh's court.[52] This adds to the impression that Arzawa was a major power indeed during the Amarna era. Other Egyptian sources refer to *Isy*, apparently the Egyptian name for Aššuwa, while *a-su-ja* in Linear A texts may be the Minoan designation for the Aššuwa League.[53] *A-si-wi-ja* and other variations probably were Linear B designations for the same region that must be situated north of the later Arzawa territories, comprising most

48. Heinhold-Krahmer 2003, 204. For the purposes of this research, only texts that are generally well understood are used. Minority views are referred to in footnotes. Unintelligible texts have been ignored.

49. KUB XXIII 11; KUB XXVI 91; KUB XL 62 I+ XIII 9; KUB XXXIV 43:10; and a text on the "Mycenaeanizing" sword found at Hattuša. Another text, KBo XII 53 rev. 7', has little relevance, although some reference to Aššuwa is made.

50. Cf. Heinhold-Krahmer 1977, 84–88.

51. KBo V 4; KUB XIX 49; KUB XIX 50; KUB XXXI 83 1'–26'; KUB XXVI 59 + KUB XIV 26.

52. *EA* 31 in Moran, 1987, 192–93; *EA* 32 in Moran 1987, 195.

53. Cline 1997, 191.

Map 4: Western Anatolia in the Late Bronze Age

of west and northwestern Anatolia, although some overlap with the Arzawa lands is possible.[54]

In this politically unstable region, Ahhiyawan activity was to haunt Hittite aspirations for superiority over western Anatolia over the course of almost two centuries. From the scraps of the Hittite texts, one can recall a story of continual Ahhiyawan interference in Anatolian affairs, of support to anti-Hittite uprisings, and of raids on various Hittite vassal cities, including Troy. Although not all Ahhiyawan actions met with unqualified success, it appears that the kings of Ahhiyawa were generally able to exercise rule over at least one center on the Anatolian coast, Millawanda, now generally accepted to be the Hittite name for Miletus.[55] Despite several Hittite incursions into the area, Millawanda appears to have been the major Ahhiyawan foothold in Anatolia from where, presumably, Ahhiyawan armies roamed the regions on the Anatolian west coast. The first of these armies was headed by an Ahhiyawan king with a familiar name.

Around 1400 BC, the Hittite king Arnuwanda dictated a text to his scribe that is now generally known as "The Mischief of Madduwatta" or "The Indictment of Madduwatta."[56] The text deals with the deeds of one Madduwatta, possibly an Arzawan prince and certainly a troublesome Hittite vassal,[57] who had come into conflict with a man from Ahhija (an older form of Ahhiyawa) named Attariššija (Madd. §1.1).

> Attariššija, the man from Ahhija, chased [you], Madduwatta, out of your land. Then he harassed you and kept chasing you. And he continued to seek an [evil] death for you, Madduwatta. He [would] have killed you, but you, Madduwatta, fled to the father [of My Majesty], and the father of My Majesty saved you from death. He [got] rid of Attariššija for you. Otherwise, Attariššija would not have left you alone, but would [have killed] you.
>
> KUB XIV 1, §1, 1–5. Adapted from Beckman, 1996.

Apparently Attariššija had come into armed conflict with Madduwatta, causing the latter to flee for safety to the Hittite court. The father of Arnuwanda, the Hittite king Tudhaliya I, installed Madduwatta as a

---

54. Chadwick 1976a, 80; Cline 1996, 141–42.
55. Niemeier 2002, 296; Hawkins 1998, 30.
56. KUB XIV 1; Cf. Götze 1968.
57. Bryce 1998, 141; Götze 1968, 40.

vassal in the country of Zippasla with, as a later addition the territory known as the Siyanti Land, part of the former kingdom of Arzawa.[58] Although Madduwatta now was a vassal of the Hittite king, the man from Ahhija attacked a second time. Madduwatta was forced to flee again, to be saved by a Hittite expeditionary force.[59]

> But [later] Attariššija, the man from Ahhija, came and was plotting to kill you, Madduwatta. But when the father of My Majesty heard, he dispatched Kisnapili, infantry, and chariotry in battle against Attariššija. And you, Madduwatta, once more did not resist Attariššija, but broke ranks before him. Then Kisnapili came and took charge of you [...] from Hatti. Kisnapili went in battle against Attariššija. One hundred [chariots and ... infantry] of Attariššija [drew up]. And they fought. One officer of Attariššija was killed, and one officer of ours, Zidanza, was killed. Then Attariššija [...] to Madduwatta, and he went off to his own land. And they installed Madduwatta in his place once more.
>
> KUB XIV 1, §12, 60–65. Adapted from Beckman, 1996.

According to the text, Madduwatta was later found raiding the coast of Cyprus. This act aroused the anger of his Hittite overlord, as Cyprus was considered subject to the Hittite crown (Madd. §36.85).[60] In this context Attariššija is mentioned again, also raiding the Cypriote coast together with "a man from Piggaja." The Madduwatta text represents the first textual evidence for Greek incursions into the Anatolian mainland. Excavations at Miletus suggest that Mycenaeans settled there already during LH IIB (*ca.* 1450 BC),[61] although Mycenaean prevalence at Millawanda came about only later, possibly as a result of new waves of immigration.[62] It is likely that Attariššija had a base on Anatolian soil, although Hawkins notes that Ahhiyawa itself at this time must be situated "across the sea" and that Arzawa represented its point of contact with Anatolia.[63] Ahhiyawa proper, without a doubt, must be somewhere off the Anatolian mainland, but this does not exclude the possi-

58. Hawkins 1998, 22 ff.
59. Bryce 1998, 141.
60. Güterbock 1983, 134–35.
61. Niemeier 1998, 142.
62. Niemeier 2002, 295; see below for the archaeological evidence.
63. Hawkins 1998, 30; *KBo* III, 4 iii 1–6.

bility that already at an early stage Mycenaeans used Millawanda as a base for further action.[64] They evidently did so during later years.

The activities of Attariššija in western Anatolia and, later, Cyprus take place roughly at the time of the Hittite invasion of Aššuwa, around 1430 BC. Before its fall to the Hittites, Aššuwa had been the major power in western Anatolia and a serious threat to Hittite hegemony in Anatolia. The best testimony to this can be found in the annals of the victorious Hittite king Tudhaliya I/II.[65] According to the annals, after defeating his enemy the Hittite king deported 10,000 Aššuwan soldiers and 600 teams of horses with their charioteers, along with the Aššuwan king Piyama-^{d}KAL and his son Kukkuli, to the Hittite capital.[66] Although these numbers may have been exaggerated, it is clear that Aššuwa had been a formidable power. It has been proposed that the upheavals in western Anatolia around 1400—clashes between the Hittites and Aššuwa and probably the first Greek intrusions—were the source of various pre-Trojan War legends, including Achilles' failed expedition in Teuthrania, a region at the mouth of the Caicus River.[67] Although this is far from proven, the "Mycenaeanizing" sword dedicated to the storm-god in the Hittite capital Hattuša after the Hittite victory over Aššuwa may relate to some Mycenaean involvement.[68]

After the reign of Tudhaliya I/II, Hittite resources were increasingly drawn to the east, where Hurrian expansion proved itself a serious

---

64. Mountjoy 1998, 51.

65. Due to poor understanding of the sequence of the earliest Hittite kings, there is some uncertainty concerning Tudhaliya. Some discern two separate kings, reigning shortly after each other, whereas others see only one. Without choosing between these options, I refer to Tudhaliya I/II in this case for simplicity's sake.

66. Cf. Cline 1997, 191.

67. Cline 1997, 202 ff. The legend deals with the slaying of Eurypylos, son of Telephus and prince of the Ceteians, by Neoptolemos (see for example Quintus of Smyrna VIII, 133–220). Huxley (1960, 40) proposed that Telephus might be the Hittite name Telepinu, while "Ceteians" (Κητειοι) remarkably resembles "Khatti," the Hittites. The Caicus River is most likely to be identified with the Seha River known from Hittite texts (Gurney 1992, 221), which means that these legendary events happened in the region just south of Hittite Wiluša, now generally seen as the Greek Ilion (Bryce 1998, 395; Starke 2001, 34).

68. Cline 1996, 137–51; Hope Simpson 2003, 205.

threat to Hittite interests. During this time the kingdom of Arzawa filled the vacuum left in western Anatolia. With the Hittites busy elsewhere, Arzawa challenged Hittite dominance in Anatolia and its armies are believed to have made incursions into the Hittite heartland. The capital of Arzawa was Apaša, generally equated with later Ephesus.[69] As such, it must have been the seat of Tarhundaradu, the king of Arzawa known from the Amarna letters.[70] Under his sway, the kingdom for some time was considered a Great Power, at least in Egyptian eyes.

Ahhiyawan relations with the Hittites remained hostile over the course of the fourteenth century. When, around 1315 BC, the Hittites returned from the Hurrian front to re-establish their rule in western Anatolia, we find the king of Ahhiyawa supporting the king of Arzawa against the Hittites. The relevant text, KUB XIV 15 I, 23–26, is rather fragmentary, but what can be discerned refers to the mobilization of troops, the land, and the king of Ahhiyawa, as well as the king of Arzawa, Uhhaziti. Although the exact meaning of this text is a matter of dispute,[71] the text indicates that the center of Millawanda was now part of the Ahhiyawan realm.

Around the same time, Ahhiyawa is reported to have seized various islands, presumably in the Aegean. Although the relevant text does not specify which islands had been seized, it adds to the impression of Greek encroachment in western Anatolia during the later part of the fourteenth century BC.[72] This impression is supported by archaeological evidence. A destruction layer at the site of Miletus/Millawanda has been interpreted as the result of a Hittite attack in retaliation for Ahhiyawan support of the Arzawan cause.[73] Even if this interpretation is

69. Cf. Bammer 1986–87, 32.

70. *EA* 31, *EA* 32; Moran 1987, 101–3.

71. Some have proposed that it was the Ahhiyawan king who summoned his troops to quell a rebellion (see, e.g., Sommer 1932, 307), but another reading, now favored by most scholars, suggests it was not the Ahhiyawan but the Hittite king Muršili (see Bryce 1989b, 299; Güterbock 1983, 135).

72. KUB XXVI 91; Sommer 1932, 268–71. The text is dated to the reign of Muršili II or his successor Muwatalli. Cf. Easton 1985, 192; Gurney 2002, 136. I will return to a newly proposed reading of this text below.

73. In KUB XIV 15, Millawanda is reported to have been sacked by a Hittite strike force sent by Muršili II under the command of the generals Gulla

correct, the Hittites evidently did not consolidate their grip on Millawanda, since, in later texts, the center appears to have been firmly in Ahhiyawan hands.[74]

One of these later texts is the so-called "Tawagalawa Letter," a letter sent by a Hittite king, probably Hattušili III, to an unnamed king of Ahhiyawa.[75] It refers to several problems on the western fringe of the Hittite empire, apparently the result of Ahhiyawan activity in the region, centering around two men: Piyamaradu and a certain Tawagalawa. In the letter, Tawagalawa is regarded as the brother of the Ahhiyawan king and appears to be operating in and around the Ahhiyawan dependency Millawanda, recruiting Anatolians for labor in Ahhiyawa.

It has been suggested that the recruitment of Anatolian laborers referred to in the Tawagalawa letter relates to the inception of various monumental building projects in Greece, such as the extension of the

---

and Malliziti (cf. Güterbock 1983, 135; Bryce 1989b, 299). This "kriegerische Zerstörung" is also adduced to by Schiering (1959–60, 12–13), who notes the rebuilding of Miletus immediately after the destruction and the construction of a defensive wall with features resembling Hittite fortifications at Hattuša. Cf. Schiering 1979, 80–82; Mee 1978, 135. For an extensive discussion of the archaeological evidence, see below.

74. Given the fact that around 1315 BC, Muršili II had conquered the center because of its support of the Arzawan uprising, somewhere between Muršili's early years and the reign of Hattušili III, when Millawanda is reported to belong to the king of Ahhiyawa (see below), the Ahhiyawans must have taken control of the center. Bryce (1989b, 302) suggested that the Hittite king Muwatalli II ceded the center to the Ahhiyawan king with the understanding that this would still his hunger for territory on the Anatolian coast. Indeed, the concept is attractive, if only because, as Bryce rightly points out, Ahhiyawa is omitted in the so-called Aleksandu treaty (CTH 76). This text is dated to the reign of Muwatalli II and is of interest because it signals the formal incorporation of the kingdom of Wiluša, situated in the Troad, into the Hittite empire. In it, one would expect references to other powers in the region, especially to the formerly troublesome Ahhiyawans. As this is not the case, Ahhiyawa apparently was of no threat to the Hittites at that time, which could be achieved only by means of some kind of understanding. If we assume the reality of Bryce's hypothesis, it is of interest to note that once Ahhiyawa had been tamed by political means, the Hittites lost interest in it and did not even bother to mention the land in a treaty with Wiluša, a country close to the Greek sphere of influence.

75. KUB XIV 3; cf. Singer 1983, 209–10; Güterbock 1983, 133–38.

fortifications at the citadels of Mycenae and Tiryns—it has been proposed that especially at the latter site there are architectural parallels with Anatolia and the drainage of the Nemea Valley and the Kopaïs basin.[76] Although there is no definite proof of any relationship between Anatolian and Mycenaean architecture, the Tawagalawa letter certainly shows that there were personal ties between Ahhiyawan and Hittite nobility, as Tawagalawa, the brother of the Ahhiyawan king, is reported to have stood in a chariot with the personal charioteer of the Hittite king himself (Taw.§8,59–62). While it is beyond doubt that Tawagalawa was a major political figure at that time,[77] his actions appear to have been less important to the Hittite king than the deeds of Piyamaradu.

Piyamaradu seems to have been of Anatolian origin and must have been a man of some stature.[78] The Tawagalawa letter is too fragmentary to inform us on the exact nature of his deeds (though a roughly contemporary text provides us with much more information; see below) but whatever it was, the Hittite king demanded the extradition of Piyamaradu, who had by now found refuge at the Ahhiyawan center Millawanda. According to the Tawagalawa letter, Millawanda at that time was governed by Atpā, a representative of the king of Ahhiyawa, who is known to have been the brother-in-law of Piyamaradu (Taw.I §5.64). On hearing the demand of extradition, the Ahhiyawan king is reported to have sent his governor orders to hand over Piyamaradu to the Hittite king (Taw. I §5, 53–56):

> GIM-an-ma-mu [^{LÚ}*TE-MU ŚA* ŠEŠ.*I*]*A*? an-da ú-emi-ia-at
> nu-mu *Ú-U*[*L* aš-šu-la-an ku-in-ki] ú-da-aš *Ú-UL*-ia?-⌈mu⌉ up-pí-eš-šar
> ku-it-ki [ú-da-aš ki-iš-ša-an-m]a *IQ-BI A-NA* ^{I}at-pa-ua *IŠ-PUR*
> ^{I}pí-i[a-ma-ra-du-un-ua-ká]n? *A-NA* LUGAL ^{URU}ḫa-at-ti ŠU-i da-a-i
>
> And when [the messenger of m]y [Brother] arrived,
> he did not bring me any greeting nor did he bring me any gift,

---

76. Bryce 2003b, 203; Sandars 1978, 63–65.

77. The name Tawagalawa has been the subject of much debate concerning the equating of Tawagalawa with Greek Ete(w)okles (and therefore should Ahhiyawa proper be located in the Thebaid?). Cf. Niemeier 1998 with references.

78. Götze 1986, 40; Houwink ten Cate 1983, 37; Hawkins 1998, 17.

but thus he spoke: he has written to Atpā:
Place Piyamaradu in the hands of the king of Hatti!

transcription from Sommer 1932, 4;
translation adapted from Sommer 1932, 5.[79]

The king of Ahhiyawa appears to have had near direct control over Millawanda, sending orders to his attaché Atpā.[80] This, if anything, attests to our lacunal understanding of the Mycenaean world on the basis of Linear B texts only, as no such orders have been found in the various Linear B archives. Moreover, there is no reference in any Linear B text to a sizable Mycenaean center as a dependency of a Mycenaean palace. The high degree of control of the Ahhiyawan king over his overseas territories is further attested by the presence of his own brother in the area, a practice that seems to find its parallel in the Hittite world, where important members of the royal family were often installed as governors over important provinces.[81]

The time needed to send a messenger to and from Ahhiyawa was enough to let Piyamaradu escape by ship to the Ahhiyawan-held isles of the Aegean. Hattušili's eagerness to apprehend Piyamaradu becomes understandable when we read KUB XIX 5, better known as the "Manapa-Tarhunda Letter," which dates to around the same time as the Tawagalawa letter.[82] Manapa-Tarhunda was the king of the Seha River Land, a vassal of the Hittites in western Anatolia, and had, according to his letter, just suffered a "humiliating defeat" at the hands of Piyamaradu. Piyamaradu's victory over the Hittite vassal was crowned with the armed takeover of the island of Lesbos (Lazpa in the Hittite texts), which was subsequently handed over to the king of Ahhiyawa. Prior to that, Piyamaradu had been ravaging the land of Wiluša, a Hittite vassal state in northwestern Anatolia, now generally equated with Greek

79. I thank W. Waal for her help concerning this text.

80. That the king of Ahhiyawa wrote not only to his attaché, but also to the Hittites, is indicated by the fragmentary text KUB XXVI 91 (CTH 183), in which a letter from the Ahhiyawan king is quoted (Gurney 2002, 135). Even if one argues that *IŠ-PUR* does not necessarily mean "writing" but more generically "sending" (and that, consequently, this could also mean "sending a messenger"), the point remains that clearly Linear B texts failed to cover this (political) aspect of Mycenaean society.

81. Cf. Kelder 2004; 2005b.

82. Cf. Houwink ten Cate 1983.

(W)ilion.[83] This appears to have been the cause of Manapa-Tarhunda's intervention and the occasion of his defeat at the hands of Piyamaradu.[84]

It is clear that Piyamaradu was a direct threat to Hittite interests in the region. The seizure of Lesbos and its subsequent incorporation into the Ahhiyawan state, the personal ties between Atpā and Piyamaradu (brothers-in-law),[85] and Piyamaradu's ability to retreat to Ahhiyawan-held territory all strongly suggest that Piyamaradu was acting on behalf of, or at least with the blessing of, the Ahhiyawan king. Moreover, the army at his disposal must have been a considerable force, since Piyamaradu is able to overrun the kingdom of Wiluša, defeat the neighboring Seha River Land, embark for Lesbos, conquer the island, and establish permanent control over it before leaving for Millawanda.[86]

There can, as a result, be no question that Ahhiyawa at that point in time posed a serious threat to Hittite hegemony in western Anatolia, a fact actually stressed by Hattušili himself, who notes that, although in the past he had gone to war against the Ahhiyawan king over the land Wiluša, now a "war would be wrong for us!" (Taw.IV §12.10). Claims that Hattušili's apparent respect for the king of Ahhiyawa was the result of temporary Hittite weakness or preoccupation with troubles elsewhere[87] not only remain hypothetical, but also miss the point. Around 1250 BC, the Hittites were faced with the reality of Ahhiyawan military might,[88] and they dealt with it in the established political manner. The king of Ahhiyawa now belonged to that Club of Great Powers and was considered a Great King, at least as far as the Hittites were concerned.

It was now 150 years after the first military actions of Ahhiyawan forces on Anatolian soil and clearly those years had not been without

83. Cf. Hawkins 1998, Latacz 2001b, but see Heinhold-Krahmer 2003.

84. The exact order of events is unclear, but it likely that Manapa-Tarhunda was defeated while attempting to relieve Wiluša, rather than during an invasion of the Seha River Land itself. Cf. Bryce 1989b, 302–3; Easton 1985, 192; Güterbock 1984, 117–18.

85. Taw.I §5.64; Cf. Houwink ten Cate 1983, 37.

86. Kelder 2005a.

87. Cf. Singer 1983, 209–10; Güterbock 1983, 133–38.

88. Güterbock 1983, 136; Klengel 2002, 73; Meier 2000, 166–67.

success. But, toward the end of the thirteenth century, the eastern Mediterranean began to experience the first signs of trouble. Already during the reign of the Egyptian king Ramesses II the coast of Egypt had been subject to occasional raids of marauding peoples, which were to increase over the course of the last half of the thirteenth century. Elsewhere, the growing power of Assyria caused a constant drain of Hittite military resources, while the unruly Kaska people in the north of Anatolia remained a looming threat to the Hittite heartland. The picture in Greece is less clear, but around the time when the Tawagalawa letter was written things were not going well in Central Greece. In Boeotia, the hitherto flourishing center of Thebes was destroyed (though subsequently rebuilt), a fate shared by several smaller and larger centers in the region, including the important palatial center of Orchomenos, where palatial life did not revive.[89] Around 1220 BC, the palace of Pylos in Messenia shared a similar fate.[90] The archaeological data will be further discussed below, but the troubles Greece experienced during the latter part of the thirteenth century BC may be reflected in two Hittite texts dated to the reign of the Hittite king Tudhaliya IV.

The first of these is the so-called "Millawata Letter" (Millawata is an alternative writing of Millawanda), which may indicate the loss of Ahhiyawan control over Millawanda.[91] This fragmentary letter was probably sent by the Hittite king to a vassal ruler. Though it has been suggested that the addressee was the king of Mira (a vassal of the Hittite king, Mira consisted of the rump state of what once was Arzawa), others propose it was the ruler of Millawanda to whom the letter was sent.[92] Although the final word on this matter has not been written, archaeology may indeed indicate Hittite prevalence at Miletus at this time.

Around the same time as the composition of the Millawata letter, the Hittite king Tudhaliya IV concluded a new treaty with Šaušga-

---

89. On the grounds of (impoverished) pottery styles; cf. Mountjoy 1983, 11. Discussion in Catling 1984–85, 31.

90. Cf. Bennet / Shelmerdine 2001.

91. Cf. Niemeier, 1999, 153; Bryce, 1989b, 303–4; for a different view Singer, 1983, 214–16.

92. KUB XIX 55; Sommer 1932, 198 ff. See also Niemeier 2002, 298; Niemeier 1998a, 42 with references.

muwa, vassal king over the land of Amurru. Amurru had long been a border/buffer state between the Egyptian empire and the kingdom of the Hittites, which made it a strategically important region, but it also included various thriving ports on the Levantine coast. It is hardly surprising that the treaty between Šaušgamuwa and his Hittite overlord was full of stipulations concerning foreign contacts, be it of diplomatic nature or trading encounters.[93] It is in this context that a list of foreign potentates whom the Hittite king evidently considered as equals was compiled. This list naturally included the king of nearby Egypt, as well as the king of Assyria. Originally, it also included the king of Ahhiyawa, but his name was erased, which has caused much scholarly debate. Broadly speaking, two explanations have been proposed. The first explanation for the erasure of Ahhiyawa in the treaty is that at the time when the treaty was drawn up Ahhiyawa met with some serious setbacks, archaeologically attested as the first destructions of several palatial centers and in the Hittite texts reflected in the final loss of Miletus to the Hittites.[94] The other explanation holds that Ahhiyawa was included in the list by "habit" of the scribe and that, in the end, its inclusion was deemed irrelevant for a treaty with a region so distant from the area of Ahhiyawan influence.[95]

Whatever the case, the same text reveals that Ahhiyawan ships at that time were still frequenting Levantine harbors, as it is stipulated that Ahhiyawan ships were to be prohibited from reaching Assyria (clearly, the cargo rather than the ships was meant), which points to a trade embargo imposed on Assyria.[96] It is not clear what the Ahhiyawans brought to Assyria that triggered the Hittite ban. Mycenaean pottery, which is the clearest marker for contacts with the Mycenaean world in the Levant, is absent at Assyrian Late Bronze Age sites. A similar situation occurs in Hittite Anatolia, where Mycenaean pottery is found mainly at sites on the Anatolian west coast, but scarcely at inland sites.

Though the Hittite text thus may indicate the gradual weakening of the Ahhiyawan state, there certainly is no conclusive evidence for it.

93. Šaušgamuwa treaty, KUB XXIII 1 + KUB XXXI; Sommer 1932, 320–27.

94. Bryce 2003b, 210–12 and 21 for Miletus as a prerequisite for Great Kingship.

95. Kühne / Otten 1971, 15–17; Singer 1985, 119; Wood 1985, 180.

96. Beckman 1995, 104; Bryce 1998, 350; Singer 1985, 119, against this reading Steiner 1989.

Rather, the Hittite texts indicate that Ahhiyawa around 1220 BC still was of sufficient importance to be mentioned, not so much as an important state but as an important economic factor in Hittite diplomatic texts. The last Hittite text in which Ahhiyawa is mentioned also dates to the reign of Tudhaliya IV.[97] The situation in this last reference to Ahhiyawa is similar to the preceding ones: Ahhiyawa is supporting an anti-Hittite rebellion in former Arzawan territory:

> The Land of the Seha River transgressed again for a second time (?). [They said (?): In the past (?) the great (?)-gr]andfather of his Majesty did not conquer us by force of arms. (...) [Thereafter Tarhunderadu] (the rebel leader) waged war and relied on the king of Ahhiyawa. [And] he took refuge [on Eagle Peak]. But I, the Great King, set out [and...] and raided (lit. took down) Eagle Peak.
>
> After Güterbock 1983, 138.

With the advance of Tudhaliya's army, Ahhiyawa finally disappears from the Hittite record. Shortly thereafter, the palatial centers of Greece were destroyed or abandoned. The palatial administration collapsed and with it the use of script disappeared. Not long after 1200 BC, a similar fate befell a number of other states in the Near East. In the turmoil that heralded the end of the Bronze Age, the Hittite capital Hattuša was burnt to the ground and the Hittite empire ceased to exist. Assyria experienced a period of decline, whereas Egypt lost a significant part of its Levantine empire. No further written sources on the Aegean or western Anatolia are known until well into the Iron Age.

In effect, the Hittite texts tell the story of almost two centuries of warfare between two states, Hatti and Ahhiyawa, over the lands on the Anatolian west coast. At least seven separate Ahhiyawan actions can be discerned:

1. Attariššija's campaigns against Madduwatta, *ca.* 1400 BC.
2. Ahhiyawan support to Arzawa, *ca.* 1315 BC.
3. Ahhiyawan takeover of several isles, *ca.* 1300 BC.
4. Piyamaradu against Wiluša, Manapa-Tarhunda, and Lazpa, *ca.* 1250 BC.
5. Tawagalawa in Miletus, *ca.* 1250 BC.
6. Ahhiyawan shipments of goods to Assyria, before 1220 BC.
7. Ahhiyawan support of an anti-Hittite rebellion in the Seha River Land, *ca.* 1220 BC.

---

97. KUB XXIII 13 (Güterbock 1983, 138; 1992, 235–43).

Over the course of these two centuries neither Ahhiyawa nor Hatti appears to have been able to establish secure, unchallenged authority over the region. While the Hittites generally were able to maintain a nominal overlordship over much of what used to be the Arzawan state, they were not able to prevent the Ahhiyawan seizure of several islands off the coast of Anatolia nor were they able to drive the Ahhiyawans out of their stronghold Millawanda, at least not until the very end of the Bronze Age. Elsewhere, I have argued that the sheer numbers needed for the military expeditions listed above cannot realistically be attributed to any of the Mycenaean palatial states as reconstructed on the grounds of Linear B texts, alone.[98] I had failed to sufficiently stress the large time span during which Ahhiyawa manifested itself on Anatolian soil. During that period, many Mycenaean palatial centers had suffered setbacks that, one is inclined to think, would hardly spare them the means needed for the attested Anatolian campaigns. To name just a few: Knossos, whose powers waned during the fourteenth century; Thebes, which was burnt to the ground around 1250 (or slightly later, toward the end of LH IIIB1); Orchomenos, which never recovered from a similar fate around the same time; and Gla, which was deserted in "advanced, but not late LH IIIB."[99]

These troubles notwithstanding, the Mycenaeans did not venture into Anatolia only. As has been noted, Ahhiyawan ships were not unknown in Levantine harbors and, in view of the amounts of Mycenaean artefacts (mainly pottery) at Cypriote sites, must have found their way to Cypriote shores just as well. In the introduction, I have noted that, so far, no reference to a state with the name Ahhiyawa has come from the Egyptian textual record. Mycenaean Greece, however, certainly was not unknown to the Egyptians. From the reign of Thutmoses III the Mycenaeans appear in Egyptian texts under the name *Tnj*, usually vocalized as Tanaju.

---

98. Kelder 2005a.

99. Cf. Iakovidis 2001, 145 (his "shortly before 1200 BC" is, on the grounds of pottery styles, to be read as ca. 1230–20 BC). See also De Ridder 1894. Note that Gla is not a Mycenaean palace; the melathron uncovered on the citadel appears to have been a local administrative center that fell to the palace of Orchomenos.

THE EGYPTIAN PERCEPTION

Egypt has long been considered a country that never looked far over its borders. There is some truth in this. During both the Old and the Middle Kingdoms Egyptian armies seldom operated outside Egypt, with the exception of Nubia, which was incorporated into the Egyptian state during the Middle Kingdom. As a result, Egypt never was an imperial power; it never was expansionistic and never sought to control regions beyond its borders on a permanent base. Rather, the kings of the Old and Middle Kingdoms adopted a policy based on diplomatic marriages and, if necessary, the occasional punitive raid to secure safe access to the Levantine trading routes and the import of exotic goods.[100]

The Hyksos occupation of Egypt during the so-called Second Intermediate Period changed all this. From that moment on, the Egyptian monarchs were acutely aware that the various Levantine principalities just over the border should not be left unchecked. The king responsible for the expulsion of the Hyksos and the reunification of Egypt, Ahmose, led the way in capturing the Hyksos stronghold Sharuhen in southern Palestine after a three-year siege, thereby bringing the Hyksos period to a definite end.[101] Although his immediate successors devoted much of their reigns to stabilizing the reunited country, as the reestablishment of Theban rule did not go totally unopposed (there are references to shadowy rebellions late in Ahmose's reign),[102] we find Egyptian armies campaigning in the Levant from the reign of Thutmoses I (1504–1492 BC) onward. It is plausible that this new interest in the Levant was one of the reasons for the transfer of the administrative

100. Cf. Redford 1992.

101. Bourriau 2001, 215 ff.

102. Stabilizing the country also involved the gradual extension of Egyptian control over Nubia and campaigns against the kingdom of Kush—its core roughly situated near the third cataract—attested from the reign of Ahmose onward. With the mounting Egyptian pressure, this kingdom gradually dissolved into smaller tribal entities that were gradually incorporated into the Egyptian state. During the reign of Thutmoses III, Egyptian rule extended as far as the fourth cataract, deep into Nubia. By this time, however, Nubia had already ceased to be a military threat and further expansion of Egyptian rule in the region was prompted by economics rather than military or political considerations.

center of the kingdom from Thebes in the south to Memphis, situated near the apex of the Nile delta.[103]

From the reign of Thutmoses I onward, the kings of the 18th dynasty gradually expanded their rule in the Levant, until, during the reign of Thutmoses III (1479–1425 BC), Egyptian borders were pushed to the banks of the Euphrates River.[104] It was during Thutmoses III's campaign in the Levant that he received an envoy coming from a land hitherto unknown, across the "great green" of the Mediterranean. Thutmoses' annals, describing his exploits in the Levant in considerable detail, make only a short reference to the occasion. Messengers from a land called *Tnj*, usually vocalized as *Tanaju*, came to the pharaonic court with greeting gifts for the great Egyptian conqueror. These gifts included a silver jug in *Keftiu*-style and what is usually translated as three copper cups with silver handles.[105] This reference, which dates to the 42nd regnal year of Thutmoses III (*ca.* 1437 BC), is the first attested contact between the Egyptian court and Tanaju. Thereafter, Tanaju appears only sporadically in the Egyptian sources.

---

103. The date of the establishment of Memphis as the capital is debated. Although some lean toward a date as late as Thutmoses IV, a date in the early 18th dynasty is generally preferred (Strudwick / Strudwick 1999, 31). I believe Thutmoses I to be the principal agent in this process, because of his attested activity in the Levant. A parallel with clear military and political considerations is the later shift of the administration from Memphis to Piramesse, during the reign of Ramesses II.

104. Redford 1992 provides a detailed and readable account of the Egyptian-Mittanian wars, as well as a good introduction to the organization of the Egyptian empire in the Levant.

105. Latacz 2001b, 164. Haider (1988a, 10) reads "iron" cups, which would make the gift even more extraordinary, as iron at this early stage was an extremely rare commodity, being difficult to work. It appears that the reading *bia* "iron" is now widely preferred (written communication M. Raven). It appears plausible (on the basis of analogies with preceding sections of the annals) that Tanaju was headed by a king. The text is damaged, but generally completed as "[tribute from the chief] of Tanaju." Most relevant Egyptian texts regarding Keftiu have been published in Vercoutter 1956. Tanaju appears for the first time in the Egyptian record during the reign of Thutmoses III. Almost all Egyptian references to the Aegean (Keftiu, Tanaju, and "the islands in the midst of the Great Green") are found in Cline (1994, 108–20), the most recent compilation.

The location of Tanaju has been a matter of debate.[106] However, an inscription from the reign of Amenhotep III (1427–1400 BC) indicates that Tanaju should be sought on the Greek mainland, comprising at least various regions in the Peloponnese. This inscription is known as the Kom el Hetan text, named after a village on the west bank of the Nile, not far from modern Karnak and Luxor.[107]

Kom el Hetan is the site of what was once the mortuary temple of Egypt's "roi soleil," Amenhotep III. Although little of it remains today, the complex once boasted an impressive array of pillared halls, courts, and monumental gates, flanked by monolithic statues of the deified king. Virtually the sole survivors of this complex are the famous colossi of Memnon.

The Kom el Hetan text was inscribed on the bases of similar, but long-gone statues of the king. Most of the list described areas in Asia, mainly with regard to the traditional "nine bows," the enemies of Egypt. The lists are composed in a fairly uniform way. In one row various lands are listed, while a second row lists the cities of those lands. The "lands" of the first row seem to have been conceived of as political entities and not merely as geographical regions. This is illustrated by the listing of the great powers Hatti, Babylon, and Naharin (Mittani), and dependencies such as the Mittanian stronghold Carchemish and smaller states such as Aššur.[108] We may reasonably assume that this pattern holds true also for the last part of the Kom el Hetan list, which deals with the Aegean.

Part of the list dealt with the areas to the north, across the "Great Green" of the Mediterranean.[109] Only two lands are listed, one of which is Keftiu, the well-known Egyptian designation for Minoan Crete. The other is Tanaju. From its position in the list (after Keftiu), one could argue that Tanaju must have been situated beyond, i.e. north of,

106. Cf. Helck 1979 [rev.1995], 24, esp. note 27 with references.

107. The integral publication of the text is provided in Edel 1966. Discussions in Helck 1992; 1995; Cline 1987; 1994; 1998. See below for extensive discussion.

108. Edel 1966, 8–9.

109. "Great Green" is generally regarded as the Egyptian term for the Mediterranean Sea. Cf. Nicholson / Shaw 1995, but see Duhoux 2003 for a different interpretation.

Keftiu.[110] This is proven in the second row of geographical names, which includes such centers as Mycenae and Nauplion. Although some of the names in the Kom el Hetan text remain unidentified,[111] there can be no doubt that Tanaju lay in the Aegean and, more specifically, comprised much of the Peloponnese. Moreover, the identification of Mycenae and Nauplion has gone unopposed, whereas the inclusion of Kythera, Messenia (whether as a region or as a center), and the Thebaid appears more likely than not.[112]

Tanaju is referred to in several contemporary and later texts, but these generally are regarded as copies of geographical lists like the one mentioned above, originally dating to the reign of Amenhotep III. After Amenhotep III,[113] Tanaju in effect disappears from the Egyptian record and textual references to the Aegean in general disappear.[114]

---

110. Cf. Cline 1998.

111. Although it has been proposed that *Tnj* refers to a region in northern Syria/Cilicia (cf. Edel 1975, 63 ff.), the identification of various Mycenaean centers and regions in the list strongly indicates that *Tnj* should be sought in the Aegean (see Haider 1988b, 8 ff. for extensive evaluation of the arguments). The fact that, according to the Annals of Thutmoses III, messengers from Tanaju brought a vessel in Keftiu style may strengthen an Aegean identification of Tanaju.

Edel (1966) proposed the following identification for these names: Amnisos, Phaistos, Kydonia, Mycenae, Messenia, Nauplia(?), Kythera, Ilios(?), Knossos, Amnisos, and Lyktos. The enigmatic *dq's* (di-qa-ê-s) has been identified by some as Tegea, by others as the upper Helisson valley, by Helck (1992, 13) as Διπαιεις, and by Edel (1988, 30) as the Thebaid. Edel's identification seems to be generally accepted. The identification of Ilios with *wi-'i_4-li-ja*, however, is not (Helck 1995, 25–26). *Wi-'i_4-li-ja* has been identified also as Aulis (Goedicke 1969, 10)—which, if correct, would fit nicely with Edel's identification of *dq's* (as Aulis supposedly was the principal harbor of Thebes)—and more recently as Elis (Latacz 2001b, 163). The identifications of Amnisos, Kydonia, Mycenae, Messenia, Kythera, and Lyktos are generally accepted (cf. Haider 1988b, 9).

112. For the most recent discussion, see Latacz 2001b, 163 ff.

113. Cf. Edel 1980, 63–73. Discussion in Cline 1998.

114. With the possible exception of a number of Sea Peoples (*ca.* 1200 BC), such as the Ekwesh > Ahhiyawa, and Denyen > Tanaju (compare to the biblical tribe of Dan). Cf. Woudhuizen 2006 with references.

Let us consider the consequences of the Egyptian texts for the present subject. Although any reference to Hittite Ahhiyawa is absent in the Egyptian record, the Greek mainland certainly was not uncharted territory for the Egyptians. Analogies with other parts of the Kom el Hetan texts, referring to regions whose political structures are known, as well as the fact that gifts from Tanaju in the Annals of Thutmoses III are listed alongside gifts from other independent states—Hatti, Babylon, Assyria, "Assija" (=Aššuwa?), and Alalakh—indicate that Tanaju was an independent state, not merely a vaguely known region. The evidence from the Kom el Hetan text and the Annals of Thutmoses III, in short, indicates that the Egyptians, from the reign of Thutmoses III onward, perceived Tanaju as an Aegean kingdom, encompassing (at least during the reign of Amenhotep III) significant parts of mainland Greece, including the Argive plain, Messenia, Kythera, probably the Thebaid, and possibly Elis in the northwest of the Peloponnese. It appears likely that the ruler of this kingdom resided at one of the two centers mentioned in the Kom el Hetan text: Nauplion or Mycenae (as these are the only two centers—as opposed to regions—mentioned in that text). As shall be argued below, the archaeological record suggests that it was the latter center, though the evidence is, admittedly, somewhat patchy.

It should also be stressed that the Kom el Hetan text, if we accept Edel's identification of *dq's* as the Thebaid, suggests that eastern Boeotia was part of the kingdom of Tanaju, at least during the reign of Amenhotep III. The consequences are far-reaching, if only because, with Tanaju encompassing most of the Greek mainland, this severely limits our options in locating the kingdom of Ahhiyawa known from the Hittite texts. We will try to resolve this problem through archaeological data, as the textual evidence presented above clearly is insufficient in this respect.

ICONOGRAPHY

Before turning to the archaeological evidence, there are three pieces of evidence that are valuable to the current research, but fall somewhat in between the textual and archaeological sets of data. These are a Hittite incised potsherd from the Hittite capital Hattuša, papyrus fragments from El Amarna, and the wall paintings from the tomb of Queen Nefertari, "Great Wife" of Ramesses II.[115] The potsherd from Hattuša is of importance because it adds to our understanding of the bellicose Ahhiyawan-Hittite relations, while the other two artefacts suggest contacts between Egypt and the Mycenaean world other than trade.

The potsherd from Hattuša dates to ca. 1400 BC, i.e. the time of the clash between Attariššija and the Hittite forces. What appears to be a Mycenaean warrior carrying a sword and covered with elaborately decorated body armor is incised on its outer surface.[116] He is wearing a plumed helmet with horns, which finds its closest parallel in the helmets of a group of warriors on the (LH IIIC) warrior vase from Mycenae. Thus this incised artwork seems to be a Hittite expression of the earliest Mycenaean military incursions into Anatolia.

Depictions of Mycenaean warriors may have been found also in Egypt, on a number of papyrus fragments. These fragments were found in December 1936 by John Pendlebury, in a house (R43.2) on the eastern edge of the Central City at El Amarna, in association with (the remains of) a wooden shrine, various cultic items, a complete Mycenaean vase, and an inscription mentioning "the great statue that the king caused to be made."[117] It is likely that the building served as a chapel for the divine king (Amenhotep III or Akhenaten) and that the artefacts found inside the building played some role in that context.

Although the papyrus survives only in fragments, it appears to have been a purely pictorial papyrus, depicting a battle between Egyptians and Libyan warriors. Coming to the aid of the Egyptians are a number of warriors who, while wearing typical Egyptian white kilts, are equipped with helmets and various types of what may plausibly be argued to be leather armor. Both the helmets and the two identifiable types of armor are unique in the Egyptian iconographical record, and, therefore,

---

115. See Illustrations 1 to 4.

116. Bittel 1976, 9–14.

117. Pendlebury 1951, 140–41; Parkinson / Schofield 1994, 159–60.

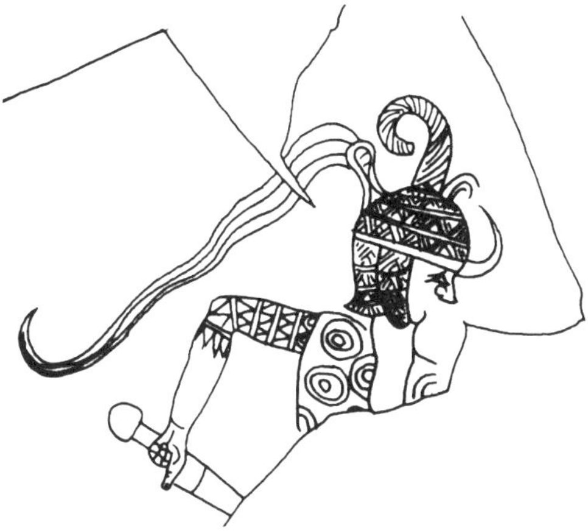

Illustration 1: A Mycenaean warrior incised on a vessel from the Hittite capital Hattuša

Illustration 2: Queen Nefertari as depicted on the walls of her tomb

She wears Aegean-style earrings, parallels of which are found at several sites on the Greek mainland, especially at Mycenae. The earrings are colored white, indicating silver. The queen is shown four times with this type of earring.

Illustration 3

Illustration 4

Illustration 3, a detail of a papyrus fragment from Amarna, possibly showing a Mycenaean warrior (courtesy Trustees of the British Museum). The helmets find their closest parallel in the boar-tusk helmet from a tomb at Dendra (near Midea) shown in Illustration 4, but also compare to the helmet shown in Illustration 1.

seem to identify a people other than those usually depicted in Egyptian paintings. It has been forcefully argued that the helmets depicted on the papyrus should be identified as boar-tusk helmets and that the armor worn by the warriors has close parallels with known Aegean types of armor. Thus the warriors depicted on the papyrus most likely represent Mycenaeans, apparently in the service of the pharaoh.[118] This identification is strengthened by the find of a piece of boar tusk, with perforations for attaching it to a leather frame, during excavations at Qantir, the site of the Ramesside capital Pi-ramesse in the eastern delta. It is likely that this piece was part of the famous boar-tusk helmets worn by the Mycenaean elite.[119] Moreover, the recent find of a metal lamella (from a suit of scale-armor) on the Greek island of Salamis, bearing the cartouche of Ramesses II, adds further weight to the possibility that Mycenaeans served in the Egyptian military. The thought of foreigners in the Egyptian military is not wholly hypothetical. For example, Egyptian kings from the Middle Kingdom onward used Nubian archers in their armies and during Ramesside times defeated Sea Peoples were incorporated into the Egyptian army.[120]

More circumstantial, but worthwhile mentioning here, is the observation that Aegean (Mycenaean) jewelry figures prominently in the wall paintings of Queen Nefertari's tomb in the Valley of the Queens. It has been proposed that the four sets of silver earrings worn by the queen may have been part of a greeting gift from the Aegean, presented to the queen on the occasion of her husband's coronation.[121] The lack of textual evidence obviously weakens this hypothesis, but four sets of finely crafted, silver earrings seem too extraordinary to have arrived at the Egyptian court other than via diplomatic missions. Aegean objects are present in the Egyptian iconographical record on various other occasions, but never with any evidence of a diplomatic connotation.

---

118. Schofield / Parkinson 1994, 157–70; Schofield / Parkinson 1995, 125.

119. Pusch 1985, 254.

120. Note in this respect the identification of two Minoans as fan-bearers on a relief from Amarna (cf. Kozloff 1977, 101–3; Haider 1996, 146, fig. 7), while it has been argued by Haider (1990, 19–22; 1996, 144–45) that Minoan shipwrights lived at Peru-nefer (long thought to have been the harbor town of Memphis, but recently identified as the harbor of Avaris [cf. Bietak 2005, 17]).

121. Koehl 1999, 424.

THE MYCENAEAN WORLD ACCORDING TO THE TEXTS

An understanding of the Mycenaean world based on the Linear B texts is wanting and fraught with problems. Most prominent among these is the absence of any reference to large, dependent centers. Miletus is mentioned several times, but nowhere is it reported to be under the sway of any of the known palaces, yet the Hittite texts demonstrate that it was controlled by the king of Ahhiyawa. Similarly, the absence of any Linear B document other than purely administrative texts is of concern, considering that the Hittite texts indicate that at least one Mycenaean king "wrote" not only to his attaché in Miletus, but also to the Hittite king himself.[122]

Moreover, the Hittite texts clearly indicate that Ahhiyawa was a threat that had to be reckoned with. It is difficult to see how any of the Mycenaean palatial states, individually, could have been responsible for Ahhiyawan actions in Anatolia over the course of some 200 years. Even though the Hittite texts may represent small snapshots of a particular period in time, they suggest a more or less continuous Ahhiyawan presence (and pressure) in fourteenth and thirteenth-century western Anatolia. Contemporary to this, several Mycenaean palaces suffered setbacks (even though, in the long run, most of the palaces during the fourteenth to mid-thirteenth century would gain rather than lose importance). Thus, equating Ahhiyawa with one specific palatial state is problematic: the continuous and increasing military pressure on Hittite western Anatolia by the Ahhiyawans seems entirely at odds with the often volatile domestic situation in many of the Mycenaean palaces. Simplistically: a burning palace seems an unlikely candidate as the seat of Ahhiyawan power.

Even without the attribution of the title Great King to the king of Ahhiyawa, we would have had reasons to doubt whether Ahhiyawa could be equated with a single palatial state. The fact that Hattušili III acknowledged Ahhiyawan might in considering the king of Ahhiyawa his equal, forces us to accept that Ahhiyawa must have had military and territorial proportions that exceeded those of even the largest Mycenaean kingdoms reconstructed on the grounds of the Linear B texts. It follows that Ahhiyawa must have been a conglomerate of several of these kingdoms.

---

122. See Koehl 1999, 32, esp. note 95.

This does not force us to totally abandon the social or territorial composition of the Mycenaean kingdoms as they appear in the Linear B texts. To the Hittites, a Great King was originally no more than a king who ruled over other kings.[123] The title did not specify the level of authority involved and, indeed, most of the Hittite vassal rulers appear to have been members of an indigenous royal house that had retained most of its former powers. In the case of the Hittites, at least, vassals usually only had obligations to aid their overlord in battle (supplying troops and assisting the Great King personally), were required to send tribute, and were restricted in their outward communication.[124] If we implement such a scenario in the Aegean, it would not be at all surprising to find scarce reference to other political entities in the Linear B texts. Indeed, there are only few references to other palatial centers in the respective palace archives.

It has already been noted that our understanding of the position and function of the *wanax* and the *lawagetas* (the only two officials in the Mycenaean palatial states active within virtually every aspect of Mycenaean society) is extremely limited. On the whole, considering his unsurpassed possessions in land and the fact that only the *wanax* is demonstrably acting (namely appointing an official), it seems reasonable to consider him the head of state. But, with the above scenario in mind, which state? Was the *wanax* the independent king of Pylos or could we, perhaps, identify him as the overlord, in which case the *lawagetas* (who seems to have been active in many of the same aspects of society as the *wanax*, but whose property, and therefore status?, was smaller) could be identified as the local vassal king? These questions appear difficult to address on the basis of our current evidence. As a result, it seems that we must content ourselves with the possibility, and no more than that, that the Mycenaean equivalent for Great King may have been the *wanax*, whereas each of his vassals may have been designated as *lawagetas* (Illustration 5).

While the presence of this great kingdom in the Aegean can be deduced from the Hittite texts, the Egyptian texts are even more explicit. That Tanaju was headed by one king is indicated in the Annals of Thutmoses III, and its territory, according to the Kom el Hetan text,

---

123. Otten 1951, 35–43; Bryce 1998, 37.

124. Bryce 2003b, 42–43.

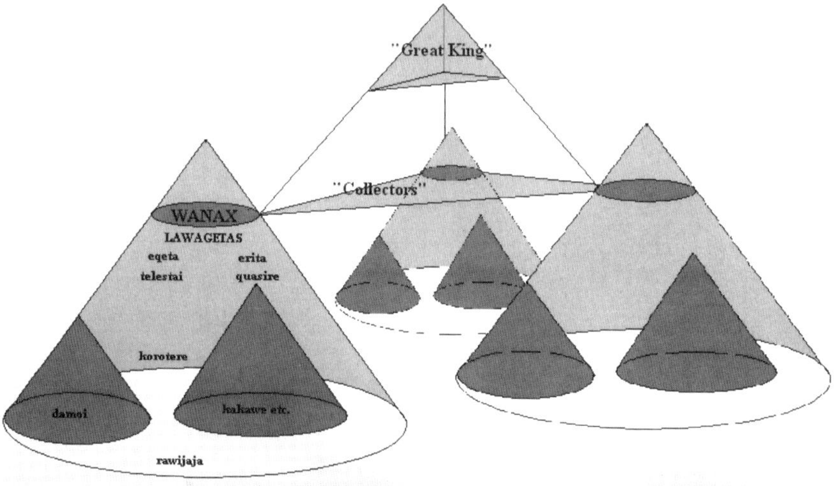

Illustration 5: The Mycenaean Social Pyramid

(adapted from Kilian 1988a)

In essence, various similar kingdoms function with their own administration, yet are subject to one Great King (himself ruling his own "core" kingdom in the same way as his vassal rulers). This Great King may have exercised control via "collectors" (high officials collecting tribute and, probably, dividing prestige gifts amongst the king's followers).

comprised the larger part of mainland Greece. Moreover, the same text strongly suggests that the core territory, the heartland of Tanaju, should be sought in the Argolid, around the centers of Mycenae and Nauplion (as these are mentioned first and are the only centers mentioned, as opposed to the regions that follow). Tanaju appears only for a relatively short period in Egyptian sources: from *ca.* 1437 BC (the 42nd regnal year of Thutmoses III) until, at the latest, *ca.* 1352 BC (the death of Amenhotep III). I have already noted that, since Tanaju covers the largest part of the map of mainland Greece, we are essentially left with two options: equate Tanaju with Ahhiyawa or look for Ahhiyawa elsewhere, on the isles or in the north of Greece. The fact that the Mycenaean kingdom Tanaju appears in Egyptian texts around the time of the first Ahhiyawan incursions into western Anatolia may suggest that the two were, in fact, one and the same.[125]

125. Tnj, Tanaju, has been equated with the ethnicon Danaoi, the name of one

Regardless of these details, the Mycenaean world bursts into the archaeological record from the early-fourteenth century BC onward, with large quantities of Mycenaean pottery reaching western Anatolia, Cyprus, the Levant, and, to a lesser extent, Egypt. The mechanisms behind the importation of these vessels almost certainly differed by region and through time.[126] Indeed, it is thought that some of these imported goods (especially those found in Egypt) should be considered in the light of diplomatic gift exchange, while other concentrations of Mycenaean artefacts (particularly those found on the coast of western Anatolia) have been interpreted as markers of Mycenaean territorial expansion.

Both of these proposed interpretations—the presence of artefacts as evidence for diplomatic gift exchange or territorial expansion—could potentially have important implications for this study and should, therefore, be reviewed on the basis of the latest (published) finds. The following pages are devoted to the evidence of Mycenaean activity in western Anatolia and Egypt.

---

of the legendary royal families in the Argolid, which came to be used as a designation for the troops under the command of Agamemnon in the Iliad (Helck 1995, 24; Latacz 2001b, 166).

126. See for discussions Crielaard e.a. 1999; van Wijngaarden 1999; 2001; 2002; Leonard Jr. 1994.

— THE ARCHAEOLOGICAL EVIDENCE —

MYCENAEAN ARTEFACTS ON THE ANATOLIAN WEST COAST

There is an archaeologically attested Mycenaean presence only in a handful of sites on the Anatolian west coast.[127] Although Mycenaean pots appear in numerous sites throughout the region, at most of those sites their number is limited and by no means sufficient to argue for anything more than trading contact. At some sites, however, Mycenaean imports—not only pottery vessels but also figurines, as well as the presence of various features that are normally connected to Mycenaean settlement (such as Mycenaean style kilns, tombs, and fortifications)—are so numerous that actual Mycenaean presence has been proposed. At least in some instances, the introduction of these Mycenaean features appears to have been quite rapid and large-scale, which has led to the suggestion that Mycenaean settlement at those sites may have been coordinated by (the rulers of one of) the larger Mycenaean centers on the Greek mainland. This is especially the case at Miletus.

---

127. The first to present a comprehensive study of Mycenaean artefacts in western Anatolia was Christopher Mee in his *Aegean Trade and Settlement in Anatolia in the Second Millennium* BC (Mee 1978, 121–55). While heavily drawing upon Mellink's successive reviews of the state of Anatolian archaeology (Mellink 1966 and later publications in the same series), Mee presented a division of Anatolia into six geographical regions (the area north of the Gediz / Hermus ("northwest Anatolia"), the area between the Büyük Menderes (Maeander) and the Gediz ("western Anatolia"), the region south of the Maeander ("southwest Anatolia"), the "south coast

This suggestion of "palatial colonization" of the western Anatolian coast calls for a close examination of the archaeological record in western Anatolia. It was precisely this region where, according to the Hittite texts, Ahhiyawan and Hittite interests and armies clashed and where there appears to be an opportunity to compare archaeological data with information from contemporary sources. Therefore, our focus is upon Mycenaean artefacts dated to the palatial period, i.e. LH II to LH IIIB2.[128]

The Hittite texts indicate Ahhiyawan activity, especially in the Arzawa lands, from *ca.* 1400 to 1220 BC. According to these texts, it appears that Ahhiyawan incursions remained confined to the coastal

---

with the lakes" ("Cilicia" and "Central Anatolia"), of which, in particular, the first three regions were prone to Mycenaean influence during the palatial period. Cilicia has yielded several sites with Mycenaean pottery, including Mersin, Kazanli, and Tarsus. Sporadic contact must have occurred during LH IIA to IIIB, but it is during LH IIIC that a dramatic increase in imports can be observed. The pottery of this period seems related to Mycenaean pottery made in Cyprus and some Mycenaean settlement in the area seems likely. No Mycenaean pottery has been found in Central Anatolia with the notable exception at Mašat. There, Pottery was found in association with spindle flasks and libation vessels, indicating that the Mycenaean imports could have arrived in a Levantine-Cypriote context (Mellink 1981, 470). See Mee 1978 for discussion and further references. Two centers on the Anatolian west coast stood out already at the time of Mee's research: Troy (Hissarlık) near the Bosporus and Miletus in the southwest had yielded considerable amounts of Mycenaean artefacts, especially pottery. Since Mee's study, the corpus of Mycenaean finds, not only at Troy and Miletus, but also at other sites, has grown. Despite that, these two sites still stand out as the largest concentrations of Mycenaean ware on Anatolian soil and although extensive Mycenaean settlement at Troy is still far from proven, it is now beyond doubt that the northwestern coastal region of Anatolia, culturally speaking, belonged to the Aegean just as much as to Anatolia (the so-called East Aegean, West Anatolian Interface; cf. Mountjoy 1998, 33–67), which, if anything, indicates at least frequent contacts between bearers of the Mycenaean culture (as it manifested itself in especially the Dodecanese) and bearers of (west) Anatolian culture. The sites in the catalogue (Appendix 1) are shown on Map 5.

128. Earlier and later material are listed in the catalogue (see Appendix 1) for the sake of completeness, but is of limited relevance to this study. Also, I will not deal with the material from the islands in the Aegean, as their political situation is not revealed by the Hittite texts (though "islands" are occasionally referred to).

Map 5: Mycenaean Finds in Western Anatolia
(from C. Mee, "Aegean Trade and Settlement in Anatolia," *Anatolian Studies* 28, 1978, 121–56)

regions of western Anatolia; there is no indication of deeper penetration by Ahhiyawan armies toward central Anatolia. Ahhiyawan activity was almost certainly largely sea borne and Millawanda/Miletus was, without doubt, the Ahhiyawan foothold in Anatolia.[129]

Archaeology confirms Miletus' position as an important Mycenaean center on Anatolian soil, yielding a vast array of Mycenaean features and artefacts, including kilns, houses, figurines, and pottery. There are several other sites on the shores of western Anatolian where Mycenaean settlement is suspected, especially at Müsgebi and perhaps at Clazomenae. On the whole, however, Mycenaean artefacts, if present at all, represent a minority of the total corpus of finds in western Anatolia.

It appears that a variety of sites on the Anatolian west coast received Mycenaean artefacts from circa LH II (fifteenth century BC) until well into LH IIIC (twelfth century BC). Of course, the archaeological record is not without problems; many sites have been only partially excavated, looted, or have suffered erosion. These problems notwithstanding, the present archaeological evidence suggests that the spread of Mycenaean artefacts in western Anatolia was most extensive during LH IIIA2 and especially LH IIIB1. During this period, *ca.* 1375–1230 BC, Mycenaean objects appear at well over a dozen sites throughout the region. The finds are mainly comprised of pottery, but at some sites the range of artefacts is wider, including figurines and metal objects.

The sites Troy, Ephesus (region), Miletus, and Müsgebi stand out for their quantity and variety of Mycenaean objects and for the time span of Mycenaean import. However, we will not deal with Müsgebi directly, as its Bronze Age name is unknown and, consequently, a synthesis of archaeology and texts cannot be made. The three other sites will be presented in a roughly chronological order, that is "in order of appearance" in the Hittite texts regarding Ahhiyawan activity. As noted above, the first Ahhiyawan activity in western Anatolia attested in the texts is dated *ca.*1400 BC, with the incursions of Attariššija into western Anatolia, in the land of Zippasla (the original realm of Madduwatta).[130]

It is around that time that Miletus became fully "Mycenaeanized," at least in terms of material culture, with domestic architecture, metal kilns, and a wide range of objects with clear Mycenaean parallels. The sudden Mycenaean dominance over what previously was a Minoan

129. See Map 6 for Ahhiyawan incursions into the relevant area.

130. Madd. §8, obv. 42–48; cf. Beckman 1996, 146 ff.

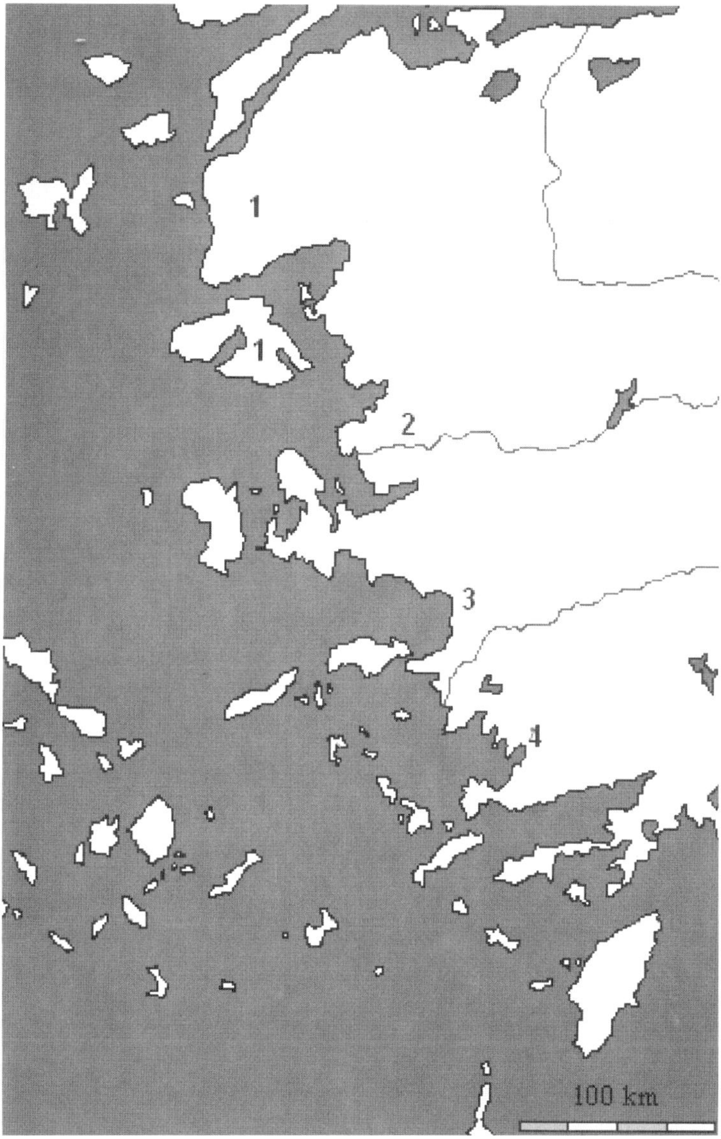

Map 6: Ahhiyawan Activity in Western Anatolia

1. raids of Piyamaradu in Wiluša and Lesbos ca. 1260 BC.
2. Legendary incursion of Achilles in the Caicus region.
3. Ahhiyawan support of Tarhunderadu.
4. Piyamaradu and Tawagalawa in Millawanda.

(copyright Daniel Dalet)

colony has been explained to be the result of a Mycenaean takeover organized by the palaces of the Greek mainland, i.e. the implantation of mainland Mycenaeans into a Minoan center.[131] Indeed, the years prior to the "Mycenaeanization" of Miletus are characterized by a steady increase of Mycenaean features on the isles in the Aegean, many of which previously were Minoan colonies or trading posts. Whatever the case, there is no indication that the step from Minoan to Mycenaean at Miletus was a violent one; there are no destructions, no trace that the Mycenaeans actually invaded the center with military force.[132]

Although the first Mycenaeans at Miletus may have settled peacefully, according to the Hittite text Attariššija's raids in western Anatolia appear to run parallel with the archaeological picture of increased Mycenaean presence on the Anatolian west coast during the LH IIB phase. The Mycenaean warrior depicted on a potsherd in Hattuša (see above) points in a similar direction: the final years of the fifteenth century BC marked the advent of the Mycenaeans in Anatolia.

From the scanty sources arises a picture of Ahhiyawan raids and, initially, only limited settlement in western Anatolia. Attariššija is reported to have raided the lands of Madduwatta with some one hundred chariots and a number of infantry (the text is destroyed at that point), but, in the end, he retreated to his own land, Ahhija. The sherd from Hattuša stresses the military character of the first Ahhiyawan incursions. It is likely that the Mycenaeans around this time were raiding the coast of Anatolia in much the same way the Vikings were to raid the coastal regions of Northern Europe in early Medieval times: small-scale, seaborne attacks on preferably weak but rich targets, and a quick retreat before stronger foes came to meet in battle. Actual settlement in the affected regions was originally limited.[133] The same seems to hold for the first Mycenaean activity in Anatolia. Miletus appears to have been

131. Niemeier 2002, 296; 1998, 29–30; Mountjoy 1998, 34 ff. on the spread of Mycenaean culture on the isles.

132. In fact, the first Mycenaean stratum at Miletus still shows a host of Minoan features, including Minoan houses and kilns, which leads to the impression that the original Minoan inhabitants did not leave the settlement, but stayed to live side by side with the Mycenaean newcomers. Cf. Niemeier 1998, 31; Mee 1978, 135.

133. Cf. Turchin 2006 for a discussion on Viking incursions into Frankish Europe.

the only Mycenaean settlement on Anatolian soil during LH IIB, although small quantities of Mycenaean pottery appear at some other sites as well.

Presumably, as with the Vikings, small-scale raids over time increased in frequency and in scale, until, at some point, the raids became true invasions, with permanent settlement in the conquered territories. From *ca.* 1400 BC onward, Mycenaean objects increasingly found their way to sites in western Anatolia: at Miletus Mycenaean culture almost completely supplants the last Minoan traits, while elsewhere Mycenaean pots reach Anatolian centers in ever greater quantities.[134]

In particular, the region around Ephesus received a good variety of Mycenaean artefacts by LH IIIA1. Over the course of the fourteenth century BC, the corpus of Mycenaean artefacts at Ephesus came to include open- and closed-shaped pottery and various types of figurines, including relatively large specimens such as the head resembling the Lord of Asine. Indeed, the variety of Mycenaean artefacts in the region of Bronze Age Ephesus has given rise not only to the suggestion that the center was home to Mycenaean residents, possibly even with their own sanctuary, but also to the theory that Mycenaeans exercised significant control over Arzawan politics.[135] The variety of Mycenaean objects, including the LH IIIA1 rhyton and various figurines, indeed argues for at least some degree of Mycenaean ritual life in the area. And although Mycenaean interference in Arzawan politics cannot be proved by archaeological evidence, a Hittite text does argue for Ahhiyawan interest in the fortunes of the Arzawan kingdom, referring to Ahhiyawan support for the king of Arzawa, Uhhaziti, against the Hittite invasion of Muršili II.[136]

Mycenaean artefacts in the Ephesus area occur only during LH IIIA1 and LH IIIA2, in other words, most of the fourteenth century BC.[137] After LH IIIA2, Mycenaean material is absent from the region,

---

134. See Table 3.

135. Cf. Bammer 1990, 142 for a Mycenaean sanctuary at Ephesus; Schachermeyr 1986, 21; Bammer 1986/1987, 21 for Mycenaean political influence in Arzawa.

136. Cf. KUB XIV 15 I, ll. 23–26 (*supra*).

137. LH IIIA2 is now thought to have lasted until the very end of the fourteenth century BC. Cf. Hope Simpson 2003, 205.

only to return in the post palatial, LH IIIC, period (although there may be some LH IIIB-C material at Kolophon). This may be significant, as LH IIIA1 and LH IIIA2 fall exactly in the period of Arzawan independence, whereas LH IIIB coincides with the period of Hittite dominance over the kingdom. As a result, Mycenaean artefacts appear to have found their way to Apaša exclusively during the years of independence. After the collapse of Arzawa under the Hittite onslaught, Mycenaean objects would not appear at Apaša for over almost a century, until the closing years of the Bronze Age, yet the center remained inhabited. The absence of LH IIIB material is all the more notable elsewhere in Anatolia. LH IIIB1 appears to have seen the pinnacle of the spread of Mycenaean artefacts, as, for that matter, is the case elsewhere in the entire Eastern Mediterranean.[138]

Whereas Mycenaean artefacts, mostly pottery, occur with increasing frequency along the shores of western Anatolia during LH IIIA2 and especially LH IIIB1, the material occurs rarely at inland sites.[139] The confinement of Mycenaean artefacts to the coastal regions seems to reflect the scope of Ahhiyawan military actions around the same time. Both Tawagalawa and Piyamaradu, active during the first half of the thirteenth century BC, appear to have been active on the coast of western Anatolia only; there is not a single reference to any Ahhiyawan incursion into the Anatolian hinterland.[140]

It has been proposed that the adoption and subsequent adaptation of the Mycenaean style in the pottery production at western Anatolian centers, effectively beginning during LH IIIB1 and flourishing in LH IIIC as the East Aegean, West Anatolian pottery koinè, was related to the dissolution of the kingdom of Arzawa.[141] The collapse of that kingdom would have created a vacuum in western Anatolia that could not be filled by any of the Hittite vassal states carved out of the Arzawan territories, which would have facilitated increased Ahhiyawan control over the region. Although Penelope Mountjoy points out that "pottery

---

138. See Table 3; for Egypt, see below.

139. Cf. Mee 1978.

140. This is in marked contrast to Hittite references to Arzawan incursions threatening the heartland of Hatti itself. See especially the "Deeds of Šuppiluliuma" (CTH 40); cf. Hoffner 1997, 185ff.; Güterbock 1956.

141. Mountjoy 1998, 51.

is not a political indicator," her suggestion that the rise of the East Aegean, West Anatolia pottery koinè is related to the increase of Ahhiyawan power (and wealth) basically implies the opposite.[142] Moreover, there appears to be no solid textual evidence that Ahhiyawa grew increasingly powerful in western Anatolia, as Mountjoy seems to suggest. The impression from the Hittite texts that deal with Piyamaradu's exploits is that Ahhiyawan armies were roaming the Anatolian coastal regions in much the same way they had in the time of Attariššija: sea-borne raids, followed by quick retreat. Only the capture of Lesbos deviates from that "standard" paradigm; but Lesbos was an island, not a mainland entity prone to Hittite retaliation. It certainly is true that the king of Ahhiyawa was addressed as a Great King in the Tawagalawa letter, but then this was also the first (and only) letter directly addressed to any Ahhiyawan king and, consequently, the first time there was any need to specify Ahhiyawan status. Note in this respect that already in the "Indictment of Madduwatta" the king of Ahhija is specifically referred to as a being independent of Hatti, which is the basic prerequisite of Great Kingship.

Although Hittite-Ahhiyawan relations remained strained over the course of the thirteenth century BC, this certainly did not involve a permanent state of war. The Tawagalawa letter basically tells us that much and the absence of Ahhiyawa in a treaty between the Hittite crown and the king of Wiluša may suggest that, at least periodically, Ahhiyawa and Hatti were at peace with each other. It may be in this context of "volatile peace," rather than being a result of Ahhiyawan incursions, that we should consider the spread of Mycenaean pottery in western Anatolia.[143] Gradual diffusion of Mycenaean pottery and pottery styles in western Anatolia appears more likely to have been the result of trading encounters and, indeed, the sheer proximity of Mycenaean centers (such as Miletus, but also centers such as Seraglio on Kos and Ialysos on Rhodes) to the Anatolian entities, than the result of an occasional Ahhiyawan raid.

---

142. *Ibid.*, 50.

143. Although Bryce (2003a, 62) observed that anti-Hittite rebellions in western Anatolia would not have furthered trade, the spread of Mycenaean pottery in western Anatolia (and elsewhere) appears to have decreased only during LH IIIB2, a decline that cannot plausibly be connected to Ahhiyawan-Hittite conflicts (but rather to domestic issues in Ahhiyawa; note that the first major destructions in the Aegean fall within LH IIIB2).

If trade were responsible for the gradual diffusion of Mycenaean objects in Anatolia, one would then expect Anatolian objects, in turn, to occur in the Aegean. However, this is not the case. The fact that very few objects in the Aegean have been securely identified as Anatolian in origin presents a problem for the trade hypothesis. Elsewhere in the eastern Mediterranean, the thirteenth century BC certainly was a period of increased stability and, as a result, of increased prosperity through trade. It was the period during which the Hittite-Egyptian tensions over control over Syria were settled with a peace treaty (around 1258 BC) and when long-distance contacts flourished. To this testifies the abundance of imported goods all over the eastern Mediterranean, not only in western Anatolia (with increasing numbers of Mycenaean pottery), but also in the Levant, Cyprus, Egypt, and the Aegean, dating to this period. Yet Hittite objects are conspicuously rare, not only in western Anatolia, but also in the Aegean and even in Egypt. This is remarkable, as we know of direct diplomatic contact between Egypt and Hatti and between Hatti and Ahhiyawa. The only plausible explanations for the scarcity of Hittite artifacts outside Anatolia are, as far as I can see, that these objects either have not been recognized as such or were of a perishable nature.

As has been observed above, the diffusion of Mycenaean artefacts in western Anatolia and the scope of Ahhiyawan military activity ran parallel, but were not the result of each other. Both phenomena were confined to the fringes of actual Mycenaean settlement. The corpus of Mycenaean pottery at Troy may also be seen in this light; as a result of (trading) contacts with the nearby Mycenaean centers in Anatolia and on the islands in the Aegean. While Troy's exact importance to the Mycenaeans is unclear,[144] Mycenaean pottery appears at Troy from LH IIA onward, well into LH IIIC, suggesting contacts between Troy and

144. Korfmann (2001c, 355 ff.) suggested Troy was a vital chain in (Aegean) trade with the Black Sea area, but conclusive evidence for extensive contact between that area and any region in the LBA Mediterranean is lacking (cf. Easton / Hawkins / Sherratt / Sherratt 2002, esp.101–6; but see Hertel / Kolb 2003, 73 ff.). Mee (1978, 148) suggested that Troy was important as a harbor for yearly fishing expeditions, but evidence for this is lacking. For our purposes, it suffices to note that the size and the "monumentality" of the Trojan citadel, as well as the wealth displayed in the artefacts found at the site, indicate that Troy was an important regional center and therefore an interesting port of trade (and potentially, a target for raids).

the Mycenaean world from the fifteenth century onward. Troy certainly was part of the East Aegean, West Anatolian Interface koinè, as indicated by the abundance of locally produced Mycenaean-style pottery. Although the corpus of Mycenaean pottery at Troy does not suggest extensive Mycenaean settlement—one would expect a larger variety of Mycenaean objects and features—it does indicate Troy's acquaintance with the Mycenaean world. Though Hittite texts indicate that at least on one occasion Wiluša was invaded by Ahhiyawan forces,[145] the distribution of Mycenaean pottery appears unrelated to Piyamaradu's invasion of Wiluša.

It has been proposed that the limited diffusion of Mycenaean artefacts (especially pottery) toward the Anatolian hinterland was the result of a Hittite embargo. This concept has mainly been informed by the above-mentioned Šaušgamuwa treaty, in which the vassal king of Amurru is ordered not to let Ahhiyawan ships pass to Assyria.[146] However, as I noted above, there is little to suggest that the diffusion of Mycenaean pottery in western Anatolia was in any way hindered or furthered by Ahhiyawan or Hittite military or political enterprises; indeed, LH IIIB1, the time of Piyamaradu's raids in western Anatolia, witnessed the greatest spread of Mycenaean pottery throughout the very same region.

As military or political upheavals thus appear unrelated to the spread of Mycenaean objects, there must be another explanation for the dearth of Mycenaean pottery in central Anatolia. One such explanation is that Mycenaean pottery, especially such vessels as stirrup jars and amphorae, was deemed unfit for transport overland.[147] Indeed, this theory holds some attraction, as virtually all corpora of Mycenaean pottery throughout the Mediterranean are found in close proximity to the shores of either the sea or a major waterway.[148]

---

145. For the equation Wiluša = Troy, see Hawkins 1998; but see Heinhold-Krahmer (2003b) for criticism.

146. Cf. Cline 1998, 249 (*supra*).

147. Bryce 2003a, 61.

148. See Map 7. This certainly holds for Egypt, where all corpora have been found in the delta or along the Nile (although, admittedly, most Egyptian sites where clustered in the delta and Nile Valley anyway).

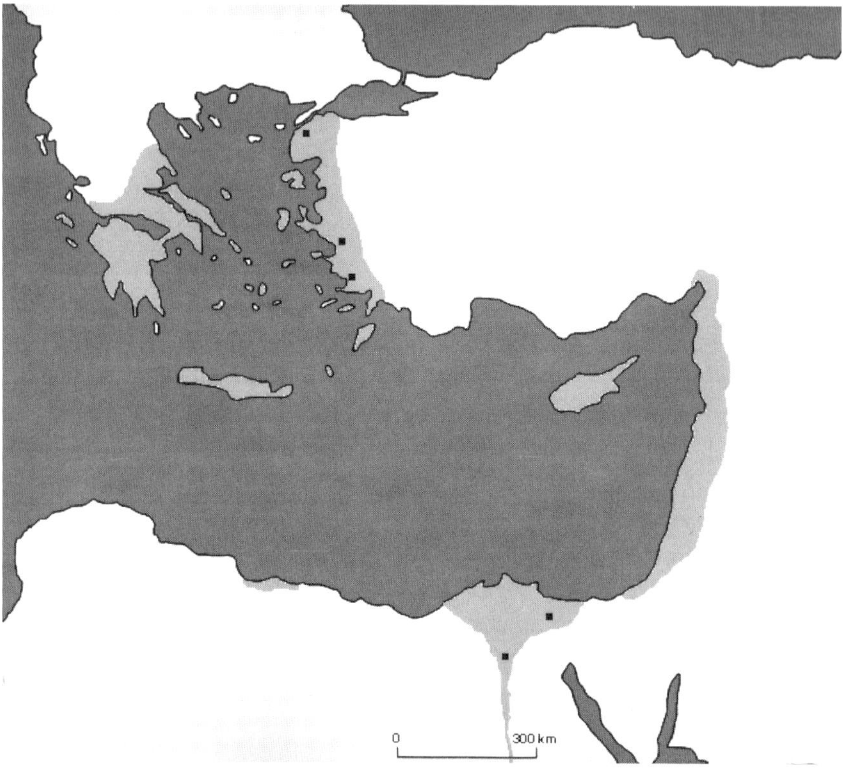

Map 7: The Eastern Mediterranean

The gray areas represent the regions where Mycenaean pottery has been found. The black squares represent the sites specifically investigated in the text; i.e. Troy, Ephesus, Miletus, Pi-ramesse, and Memphis.

(with the permission of Daniel Dalet)

AHHIYAWA IN WESTERN ANATOLIA

The archaeological data thus support the impression given in the Hittite texts of increased Mycenaean presence in Anatolia from the late fifteenth century BC onward. Archaeology indicates also that Miletus indeed was the only truly significant Mycenaean settlement in Anatolia, although small quantities of Mycenaean objects (mainly pottery) did find their way to the north, to the Arzawan lands and beyond. The fourteenth century may have seen some Mycenaean settlement in the region of Ephesus, at the same time of the *floruit* and subsequent collapse of the Arzawan kingdom with Apaša/Ephesus as its capital. The presence of, usually small, quantities of imported Mycenaean pottery at various sites in western Anatolia and especially the rise of the East Aegean, West Anatolian koinè in LH IIIB1 indicate the close relationship between western Anatolia and the Mycenaean world.

Whereas both the Hittite texts and the archaeological evidence indicate that only Miletus and its surroundings firmly fell under Ahhiyawan control, the rest of western Anatolia clearly belonged to a sphere of strong Mycenaean cultural influence. Although there is no evidence for Ahhiyawan control over it, the area occasionally fell victim to Ahhiyawan raids. The Tawagalawa letter suggests that at least one of the aims of these raids was the acquisition of labor, which may be reflected in various Linear B texts mentioning slaves of Anatolian origin.[159]

Western Anatolia appears to have been an unstable and fragmented region, ground between the colliding interests of Hatti and Ahhiyawa, much as the Levant appears to have been a conflict zone between Egypt, Mittani, and Hatti. As was the case in the Levant, the unstable political situation did not prevent trade from occurring, even flourishing. But unlike the Levant, equilibrium was never achieved in western Anatolia, where the situation remained unstable until the very end of the Bronze Age. Mycenaean pottery reached various sites in the region until the post-palatial period, but it appears to have been unrelated to the gains or losses of either Ahhiyawa or Hatti in the region.

The contacts between the Hittite court and the Ahhiyawan king, as evidenced by Hittite texts, must have involved the exchange of objects other than pottery. The exclamation of the Hittite king in the Tawagalawa letter that the messenger of the king of Ahhiyawa did not bring him

149. Cf. Ergin 2007 (forthcoming); Woudhuizen 2004–5.

any greeting gift indicates that the exchange of prestige objects was standard protocol.[150]

In conclusion, the distribution of Mycenaean objects throughout western Anatolia supports the picture from the Hittite texts of Ahhiyawan activity in the coastal region. It does not indicate where Ahhiyawa must be situated, although the prevalence of Argive wares among the imports at sites such as Müsgebi and Ialysos on Rhodes may suggest that we should look to Mycenae, but at the same time, only very few corpora of Mycenaean pottery in western Anatolia have been properly analyzed.

MYCENAEAN ARTEFACTS IN EGYPT

Contacts between Egypt and the Aegean are attested from the final Neolithic onward. Egyptian proto- and early-dynastic artefacts have been found at a variety of sites on Crete, whereas objects from the Cycladic islands and Crete have been found at various early-dynastic sites in Egypt.[151] Contacts between Egypt and the Greek mainland are attested only at a later stage, but during the Late Bronze Age Mycenaean objects clearly found their way to Egypt and Egyptian objects made their way the other direction. Despite the abundance of Mycenaean vessels at various sites throughout Egypt and the presence of a significant corpus of Egyptian artefacts at Mycenae, it has been argued that there never was any direct contact between the Greek mainland and Egypt during the Late Bronze Age and that objects from both lands arrived at their place of deposition via middlemen in the Levant and/or Cyprus.[152] Considering that no unequivocal evidence has been offered to support this hypothesis and that the two Egyptian texts cited above (i.e. the Annals of Thutmoses III and the Kom el Hetan text) strongly suggest that there was at least some direct diplomatic contact between the Mycenaean world, in this case the kingdom of Tanaju and the Egyptian court, I will not delve into the topic of trade and exchange mechanisms.[153] For the purpose of the current research, it suffices to

150. Taw. §5. 54–55. Cf. Sommer 1932, 5.

151. Cf. Karetsou 2000; Cline 1994; Pendlebury 1930.

152. Cf. Merrillees 1972, 180–81; 2003, 37; but see Podzuweit 1994, 468, esp. note 68, for criticism.

153. But see for a discussion of the relation between trade and diplomacy Cline 1995c, esp. 146, with references.

state that textual evidence suggests a near total monopoly of the state (i.e. the court) on the import of exotica, such as timber from the Lebanon and copper.[154] Apart from the proscribed limitations preventing unchecked exchange across Egyptian imperial borders, equipping a merchant ship, let alone a flotilla, was an affair so costly that one can hardly think of anyone except for high courtiers or the larger temples as being able to do so. As a consequence, it appears unlikely that ships, whether Egyptian or not, coming from abroad could dock in Egyptian harbors without the pharaoh's explicit consent; even trade between visiting foreigners and individual Egyptians is unlikely to have occurred more than occasionally und must have been of a very limited nature.[155] The distribution of the foreign goods brought by royal missions within Egypt was closely monitored by the palace: as soon as foreign goods reached Egyptian shores, they were taken and further distributed by the royal administration.[156]

---

154. Only during the Late Ramesside period are there indications that the royal monopoly gradually gave way to a more general accessibility to foreign markets. Especially temples, such as the temple of Amun (Thebes), appear to have acquired the right to send merchant flotillas to the Levant, even with a tax exemption. The wealth needed for carrying the costs of such expeditions was generated by the temples' extensive landholdings scattered throughout the empire and farmed on a complex rental basis, with up to 30 percent of the crop paid to the temple in rent. Cf. Bickel 1998, 166; for the latter, Kemp 1989, 191; Baer 1962, 25–45.

155. Cf. Hankey 1993, 110.

156. There is no point in dealing extensively with the Egyptian bureaucracy of the New Kingdom here, but in general, it appears that all goods were distributed to various major centers in the provinces, where they were stored, for example, at major temples dedicated to the cult of the divine king. Apart from luxury imports, this also included more mundane products, such as grain. Major storage facilities for the latter have been found at several royal mortuary temples, including the Ramesseum near the modern town of Luxor, in southern Egypt. It is calculated that the storage capacity of the Ramesseum alone would suffice to feed the population of a medium-sized city (cf. Kemp 1989). Temples such as the Ramesseum, or the nearby (and slightly later built) mortuary temple at Medinet Habu, served as local distribution points from where the salaries of the state's employees were paid. It is around the temple of Medinet Habu, for example, where the workmen from "the Village," now known as Deir el-Medina, gather in protest after the state's repeated failure to pay them their wages (in grain). This strike (the first attested strike in world history) is exemplary for

The distribution of Mycenaean artefacts throughout Egypt thus is irrelevant for the present aim of establishing whether there are grounds on the basis of the archaeological data to assume that messengers were indeed, as the texts suggest, sent across the Great Green of the Mediterranean. Instead, we should focus on anomalies: single, but especially groups of objects of extraordinary quality, homogeneity or function, or objects in extraordinary contexts. Unlike the case of (western) Anatolia, the Egyptian story goes two ways and, when possible, we will deal both with relevant Mycenaean objects in Egypt and with Egyptian objects on the Greek mainland.

The following discussion should not be understood as an attempt to characterize the typical relation between the Greek mainland and New Kingdom Egypt, but solely as an argument that there was direct, indeed directed, contact between the two lands, between the pharaoh and the king of Tanaju. To that purpose, focus is directed toward the corpora of Mycenaean pottery at El-Amarna (ancient Akhetaten), Deir el-Medina (the ancient Theban workmen's village), Mit Rahina and Saqqarah (ancient Memphis and its cemeteries), and Tell el Dab'a and Qantir (ancient Avaris / Pi-ramesse), as shown on Map 8.

In Support of Direct Contact

The theory that Mycenaean pottery, or at least some of it, found at Egyptian sites may indicate direct contact between Egypt and the Mycenaean Greek world is not a new one. Already during his excavation at El-Amarna, Petrie was struck by the quantity of Mycenaean sherds he found in the so-called Central City, a district where most of the state's institutions were housed during the reign of King Akhenaten. Petrie calculated that the sherds belonged to about 600 Mycenaean vessels, a significant number and, to this day, the largest corpus of Mycenaean pottery in Egypt.[157] During later excavations, Pendlebury found an additional number of Mycenaean sherds in various other districts of Akhetaten, including what is now known as the northern suburb, a residential area where Akhetaten's "middle class" lived.

---

the failure of the royal administration at the end of the New Kingdom. See especially Romer 1984.

157. Petrie 1894, 17. See Map 9 for an overview of El Amarna. See the next chapter for extensive discussion.

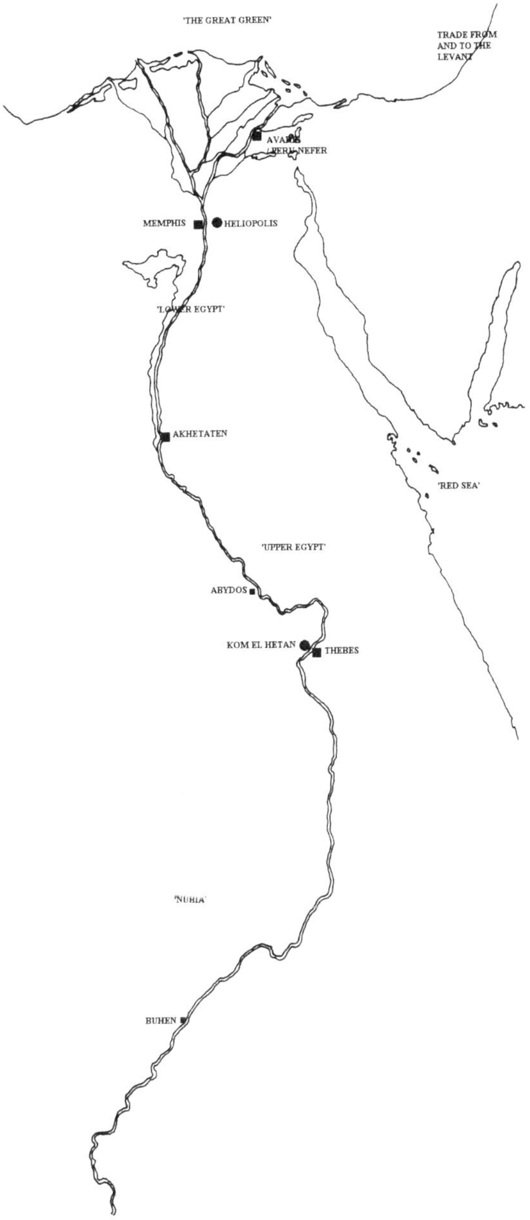

Map 8: New Kingdom Egypt

Big black blocks stand for capital centers; small blocks stand for significant provincial centers. Black dots represent sites where textual evidence referred to in the text has been found. Text between quotation marks designates geographical areas.

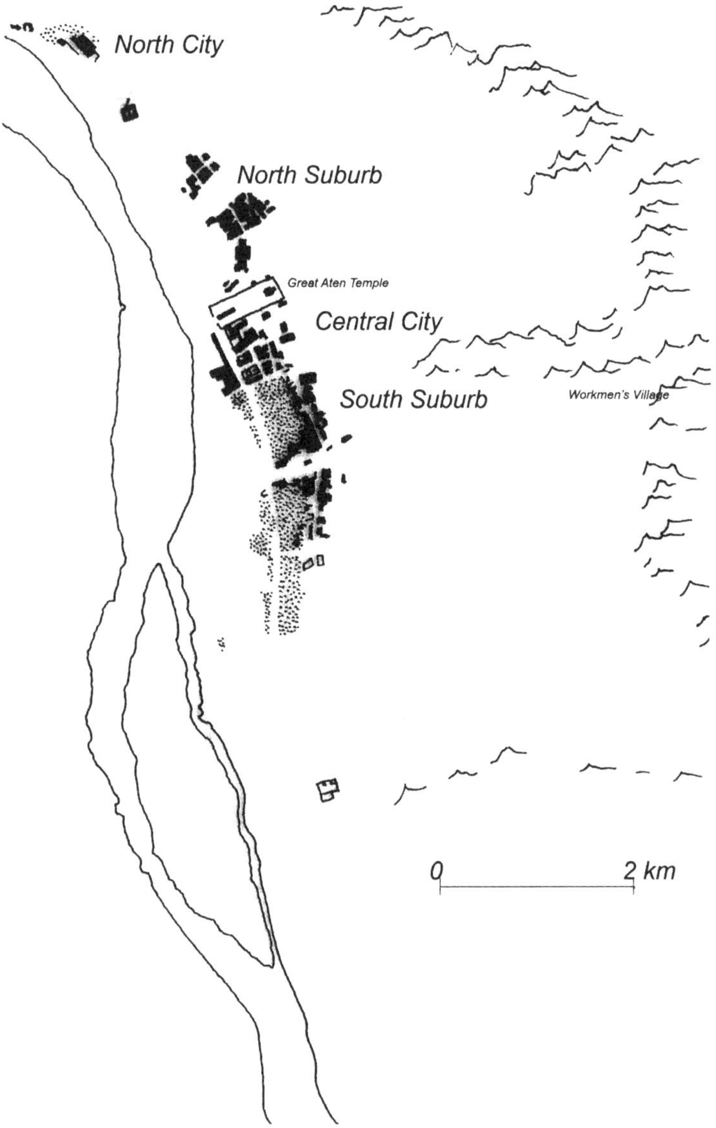

Map 9: The Site of El-Amarna

City boundaries were marked with boundary steles. The city itself fell apart in several quarters, connected by the "Royal Road." By far the largest structure in the capital was the great Aten temple, roughly opposite the remains of the royal palace.

This area yielded about 30 sherds, concentrated in and around a house in the western part of the district. The house, T.36.36, displayed a number of architectural features, such as what is described as a "light well," that were considered to be "Aegean" in origin. Although the number of Mycenaean sherds in the northern suburb in no way compared to the more than 1300 sherds that had been found in the Central City, Pendlebury dubbed the house in question "the house of the Mycenaean Greek" and the street facing it "Greek Street."[158] Although Pendlebury clearly believed that there were Mycenaean residents in Akhetaten, he did not substantiate this hypothesis nor did he explain how and why these Mycenaeans would have come to Akhenaten's royal city.

In *The Aegean Interest in El-Amarna*, Vronwy Hankey presented the first model explaining the presence of the exceptionally large quantity of Mycenaean pottery at El-Amarna.[159] According to Hankey's reconstruction of events, contact between Egypt and the Mycenaean world was initiated by King Amenhotep III (1390–1352 BC), the father and predecessor of Akhenaten (1352–1336 BC). Late during his reign, he sent an official mission to the north, including the Peloponnese. Upon reaching the Mycenaean port of Nauplion, Amenhotep's messengers travelled to the north, toward Mycenae, where they met the king of Tanaju. Here, they followed the Near Eastern practice of gift exchange, presenting the Mycenaean king with faience plaques, stamped on both sides with the king's royal cartouche. In return, the Mycenaean king not only allowed the Egyptians to travel through his realm, but also gave them a shipment of Mycenaean pottery, presumably containing perfumed olive oil. With this cargo, the Egyptian envoys embarked on their voyage home, only to hear upon their arrival that the king had died and that his son had moved the court from Thebes to the new city of Akhetaten. After leaving a description of their voyage at the dead king's mortuary temple at Kom el Hetan, they made their way to the new capital and delivered the Mycenaean vessels at the royal court.

Hankey's scenario has received criticism, but for the wrong reasons. Wachsmann's argument that the Kom el Hetan text is an Egyptian translation of a Minoan text and, therefore, does not reflect an Egyptian

158. Pendlebury 1933, 46.

159. Hankey 1981.

voyage is not sustained by any evidence. The importance of the recent assessment that we are probably dealing with as many as eleven faience plaques on the citadel of Mycenae can hardly be overstated. Plaques like these have not been found elsewhere outside Egypt nor, in fact, have they been found within Egypt itself. Various similar plaques (with cartouches on only one side) have, however, been found in Egypt, where they appear exclusively in a royal setting, within palace grounds or as temple deposits. Not only does this make the argument that these were just some wandering souvenirs extremely implausible, but it also strongly indicates some very special status for Mycenae.[160] Considering the extraordinary nature of the plaques, the burden of proof lies with those claiming that these plaques, and the contemporary Kom el Hetan text, do not reflect an Egyptian diplomatic mission to the Aegean.

Though an Egyptian mission to the Mycenaean world during the reign of Amenhotep III thus appears more likely than not, Hankey's notion that the vessels at Amarna are the result of that same mission appears unlikely. Not only is it extremely unlikely that the Egyptian envoys would not immediately have been informed upon their return in Egypt of the change of regime and thus would have sailed directly to the new capital Akhetaten, but on their very way toward Amenhotep III's palace at Thebes they would have actually passed the new capital and would have stopped there. There thus would be no reason to leave an account of their voyage in the temple of the deceased king. A connection between the mission under Amenhotep III and the Mycenaean vessels at Amarna thus cannot be supported. Consequently, the Amarna corpus must be understood in a different light.

Akhetaten: The Horizon of the Solar Disk[161]

The Amarna corpus comprises a relatively large number of Mycenaean sherds, estimated between 1500 and 2000 and thought to repre-

---

160. For criticism on the Hankey scenario, see Wachsmann 1987, 113. For a recent study of the faience plaques, see Phillips / Cline 2005, 327. It is noteworthy that the Mycenaeans appear to have been relatively "aware" of the plaques' cultural meaning in Egypt, since the deposition of one of the plaques (the context of the others is less clear) at the cult center, close to the palace, appears to reflect Egyptian practice.

161. See Table 4 for a complete list of the Mycenaean pottery found at that site published to date.

sent at least 600 whole pots. Hankey, in 1981, had noted that the corpus of Mycenaean pots at El Amarna was exceptional, both in size and homogeneity. The types of vessels present in the corpus are virtually all of closed shape, with pilgrim flasks and stirrup jars (Illustration 6) predominating. Compared to the then-known corpora in the Levant, the prevalence of closed shapes in the Amarna corpus was remarkable, since the Levantine corpora usually displayed a more diverse range of shapes, including open-shaped vessels (such as kylikes, rhyta, and kraters). However, more recent research elsewhere in Egypt has demonstrated that all corpora in Egypt are dominated by closed-shaped vessels (especially stirrup jars) and that the Amarna corpus, in this respect at least, does not stand out as much as had been previously thought.[162]

Illustration 6: A Mycenaean stirrup jar from Amarna
(in the collection of the University College Dublin)

162. Podzuweit 1994, 466.

The vast majority of Mycenaean pottery at El Amarna has been found in the waste heaps of the Central City, an area reserved for official appearances of the king and his followers and the center of the royal administration.[163] Though the exact use of these ceramics remains a matter of debate, it is clear that they were used in an official, royal context. The extremely limited occurrence of Mycenaean pottery elsewhere in the city stresses the fact that, at El Amarna at least, Mycenaean pottery was closely related to royal activity.[164]

Amarna does not represent the first Mycenaean pottery in Egypt, although it certainly is the first time that Mycenaean pottery appears there in large quantities. The Mycenaean pottery found at El Amarna generally belongs to the stylistic phase of LH IIIA2, although one or two pots may date to LH IIIB1.[165] Earlier attestations of Mycenaean pottery in Egypt include LH IIA/LM IB pottery at Saqqarah, Abydos, and Dra' Abu el-Naga; LH IIB pottery at Saqqarah, Memphis, Kahun, Gurob, Gurnah, and Malqata; some LH II material at Deir el-Medina; and some LH IIIA1 material at Gurnah, Deir el-Medina, and (one sherd) Malqata.[166] Though Mycenaean pottery evidently did find its way to Egypt before the Amarna era, the quantities are very small, rarely more than a few pots per site. Amarna really marks the advent of the Mycenaean world in the Egyptian archaeological record, after which Mycenaean pottery is found at sites throughout Egypt until the end of the twelfth century BC. Quantities vary, and most sites yielded only a dozen or so pots, though several major sites yielded larger amounts.

---

163. Cf. Petrie 1894; Kemp 1989.

164. Hankey 1981, 41.

165. For an extensive discussion, see Hankey, Kelder, Leonard Jr., van Wijngaarden, in preparation. The Mycenaean pottery found at El Amarna is presented in Petrie 1894, 17; Borchardt 1907, 29–52; 1913, 23; Peet 1923, 15 ff.; Pendlebury 1933, 8 ff.; 1951, 38 ff., and Rose 1987, 119. An overview with primary references is provided in Table 4. Since these articles appeared, more Mycenaean material has been found in Amarna, though the general pattern of distribution (with a clear concentration in the Central City) has not changed (B. Kemp, personal communication). The best introduction on Akhetaten and the relations between the various quarters of the city is found in Kemp 1989.

166. Hankey 1993a, 114; 1981, 46; for Deir el-Medina, see Bell 1982. More LH IIIA1 material (but as yet unpublished) may be found at Tell el Dab'a; see below.

After Amarna: The Late 18th Dynasty and the Early 19th Dynasty

The "boom" of Mycenaean vessels at Amarna thus marked the beginning of an era during which Mycenaean vessels regularly made their way to Egypt. Following the Amarna period, this was particularly true at Deir el-Medina, which in ancient times was simply called "the Village." The Village was the place where the workmen lived who constructed the tombs of the pharaohs. It was a remote place, away from the arable land near Thebes, amidst the cliffs of the eastern delta and not far from "the Great Place," the Valley of the Kings. The Village was abandoned during the reign of Akhenaten, but inhabited again during the reign of Tutankhamen (1336–1327 BC). An unspecified number of Mycenaean sherds, thought to represent over 120 vessels, has been found in the Village and its adjacent tombs.[167] Although there is some LH II material at Deir el-Medina,[168] the majority dates to LH IIIA2 and LH IIIB.[169] It follows that the LH IIIA2 and LH IIIB1 early material must be from the reign of Tutankhamen or his immediate successor, Aye (1327–1323 BC).

Stirrup jars are by far the most common shape at the Village and even appear to have been copied by Egyptian potters, a phenomenon that can be observed elsewhere in the Egyptian empire, e.g. Buhen.[170] Little can be said about the social value/appreciation of the Mycenaean pottery at the Village, but it appears that the material was available to most inhabitants. The fact that the majority of the pottery at Deir el-Medina consists of closed shapes suggests that, as appears to have been

---

167. Cf. Hankey 1993, 114; Bell 1982. Most of the material was found during French excavations at the site and has been published by Bell (see above). Earlier excavations, directed by Georg Möller (Möller 1918, 217–27) yielded three fragments of stirrup jars, whereas Schiapparelli (1927, 3) found a stirrup jar, a horizontal flask and a vertical flask in the tomb of the architect Cha, just north of the Village.

168. Bell 1982, 154. LH II material is found in small quantities elsewhere in the Theban region as well: in the tombs of the nobles at Dra' Abu el-Naga (see above). Pendlebury (1930, 113) noted a possible LH II sherd from the tomb of Montuherkhepeshef, although this sherd was previously considered Minoan (LM II) in origin (De Garis Davies 1913, 6–7). Furumark (1950) noted a whole LH IIA pithoid jar coming from the region.

169. Bell 1982.

170. The Egyptian stirrup jars appear to follow so-called "Simple Style" originals, which are most commonly attested on Cyprus. Cf. Bell 1982, 146.

the case at El Amarna, the vessels were imported as containers, probably of olive oil. As noted above, Mycenaean pottery was found both within the Village (i.e. in a domestic setting) and in the adjacent tombs. There thus is the suggestion that Mycenaean pottery and its contents were used in day-to-day life (and life after death, which was perceived as a reflection of life amongst the living) in post-Amarna Deir el-Medina.

That is not to say that it was a common item throughout the country. Deir el-Medina certainly was not the average village and the presence of a significant quantity of pottery at the Village should not be understood as being representative of all villages throughout Egypt.[171] To this testifies the lack of Mycenaean pottery in strata from this period elsewhere in Egypt. Deir el-Medina was one of the few places where Mycenaean pottery, for whatever reason, was brought, as it was a place of state interest, where work was done to ensure the eternal life of the pharaoh.

Mycenaean pottery is found also at Saqqarah, in the tombs of several high-ranking courtiers of the late 18th dynasty.[172] Even during the reign of Akhenaten, Saqqarah had been a burial ground for Egypt's elite. It was a hallowed place, dominated by the tombs of ancient kings and their entourage. Nearby, just south of the apex of the Nile, lay the old administrative capital Memphis, allegedly founded by Egypt's first king, Narmer.[173] Despite the fact that Akhenaten and his court resided at El Amarna, many of the elite still had their tombs built in the shadow of the ancient city, instead of choosing to be buried near the new capital, Akhetaten. In the tombs of high-ranking courtiers from the Amarna and post-Amarna Age a good number of Mycenaean vessels has been recovered.

---

171. Contra Bell 1982. The importance of the Village, with highly skilled, and paid for, inhabitants, laboring on the tombs of the kings, can hardly be compared with any other town in the country. There was a massive administration responsible for the provisions and supervision of the Village, under the direct responsibility of the vizier of Upper Egypt and the Major of Thebes. There can be no doubt that Deir el-Medina enjoyed a status apart. Cf. Romer 1984.

172. Warren / Hankey 1989, 151–52.

173. Possible Mycenaean ware at Memphis was found in the vicinity of the temple of Ptah (the material had linear decoration and was described as "Aegean"; cf. Anthes 1959, 33–34).

The earliest Mycenaean pottery at the Memphite tombs dates back to LH IIA1 and was found in the tomb (1N) of two women in the cemetery around the pyramid of Pepi I. The finds include a LH IIA alabastron and a LH IIA1 late shallow ring-handled cup.[174] Though there thus is some relatively early material in the Memphite region, the majority by far consists of LH IIIA2 and B1 material. The tombs in which this material was found span the period from the early Amarna Age to the reign of Ramesses II (1279–1213 BC), i.e. the late 18th to mid–19th dynasty. This material includes, in chronological order:

In the tomb of Aperel, vizier under Amenhotep III and Akhenaten, a Mycenaean piriform jar and a stirrup jar were found.[175]

The tomb of Pay, a harem official of Tutankhamen, yielded fragments of two stirrup jars in a late 18th-dynasty context.[176]

The tomb of Maya and Merit yielded a number of pottery fragments from stirrup jars and a kylix, including LH IIIA-B1 and purely LH IIIB1 material. This material with certainty was not deposited later than the 9th regnal year of Horemheb (*ca.* 1272 BC).[177]

Nearby, in the tomb of Horemheb, several sherds from a total of seven vessels, dating to LH IIIA2 and LH IIIB early, were found, as well as a LH IIIB1 (possibly LH IIIAB2) sherd from a stirrup jar.[178]

---

174. Cf. Kemp / Merillees 1989, 253; Firth / Gunn 1926, 70, Pl. 42D. I myself am inclined to consider the alabastron as Minoan. Doubt concerning the mainland/Mycenaean origin of this vessel may also be reflected in Hankey's (*supra*) designation as LH/LM.

175. Cline 1994, 7.

176. Cf. Martin 1996, 6.

177. Warren / Hankey 1989, 152.

178. A FS 166 piriform stirrup jar, a FS 171 globular stirrup jar, two FS 178 squat stirrup jars, an unspecified stirrup jar, a FS 189 globular flask, and closed vessel, possibly a jug, could be reconstructed. The material was found in a subsidiary burial shaft, i.e. not the one originally meant to house the body of its owner (Hankey 1980, 2). With the accession of Horemheb to the throne, the tomb was left unfinished. It may have served as a center for the king's mortuary cult in Ramesside times and it has been suggested that the person eventually buried in the tomb was a daughter of Ramesses II who died during the reign of Merenptah, although this is not wholly clear (personal communication M.J. Raaven). The piriform stirrup jar and the vertical flask, Hankey notes, would have been inconspicuous among others of

The disturbed fill from the tomb of Ramose, who was the field commander under Horemheb (1323–1295 BC), yielded a number of LH IIIA2 and B1 sherds, including a fragment of a stirrup jar.[179]

In the disturbed fill from the tomb of Tia (treasurer under Rameses II) an unspecified number of LH IIIA2 and LH IIIB1 sherds were found, including one fragment from a stirrup jar.[180]

The tomb of Iurudef, who was the private scribe of Tia, yielded two fragments of LH IIIA2-B1 stirrup jars, thought to have been deposited there in Ramesside times.[181]

As noted, all these tombs belonged to high-ranking courtiers from the Amarna period to the mid-19th dynasty. Without exception, the tombs' owners were the "great men" of their age: viziers (in effect ruling half of the country on behalf of the king), royal treasurers such as Maya and Tia, members of the royal family, and high-ranking generals such as Horemheb, who eventually became king. As was the case at El Amarna, Mycenaean pottery at Saqqarah appears to have been accessible exclusively to the highest levels of the Egyptian social pyramid. It seems that, at Saqqarah a least, this situation persisted into Ramesside times.

Unfortunately we lack well-excavated tombs of the "common people." In effect, Deir el-Medina appears to be the only place in Egypt where tombs of "commoners" have been investigated properly and even there, as has been pointed out above, we are hardly dealing with the "average Egyptian" (but rather with a social class all its own, with special rights and luxuries, because of the extraordinary nature of the work done at the Village). The lack of Mycenaean pottery in the residential areas and the few excavated burial grounds of Egypt's lower classes, most conspicuously so at Amarna, but also at various provincial centers (such as Abydos and post-Hyksos Avaris[182]), strongly suggests

---

their types at El-Amarna (Hankey 1980, 3). For the LH IIIB1 (2?) sherd, see Aston / Aston 1999, 60.

179. Cf. Warren / Hankey 1989; Aston / Hankey 1990; Aston / Aston 2001, 56.

180. Warren / Hankey 1989, 151; Aston / Hankey 1990, 77; Aston 1997, 92–93.

181. Aston 1986, 21. See Aston 1991, 53 for a LH IIIB date.

182. Early references to Mycenaean pottery at Abydos (cf. Petrie 1902, 6, pl. LIV; 1901, 46; Randall-Maciver / Mace 1902, 72–75; Ayrton / Currelly / Weigall 1904, 50) could, after examination of the published material, be

that Mycenaean pottery was available only at places where there was a direct royal interest. This may also explain the appearance of a number of Mycenaean stirrup jars in tombs at Buhen, an important fortress and administrative center far to the south, in Nubia.[183] Similarly, the increasing numbers of Mycenaean pottery at Tell el Dab'a, coinciding with the foundation of the new royal residence Pi-ramesse near the old center of Avaris, strongly suggest that the increased demand for Mycenaean pottery was directly related to increased royal interest and activity in that center.

The Delta Residence

The reign of Horemheb (1323–1295 BC[184]) marked the official end of the Amarna Age and, with his death, Egypt's illustrious 18th dynasty

---

discarded. Petrie's material is now safely identified as EBA Levantine pottery, whereas the other material thought to be Mycenaean may display some vague influences from the Aegean, but is most certainly not of Mycenaean origin. The site of Tell el Dab'a, ancient Avaris, has yielded some Mycenaean pottery predating the foundation of Pi-ramesse (including some LH IIIA1 pottery) but only during LH IIIA2 and LH IIIB, roughly contemporary with the rise of the 19th dynasty, Mycenaean pottery appears to have reached the center in substantial amounts. See below for further discussion.

183. According to the first excavators of this site (Randall-Maciver / Woolley 1911, 132), "Mycenaean stirrup jars at Buhen were of fairly common occurrence." Although this fairly common occurrence is regrettably not specified in the excavation reports, later excavations by Emery, Smith, and Milard (1979) yielded another seven or so pots, five of which were stirrup jars, one pilgrim flask, and one sherd from a closed-shaped vessel. The occurrence of an Egyptian faience imitation stirrup jar next to an original Mycenaean pot in a tomb (H80) is paralleled at Deir el-Medina. Considering that all these vases came from an 18th-dynasty cemetery, it is reasonable to assume that we are dealing with LH IIIA2 pottery here, possibly with a little bit of earlier material (although, considering the scarcity of this material in Egypt itself, this seems unlikely). In a similar fashion, a small number of Mycenaean pottery has been found also at Sesebi, another important Nubian fortress.

184. In a recent (as yet unpublished) paper held at a conference on Rhodes, Van Dijk demonstrated that the reign of Horemheb cannot have exceeded fourteen years. As a result, the regnal years of the Egyptian kings given here should be taken with some measure of flexibility, though the main argument presented in this research is not affected by this new insight.

came to an end; the line of Theban kings starting with Ahmose "the Liberator" (who drove the Hyksos out of the delta around 1550 BC) and including great rulers such as Thutmoses III (1479–1425 BC) and Amenhotep III (1390–1352 BC) had finally died out. Of course, Horemheb had long served the last kings of the 18th dynasty as a high-ranking official and, during the reign of Tutankhamen (1336–1327 BC), appears to have effectively ruled the country together with the vizier Aye, who later became king. After the death of Aye, he probably was the most logical, and certainly the most powerful, contender for the throne.

Horemheb's successor was, like Horemheb himself, a man from the army, named Piramesse (ruling as Ramesses I: 1295–1294 BC). Piramesse's origins are thought to have lain in the eastern Delta and he may have been governor of the provincial town of Avaris, near present-day Tell el Dab'a. His short reign and especially that of his son and successor Seti I (1294–1279 BC) were devoted to the conquest of those Levantine territories that had been lost during the chaos following the death of Akhenaten and, as such, were essentially anti-Hittite.[185] Whereas both Ramesses I and Seti I resided at the old centers of Thebes and Memphis, Ramesses II (1279–1213 BC), who succeeded Seti I, decided to move the court to his family's old Delta estate at Avaris. He embarked on a massive building campaign, remaking the provincial town of Avaris into a giant metropolis, bursting with life and adorned with giant temples, palaces, statues of the gods, and, most of all, statues of himself. Moreover, Ramesses renamed the city after himself: Piramesse. Its splendor notwithstanding, contemporary texts make it abundantly clear that the new capital served primarily as a major military

---

185. The historical outlines of the last years of the 18th dynasty can reasonably be reconstructed on the basis of the so-called Amarna letters, Hittite texts, and Egyptian temple inscriptions. It appears that the death of Akhenaten coincided with a period of relative instability in the Egyptian Levantine empire, during which especially the vassal rulers of the kingdom of Amurru tried to carve out their own independent kingdom while playing the Egyptians and Hittites against each other. Ultimately, Hittite forces captured Amurru and several other vassal states originally belonging to the Egyptian sphere of influence. With dynastic troubles solved, Egyptian focus returned to the Levant with the advent of the 19th dynasty and resulted in Egyptian-Hittite wars that essentially lasted well into the reign of Ramesses II. Cf. Kitchen 1982; Reeves 2001; Kemp 1989; Klengel 2002, with references.

base from where campaigns to the Levant were launched. It boasted naval installations, as well as infantry barracks and the headquarters of Egypt's chariot corps. Of interest for our present research, and confirming the notion that the import of Mycenaean pottery was closely tied to royal interest, is the sudden increase in Mycenaean pottery at the site.

Over the years, Austrian and German excavations at Avaris and Pi-ramesse (present-day Tell el Dab'a and Qantir, respectively) have yielded a variety of Mycenaean material in strata ranging from the mid–18th dynasty to the late 19th dynasty.[186] Unlike the other sites discussed above (and in fact, unlike any other site in Egypt), the site of Pi-ramesse yielded an unprecedented variety of ceramic shapes, including not only stirrup jars, but also kylikes and even kraters, as well as a possible peg-top rhyton.[187] Moreover, in a pottery fragment found in what once were the royal stables of Ramesses' delta residence, a horse head was incised in such a manner that it has provisionally been identified as a Linear B sign.[188]

Though a thorough survey of the complete corpus at Qantir and Tell el Dab'a is still lacking, the overall picture seems to be that, preceding the foundation of Pi-ramesse, Mycenaean pottery appeared at Avaris, but in modest quantities. Although LH IIIA1 pottery has been found at Avaris, only during LH IIIA2 did Mycenaean pottery appear more frequently.[189] It is only during LH IIIB, however, that Mycenaean

186. I had the honor of visiting the excavations at Tell el Dab'a during the summer of 2002. Dr. D. Aston kindly showed me some of the newly found pottery, which, to me, appeared to be LH IIIA1 and LH IIIA2 material. At least part of this material was found in strata that were dated to the reign of Amenhotep III, which, if true, would be a relatively early attestation of Mycenaean pottery in Egypt (compare to pages 70–71). The Mycenaean pottery at Qantir is under study by Penelope Mountjoy. Final publication is not yet available for both the Qantir and the Tell el Dab'a corpora.

187. Pusch 1999, 29; Hankey 1993 (ref. to D. Aston), Mountjoy / Mommsen 2000, 146.

188. Pusch 1999, 29, Abb.3.

189. This would have been contemporary with the Amarna and the late Amarna period, i.e. from the reign of Akhenaten till Aye / Horemheb, although Aston (2001, 181) noted that LH IIIA2 may date as late as the early reign of Ramesses II. As we have seen at Memphis, Buhen, and Deir el Medina, Mycenaean pottery has been found in modest quantities throughout Egypt and its Nubian territories during this period, albeit always in close relation to royal activity. Our knowledge of Avaris during

pottery appears to have reached the center in substantial amounts. LH IIIB can be roughly equated with the reign of Ramesses II and although it is currently impossible to provide an exact quantity of LH IIIB material at Pi-ramesse, the occurrence of LH IIIB (and no earlier) sherds in the wider region around Pi-ramesse does suggest that this material, from the reign of Ramesses II onward, was imported on a larger scale than had previously been the case.[190] The distribution of Mycenaean pottery within Pi-ramesse is uncertain. It would appear that from LH IIIB1 onward, Mycenaean pottery is concentrated in the area of Qantir, rather than Tell el Dab'a (though it is not absent at the latter site). As Qantir seems to have been the "royal district" of Pi-ramesse, where the palaces were situated, this would further substantiate the above-presented concept that the presence of Mycenaean pottery was closely tied to royal interest.

The various corpora discussed above demonstrate that from the reign of Akhenaten onward, Mycenaean pottery was imported into Egypt on a more or less regular basis, with small quantities appearing in the tombs, palaces, and ministries of Egyptian courtiers until well into the reign of Ramesses II. We have seen that Hankey's hypothesis that

---

the 18th dynasty is still too insufficient to enable us to understand its position within the Egyptian state, although the presence of an early 18th-dynasty palace at Avaris suggests that it was at least the capital of a nome: the Mycenaean pottery found at the site may thus relate to the royal administration of the nome. If so, Avaris compares well to Buhen, which was, in effect, the administrative center of the larger part of Nubia (and as such, of importance to the crown). Moreover, it appears increasingly likely that Avaris was an important harbor town during the entire duration of the New Kingdom. As such, it was a "port of entry" and one of those places where foreign missions, whether for trade or with diplomatic aims, would anchor upon arriving in Egypt. It is, in this respect, of interest to note that Haider (1990, 19–22; 1996, 144–45) convincingly argued for the presence of Minoan shipwrights(!) at Peru-nefer, a harbor town that has recently been identified as the harbor of Avaris (Bietak 1996a). With Avaris' indisputable long-standing relations with Aegean in mind (esp. the Bull-leaper fresco, now securely dated to the early 18th dynasty; cf. Bietak 1996b, 67) the presence of Mycenaean pottery, essentially from the Amarna time onward, should hardly come as a surprise.

190. Cf. Van den Brink 1987, 14. Pusch (1999, 29) notes that at Qantir, the majority of Mycenaean pottery is dated to LH IIIB1 and LH IIIB2, though some material may be dated to LH IIIA.

Mycenaean pottery at Amarna was a result of Amenhotep III's mission to the Aegean cannot be upheld. Yet, the apparent close connection between the Egyptian court and the presence of Mycenaean pottery in Egypt, mainly at Amarna but also elsewhere, does suggest at least some sort of royal supervision in the acquisition of the pottery. This does not necessarily mean direct contact between Greece and Egypt, as the pottery may have been acquired elsewhere (i.e. Cyprus or the Levant).[191] We have seen, however, that in the years preceding the Amarna period, Egypt and Mycenaean Greece had, at least occasionally, direct contact. Therefore, it would *à priori* be rather unlikely that this had not continued in later years.

Of Olives, Pottery, and Men

One of the main arguments in favor of direct contact between the Egyptian court at Amarna and the Mycenaean world is the remarkable homogeneity of the corpus of Mycenaean vessels at Amarna. Unlike many of the other corpora of Mycenaean vessels in western Anatolia, the corpus of Amarna has been subject to various studies to determine its origin, which appears to have been the northern Argolid with Berbati, which was under the direct control of Mycenae, as a likely production center.[192] In other words, the corpus of Mycenaean pottery at Amarna derives from the kingdom of Mycenae. We should consider that the significant size and the homogeneous (Argive) origins of the corpus make it highly unlikely that the vessels had been assembled somewhere other than at the place of origin. The shipment, therefore, is most likely to have come to Egypt in a direct way. Moreover, as reconstructed from the texts, the Argolid, from where the pottery came, was the heartland of the kingdom of Tanaju, which had been known to the Egyptians from at least the reign of Thutmoses III. On at least two previous occasions, the king of Tanaju can be demonstrated to have had direct contact with the Egyptian court. Thus the Mycenaean vessels at Amarna may well have been sent as greeting gifts, from the king of Mycenae to his Egyptian colleague.

191. Cf. Sherratt 1998 on the role of Cyprus in Late Bronze Age economies; see Kemp 1989, 232, esp. 234 ff. for discussion on the nature of the Egyptian economy and the role of the state.

192. Cf. Podzuweit 1994, 157 with references.

Why did Mycenaean-Amarna relations suddenly involve the exchange of Mycenaean pottery, whereas earlier Mycenaean-Egyptian contacts did not? The answer, I think, lies in the climatic differences between Egypt and Greece and the Egyptian desire to acquire what Greece is known for even today: olives.

The Egyptian climate is not favorable for growing olives and, therefore, olives and olive oil had to be imported. It is likely that olives initially were imported from the Levant, if only because the Egyptians used a Semitic loanword to designate the fruit.[193] Considering the limited occurrence of olive stones in strata predating the New Kingdom and the absence of the olive in Egyptian texts or iconography, its importation before the Amarna period must have been sporadic at best.[194] At Amarna, however, olives are omnipresent. Olive pits have been found in the workmen's village at Amarna and in the Central City a wreath of olive twigs was found.[195] Olive twigs are also shown on the walls of the Great Aten temple, where they are offered to the sun-god by none other than the king himself.[196] Slightly later, four wreaths of olive twigs were buried in Tutankhamen's tomb in the Valley of the Kings.[197] Olives in the Amarna Age, at least, appear to have had a close connection to the king and his court.

The sudden appearance of the olive in the paleobotanical and the iconographical record at Amarna is paralleled by the importation of an unprecedented number of Mycenaean closed-shaped vessels. As has been observed, both olives and Mycenaean pottery appear virtually exclusively in an elite context. More to the point, both the pilgrim flask and the stirrup jar are known to have been used as containers of olive

---

193. Egyptian *dt* for "olive" appears to derive from West Semitic *zayt-*. Cf. Frankel 1999, 37 for the use of the olive in the Levant; see Hoch 1994, 395; Serpico / White 2000, with references, for *b3ḳ* as a designation for olive oil.

194. The olive has been attested only twice in contexts predating the New Kingdom: in 13th-dynasty levels at Kom el Rabi'a and to late Hyksos levels at Avaris. Cf. Murray 2000, 610; Newton / Terral / Ivorra 2006, 407. For a more intensive study and a proposal to re-date the introduction of the olive in Egypt, see Kelder 2009.

195. Renfrew, J. 1985, 188; Pendlebury 1951, 118, pl.LXXVIII.

196. Cf. Kelder 2009.

197. Germer 1989, 90–95.

oil.[198] The connection between olives and the Mycenaean pottery at Amarna is at hand. It now appears very likely that Akhenaten received not only Greek olive oil (perhaps perfumed, as the tablets from Pylos suggest?), but also living olive trees to be planted in his new capital.[199] The latter would also explain the king's ability to offer fresh olive twigs to his god and to appear, perhaps during religious ceremonies or festivities, donned in wreaths of olive twigs. At those occasions, while watching the king's procession, the people of Akhetaten may have inhaled an expensive Mycenaean perfume.

This scenario appears to be the best explanation for the presence of Mycenaean pottery at Amarna. The "olive hypothesis" does, of course, not exclude the possibility that there may have been other reasons for direct Egyptian (diplomatic) contact with the Mycenaean kingdom. Abroad things were rapidly changing, and distinctly not in the way the pharaoh would have wanted.[200]

In his "biography" of Amenhotep III, Eric Cline devoted a chapter to Egypt's overseas connections, especially with the Aegean.[201] He proposed that the faience plaques with Amenhotep's royal cartouche at Mycenae should be seen as evidence for an Egyptian mission, primarily meant to strengthen bonds between Egypt and Mycenae. Moreover, a strategic alliance with Mycenae, Cline posits, was intended to threaten the western flank of the Hittite kingdom (where Egypt also found an ally in the kingdom of Arzawa), while the alliance with Mittani was to keep the Hittites out of Syria.[202]

The military considerations of diplomatic ties with Mycenae may be portrayed in the papyrus fragments found at Amarna, on which Mycenaean (?) warriors, coming to the aid of a fallen Egyptian, are de-

198. Cf. Haskell 1985, 221–29 with references.

199. Cf. Hepper 1990, 16 for olive importation during the reign of Tutankhamen. For Pylian oil production, see Shelmerdine 1985.

200. The rump-state of Mittani was incorporated into the Hittite Empire, while Mittani's former vassal Assyria gradually assumed a leading position in northeastern Syria and northern Mesopotamia.

201. Cf. O'Connor / Cline 1998, esp. Cline 1998, 250.

202. In this respect, it should be noted that the first Ahhiyawan incursions into Anatolia that we know of are roughly contemporary with the reign of Amenhotep III, i.e. the first quarter of the fourteenth century BC.

picted.[203] As I have noted above, Egypt had a long tradition of incorporating foreign troops into its army. We should ponder at least the possibility that the Egyptian court during the Amarna Age employed groups of Mycenaean warriors and that these warriors came from the befriended king of Mycenae. At any rate, with the collapse of Mittani, one can see the value of strengthening ties with the remnant of an anti-Hittite alliance.

It thus appears likely that from the reign of Thutmoses III until the reign of Akhenaten, the Egyptian and Mycenaean courts, at least occasionally, exchanged messengers. In accordance with contemporary political *mores*, these messengers brought prestigious goods, such as precious metal vessels and faience plaques, while during the reign of Akhenaten these gifts would have also included Mycenaean vessels containing olive oil and possibly live olive trees and elite military forces. But what about the later years? The relationship between Hatti and Egypt would remain strained well into the thirteenth century BC and, following Cline's scenario, there thus would have been good reason to uphold the contact with the Mycenaean Greeks.

We have seen that Mycenaean pottery was imported into Egypt until the reign of Ramesses II and that it remained largely confined to the Egyptian elite. Some of the pottery following the Amarna period closely resembles the pottery at Akhetaten (such as the flask and the piriform stirrup jar found in the tomb of Horemheb) and might have come from the same source, i.e. the northern Argolid. This certainly is the case for the larger part of the one hundred sherds from Pi-ramesse that have been chemically analyzed.[204]

The corpus from Pi-ramesse deserves to be mentioned here because of the diversity of shapes. Pi-ramesse, so far at least, is the only site in Egypt where kraters, kylikes, and possibly even a rhyton have been found alongside the "usual" stirrup jars and pilgrim flasks. It clearly would go too far to jump to the conclusion that we are dealing with Mycenaeans actually living in the city (as we may just as well be dealing with changing patterns of Egyptian appreciation of the Mycenaean

---

203. See above, pp. 40–41.

204. Mountjoy / Mommsen 2000, 138 ff. Most of the pottery definitely came from the Argolid. Some material may have had its origins on Cyprus, while there also is the suggestion that some pottery may have been locally (i.e. Egyptian) made.

pottery), but it raises at least that possibility. I have discussed above the long-standing link between Avaris/Pi-ramesse and the Aegean (with Minoans living in the old city). And Ramesses II is known to have included large groups of foreigners, most notably Sea People,[205] in his army. Considering this, and keeping the Amarna papyrus in mind, the possibility of Mycenaean warriors being in the pharaoh's service and settling at Pi-ramesse is not too far-fetched. Egyptian interest in the Aegean had not waned since Akhenaten's days: the earrings of Queen Nefertari are Mycenaean (Illustration 3) and the walls of the burial chamber of Ramesses III show Mycenaean amphorae.

The accumulation of data suggesting direct contact between Egypt and Mycenae, taken together with hard textual evidence of direct contact during the reign of Thutmoses III, places the burden of proof upon those claiming that direct, diplomatic contact did not occur.

---

205. Especially the Sherden, a people thought to have come from, or later settled in, Sardinia. Cf. Woudhuizen 2005; Sandars 1978. Note that none of these groups, while we know of their presence within Egypt, has left any trace in the archaeological record that would identify them as being "foreign."

— TANAJU, THE KINGDOM OF MYCENAE — AND AHHIYAWA

SEARCH FOR THE HEARTLAND

We have seen that during the reign of Thutmoses III an Aegean kingdom called Tanaju had direct diplomatic contact, involving the exchange of prestige gifts, with the Egyptian court. The Kom el Hetan text indicates that the heartland of Tanaju was the Argolid, with Mycenae and Nauplion as its principal centers. Both the Kom el Hetan text itself and the presence of faience plaques at Mycenae with Amenhotep's royal cartouche argue for continuation of direct contact between the Egyptian court and the king of Tanaju from the reign of Thutmoses III until the reign of Amenhotep III.

As I argued above, the combination of the sudden import of Mycenaean pottery at Amarna, as well as the presence of olives, olive twigs, and the possible depiction of Mycenaean warriors on a papyrus at Amarna, is most plausibly explained as being the result of diplomatic contact between Amarna and Mycenae.

After the Amarna period evidence of direct contact between Egypt and the Mycenaean world becomes increasingly flimsy, although, as we shall see below, Mycenae in particular has yielded a substantial amount of *Aegyptiaca*, including objects from the late 19th dynasty (and perhaps even later). I believe I have demonstrated that there was continuing direct Egyptian contact with the Mycenaean world. But even if one is unwilling to accept this conclusion, it remains that at least between *ca.* 1437 (the 42nd regnal year of Thutmoses III) and *ca.* 1335 BC (the final year of Akhenaten)[206] the Egyptian court had diplomatic ties with the court of Tanaju/Mycenae. This overlaps with the first (bellicose) actions of Ahhiyawans in western Anatolia. In other words, Ahhiyawa and Tanaju must have been contemporaries.

Consequently, we are faced with the question as to where these kingdoms, both apparently able to deal as equals with contemporary Great Powers, must be situated. As for Tanaju, the Egyptian textual sources have provided ample proof that its heartland was situated around the centers of Nauplion and Mycenae, as those were the only centers specifically mentioned in the Kom el Hetan text (as opposed to the other toponyms, which appear to designate regions). Moreover, at least during the reign of Amenhotep III, Tanaju encompassed the larger part of the Peloponnese and, in all likelihood, the Thebaid. The Hittite texts however, do not provide us with such a geographical specification: the Ahhiyawan heartland must be situated "across the sea," but that is about all.

Yet this is enough. It is clear that Millawanda, Ahhiyawa's foothold on Anatolian soil, was not itself the principal center of the kingdom. That center must have been on the isles in the Aegean or on the Greek mainland itself. We may reasonably assume that the capital of Ahhiyawa must have been one of the Mycenaean palatial centers in the Aegean.

Yet, if we take a closer look at these centers, we are left, perhaps surprisingly, with a limited number of possibilities.[207] The palace of Pylos can safely be dismissed on the grounds that very little *Orientalia* has been found there, and the Menelaion cannot have been the principal center of the Ahhiyawan kingdom because of its decline in the fourteenth century. Admittedly, our knowledge of even the most significant Mycenaean centers is spotty.[208] But even those centers can, be-

206. The sporadic occurrence of LH IIIB1 pottery in the Amarna corpus argues for a late stage of Akhenaten's reign as the time of importation.

207. An extensive survey of all major Mycenaean palatial centers can be found in Kelder 2005b.

208. Most notably, the impressive rock-cut tholos tomb at Pellana in Laconia strongly suggests the presence of a nearby important palatial center, but this has not yet been located. Excavations at Dimini (near Volos) have uncovered an important Mycenaean settlement, including several megara, one of which appears to have been used for cultic activity. A palatial complex at Dimini has, however, not yet been found, although its discovery seems to be just a matter of time. The complex that was hailed as "palatial" during

cause of the lack of *Orientalia* or for reasons of size or "monumentality," be discounted as having been the capital of Ahhiyawa. Looking for an Ahhiyawan capital in one of the islands in the Aegean appears to be equally fruitless.[209]

We are left with only two plausible candidates, namely Thebes (in Boeotia) and Mycenae (in the Argolid).

---

the 2006 excavations at Salamis has still not yielded a Linear B archive or anything else that with certainty proves its dominance over the island (and beyond). For all three sites, good publications are regrettably lacking. The finds at Pellana have essentially been published only on a poster, while the findings at Salamis and Dimini are briefly reviewed in the Archaeological Reports and the Arch. Delt.

209. A site on Crete is an unlikely candidate for a number of reasons. As has been noted, Crete is known in Egyptian sources as *k-f-tj-w*, usually transcribed *keftiu*, while the name *Tnj* was used to refer to the lands beyond Crete (cf. Edel 1966, 54; Latacz 2001b, 161 ff.). Contact with Crete was quite close until the reign of Thutmoses III, after which Crete seems to have lost its importance to Egypt (cf. Wachsmann 1987). Despite a subsequent recovery at some sites, destructions at the major Cretan sites around 1450, including Knossos, make a direct association with Ahhiyawa unlikely, as Ahhiyawa for the first time appears in the Hittite records some decades later. Penelope Mountjoy (1998, 51) suggests that the capital of Ahhiyawa might plausibly be looked for at Rhodes, a thought that essentially sprang from her equation of the East Aegean, West Anatolian pottery koinè with the territorial extent of Ahhiyawa. Apart from the apparent methodological flaw, there is the additional problem that the pottery koinè flourished only at a very late stage of Mycenaean culture, during LH IIIB2 and especially C, which is difficult to relate to the contemporary decline of Ahhiyawa as in the Hittite texts (Mee 1982, 86 notes that during Rhodes' *floruit*, the island actually imported a great deal of Argive pottery; Mee 1998, 143 [without any real argument] proposes an island-based federation headed by a mainland state such as Mycenae). Essentially, it appears wisest to follow Deger-Jalkotzy (1998, 106) in stating that "there is, moreover, no evidence that any island polity could have been on a par with the leading states."

THEBES OR MYCENAE?

Thebes

In the recent update of his original 2001 *Troia und Homer*, Joachim Latacz presents an argument favoring Thebes as the capital of the kingdom of Ahhiyawa.[210] Claiming support for his views from established scholars, including Wolf-Dietrich Niemeier,[211] Latacz presents three major arguments for his identification of Thebes as Ahhiyawa.

The first of these is the apparent Boeotian prominence in Homer's Catalogue of Ships. I am unwilling to take later legends (even if their "backbone" may originally date to the Mycenaean Age) into account for this research and I will, therefore, not deal with Latacz's first argument.[212]

Latacz's second argument is, however, of relevance to our current research as it deals with a new reading of a Hittite text. The text in question, KUB XXVI 91, has already been briefly discussed above (see note 97) in the context of Mycenaean encroachment on the Anatolian west coast and is generally understood as a letter from an unnamed Hittite king to the king of Ahhiyawa. Latacz, however, refers to a new interpretation proposed by the Hittitologist Frank Starke, holding that this text was written by an unnamed Ahhiyawan king to his Hittite colleague, providing historical justification for the recent Ahhiyawan seizure of several islands before the Anatolian west coast on the grounds that these islands in the past had belonged to the Ahhiyawan's forebearer who bore the name Kadmos. It is this name, in later Greek legend closely associated with the city of Thebes, that leads Latacz to the assumption that Thebes must have been the leading center on the Greek mainland.

There are several problems with this new textual reading and, therefore, problems with Latacz's use of this interpretation to support his position. The most serious issue is that Starke's reading of the text

210. Latacz 2004; updated translation of Latacz 2001b.

211. Cf. Niemeier 2001 (quoted in Latacz 2004, 242–43). Rather than providing any indication why it should be Thebes that assumed a leading role in the Mycenaean world, Niemeier argues against the identification of the southeast Aegean as Ahhiyawa, which was not the problem, as a consequence of which he, apparently, concludes that Thebes is the only plausible option left.

212. For a discussion of those arguments, see Kelder 2007.

cannot be supported. Doubtful identifications of cuneiform signs, the improbable reconstruction of the name Kadmos in Hittite: *n*]*u-za Ka-ga-mu-na-aš-za-kán A-BA A-BA A-B*[*I-YA*, and grammatical impossibilities have triggered a flood of criticism, most recently summarized by the American scholar Joshua Katz.[213] But even if the new reading were accurate, one would need "a giant leap of faith" to identify the real Bronze Age individual named Kadmos supposedly in our text with the legendary founder of Thebes.

The third argument for Latacz's identification of Thebes as the Ahhiyawan capital is the size of the Theban territory, which is reported to have included all of central and eastern Boeotia, and at least parts of Euboea. I have briefly dealt with this issue above (see p. 9). Let it suffice here to say that the inclusion of parts of Euboea, in particular, in the reconstruction of the Theban kingdom cannot be supported. Also, as we shall see below, even this "extended" reconstruction of the kingdom of Thebes does not match the territorial extent of the kingdom of Mycenae, which included a number of extremely important citadels (such as Nauplion, Tiryns, and Midea).[214]

Latacz's arguments, in sum, are unconvincing. If we were to argue for Theban dominance over Mycenaean Greece and that it is the Theban kingdom that should be identified as Ahhiyawa, it would be better to compare the archaeological remains found at Thebes to those at Mycenae. This, admittedly, is a difficult task, if only because of the extremely lacunose state of research on the Kadmeia hill, even when compared to the state of the investigations at Mycenae.

Unlike Mycenae, which dwindled into insignificance in the Classical era, Thebes was a significant center in the Classical era and has remained inhabited up to the present day. Unfortunately modern building activities at Thebes have been extremely harmful to the archaeological record. Indeed, at several spots modern foundations have been dug down to the bedrock, destroying everything ancient in the process. Nonetheless, excavations in the city center have uncovered a sizable Mycenaean center, including two structures that have been identified as palatial. Though there may be some overlap, it appears that these structures functioned at different times. The older of them, commonly

---

213. Cf. Katz 2005 with references.

214. Contra Godart / Sacconi 1999, 545.

known as the "Old Kadmeion" but also referred to as "the House of Kadmos," was probably destroyed by fire during the early phase of LH IIIA2.[215] The younger is called the "New Kadmeion" and was built during LH IIIB1.[216] This complex covered some 2.1 hectares, including what has been understood to be a large courtyard, resembling those of the Minoan palaces on Crete.[217]

The New Kadmeion appears to have had no significant demarcation from the rest of the settlement. Unlike the major centers in the Argolid and unlike the center on the acropolis at Athens, there was no cyclopean wall to demarcate (or protect?) the residence of the ruling elite from its surroundings. The settlement as a whole, however, may have been fortified with a wall, roughly following the course of the later, Classical fortifications. Though it has been proposed that this wall included seven gates (as in Sophokles' *Antigone*, 141–43) on the spots of the modern exit roads of the town,[218] later research suggests a more modest course of the wall.[219] The wall itself, again unlike the centers in the Argolid, may not have been of cyclopean masonry.[220]

Despite its defenses, Thebes met with violent destructions on at least two occasions during the Mycenaean period: one at the end of the LH IIIB period (like most of the major palatial centers of the Mycenaean world) and one earlier. The exact date of this earlier destruction has been the subject of debate, with some arguing for a LH IIIB2 late date, while others suggest an earlier date, during LH IIIB1.[221] It appears that a LH IIIB1 date is now more or less generally accepted,[222] but the question

215. Cf. Κεραμόπουλος 1909, 57 ff.; Symeonoglou 1985, 49 for LH IIIA2; Dakouri-Hild, 2001, 101 for LH IIIB1.

216. Symeonoglou 1973, 75.

217. For Minoan, Theban contacts, see Symeonoglou 1973, 74.

218. See Κεραμόπουλος, *supra*.

219. Cf. Demakopoulou / Konsola 1981, 20–22; Symeonoglou 1985, 26–32. The wall would still have a length of approximately 1700 meters, protecting an area of 19.2 hectares.

220. Cf. Dickinson 2006, 25 with references.

221. For a LH IIIB2 late date, Snodgrass 1975, 314; Dakouri-Hild 2001, 106–7; for a LH IIIB1 date, see Symeonoglou 1985, 60.

222. "There are some grounds for believing that part, if not all, of the later so-called 'New' Palace at Thebes was destroyed at this [LH IIIB early] time, although not by fire" (Rutter 2004). This means no later than 1230 BC.

whether this LH IIIB1 destruction also meant the end of the palatial administration, as Symeonoglou argues, has not yet been resolved.[223]

The Mycenaean settlement on the Kadmeia hill was thus a sizable town, fortified in its entirety by a wall and dominated by a palace of considerable size. Yet for all its glories, Thebes was destroyed sometime during the mid-thirteenth century BC.[224] I have already noted that Thebes was not alone in its misfortune: around the same time the whole of Boeotia suffered a setback, characterized by destructions at Orchomenos and the abandonment of the important center at Gla/Kastri (ancient Arne?). As a consequence of this, the complex system of waterworks draining the Kopaïs basin fell into disuse, with the subsequent flooding of large stretches of agricultural land and, probably, of several major settlements as a result.[225] Even if the palatial administration at Thebes had survived these upheavals (or was revived afterward), the rest of Boeotia clearly did not.[226] This hardly fits the picture of an Aegean Great Power, operating as an equal with the Hittites at exactly that time.

There is still more that argues against the identification of Thebes as being the kingdom of Ahhiyawa. Troubling for those who wish to see Thebes as the leading center of Mycenaean Greece must be the lack of monumental architecture, not only in the city itself but also in its surroundings. Although the surroundings of Thebes include various

---

Shelmerdine (2001) considers the discussion closed in favor of a destruction at the end of LH IIIB1, and a later one at the end of B2.

223. Symeonoglou *supra*.

224. I am aware of the difficulties involving Aegean Bronze Age chronology and absolute dates. In general, I tend to follow the "classical" chronology as proposed in Warren / Hankey 1989. However, even if one is not to follow the data proposed in that volume, LH IIIB1 is, by any standard, unlikely to have lasted later than 1230 BC.

225. There is no point to delve deeper into the topography of Mycenaean Boeotia here. German surveys have, however, located several settlements daring to the Mycenaean period in the Kopaïs basin, including one in the fields surrounding Gla. Cf. Knauss *et al.* 1984, 216–19; 1987, 21, esp. ill.6.23; Fossey 1980, 155–62.

226. Orchomenos most certainly never recovered from the destruction. Although the center has been poorly investigated, pottery study suggests a *floruit* during LH IIIB1, followed by a marked decline in LH IIIB2. Cf. Mountjoy 1983, 11 ff.; see for general observations Bulle 1907, 61; Catling 1984–85, 31; Iakovidis 2001.

cemeteries from the Mycenaean era, no monumental tombs have as yet been found. Various chamber tombs are known, including a tomb with a double *dromos*, two chambers, and painted doorjambs.[227] This tomb is usually described as "royal," but this identification appears to be more the result of a lack of truly monumental tombs in the area rather than of any evidence of a royal burial in this specific tomb. The excuse that the area has been inhabited ever since Mycenaean times and that, therefore, much of the architecture may have been destroyed is, of course, valid to some extent. But then, one should consider that even at Athens(!) there is evidence for a tholos tomb.[228] In fact, Thebes appears to be the only major Mycenaean center where no tholos tomb has been found, yet it is precisely that type of tomb that is generally considered to be the royal tomb *par excellence*.[229] This should not be misunderstood. I am not arguing that there never were *any* tholos tombs at Thebes. I am arguing that there cannot have been *many* of these royal tombs in the Theban region. This stands in contrast to the abundance of tholos tombs in the Argolid, especially at Mycenae, where there is, in fact, a whole sequence of tholos tombs dating from LH IIA to LH IIIB.[230]

All this does not mean that the lords of Thebes were without power or prestige. Finds from the destruction layer of the palace include a variety of rare artefacts, including ivory legs to a throne, smaller ivory carvings, an abundance of jewelry, and pottery (a remarkable amount coming from Crete), which testify to Thebes' contacts with Cyprus and the Levant.[231] Egyptian artefacts are rare and I am aware of only one

227. The tomb originally dated to LH IIIA2 but was extended in LH IIIB. Cf. Leekley / Efstratiou 1980, 37.

228. Cf. Hurwitt 1999, 76.

229. Cf. Bennet 1998, 125 ff.; Pelon 1976; Hood 1978, 557.

230. Dickinson, unpublished but quoted in French 2005.

231. Cf. Cline 1994; Lambrou-Phillipson 1990; Kelder 2005b, 151–56. Of special interest are 39 lapis lazuli cylinder seals found together in a room of the palace. Edith Porada devoted a thorough study to these remarkable pieces, a majority of which seems to have been of Kassite origin, and proposed that they had been sent as a greeting gift by the Assyrian king Tukulti-Ninurta I, after his conquest of Babylon, to the king of Thebes (Porada 1981–82, 69). The fact that these seals in total weigh approximately one *mina*, which appears to have been the standard measure of a greeting gift of lapis lazuli in the Amarna letters, lends some credibility to this proposition, but the late date of Tukulti-Ninurta's reign (1233–1197 BC) is problematic as the

artefact that might be of Anatolian origin.[232] A collection of Babylonian cylinder seals has been taken as evidence of Theban prominence in Greece, but while this assemblage clearly demonstrates the prestige that the Theban lords must have enjoyed while their palace was still standing, the fact remains that at the apparent pinnacle of Ahhiyawan power (as indicated by the Tawagalawa letter) Thebes and its Boeotian hinterland experienced a series of setbacks, which makes the identification with Ahhiyawa implausible.

Although one can reasonably say that Thebes was a significant regional center with contacts to the Levant and Cyprus, there just is too little evidence for positing more than that. Neither archaeology nor contemporary texts has produced a single convincing piece of evidence that would allow for its identification with Ahhiyawa.

Mycenae

Unlike Thebes, Mycenae lost its importance in the last century of the Bronze Age, never to regain it. Although it remained an independent *polis* until the fifth century BC, habitation seems to have declined significantly from the early twelfth century onward and consequently there was little (building) activity thereafter. The archaeological record, as a result, has been left relatively intact. Excavations have, over the years, revealed the larger part of the Bronze Age acropolis (Illustration 7), as well as the occupation immediately around it. Moreover, more than 200 chamber tombs have so far been identified in the hills surrounding the citadel—surpassed only by the supposed number of chamber tombs at Nauplion—and it is generally assumed that these cemeteries mark the limit of the inhabited area.[233] The settlement around the citadel would, as a consequence, have covered some 32 hectares.[234] Its size, unsurpassed in the Mycenaean world, is a clear

---

Theban palace by that time would have been but a smoking heap of rubble. The fact that the seals were found in close proximity to a lapis lazuli workshop (as already pointed out by Porada) suggests that the seals were used as raw material. That ten of these seals appear to have been of Cypriot provenance may suggest that we are dealing here with an assemblage of seals, rather than with a single shipment of greeting gifts.

232. Cf. Lambrou-Phillipson 1990, 46–49.

233. French 2005, 125.

234. Wardle / Wardle 2001, 17.

Illustration 7: The citadel of Mycenae

To the left the bastion of the Lions Gate; "houses" in the forefront.

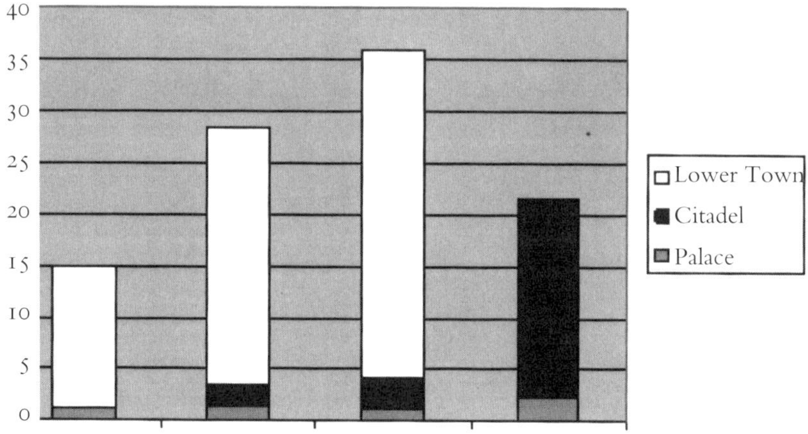

Illustration 8: The size of Mycenaean palatial centers

Note that for Thebes, the whole of the Kadmeia hill is taken as the "citadel," though this includes the larger part of the Theban settlement (i.e. also the dwellings of the populace). For Tiryns, the LH IIIC size has been taken, as the extent of the settlement in earlier periods is not well established (although almost certainly smaller).

indication that Mycenae was a center of extraordinary status.[235] Yet it is not only the size of its settlement but also a whole range of unique features that cause Mycenae to stand out among the palatial centers of Late Bronze Age Greece. Most notable among these features is the size of Mycenae's megaron and the monumental approach to the palace, but other features include (following French):[236]

- The quantity and range of the grave goods and degree of wealth in the shaft graves of Grave Circle A;
- The nine tholos tombs, forming a sequence of increasing fineness and elaboration and of which six belong to a single period, LH IIA;
- The early construction of cyclopean walls (with Tiryns);
- The "houses" outside the walls, containing Linear B tablets;
- Craft production, including stone bowls, faience and metal-inlay;
- Stone relief work on a large scale;
- Pottery manufacture and export;
- Roads and bridges.

Although the wealth displayed in the shaft graves does not settle the argument as to whether Mycenae was Greece's leading center during the last centuries of the Mycenaean period, it does testify to the early prosperity and thus power of the lords of Mycenae. As we shall see below, this observation, combined with other archaeological evidence, needs to be considered when reconstructing the rise of Mycenae to become the leading center in the Peloponnese.

Mycenae's continuing prosperity can be deduced from the sheer "monumentality" of the tombs of its ruling elite in the years following the shaft grave period. The unprecedented number of large tholos tombs, of which the majority is usually considered to have been built in LH IIA, indicates Mycenae's extraordinary status already in the early Mycenaean period. Moreover, the early fortifications, with the earliest cyclopean walls erected as early as LH IIIA,[237] suggest a continuing desire and ability of its leading elite to impress and demonstrate its

235. See Illustration 8.

236. French 2005, 125.

237. Kilian 1988b, 134; Iakovidis 1983, 57.

power and influence, extending from the period of the shaft graves right down to the palatial period.

While we can only guess how the lords of Mycenae acquired such wealth and status, there is reason to suppose that their rule extended not only over the valley around Mycenae but that Mycenae's realm included the whole of Korinthia, even at a very early stage. This hypothesis is mainly informed by survey results, which also indicate a lack of significant settlements and the absence of monumental tombs, suggesting that Korinthia's seat of power must be sought elsewhere.[238] Considering the close proximity of Mycenae, as well as the presence of a Mycenaean road connecting Mycenae with the isthmus,[239] it is difficult to propose that some center other than Mycenae could have controlled this region. The same can be said for Achaea, where I know of no significant center until the very late palatial period (with the rise of the center at Teichos Deimaion).

A similar argument can be made for the inclusion of the Argive plain in the kingdom of Mycenae. The whole system of Mycenaean roads as attested or reconstructed in the Argive plain, including the bridge at Kazarma leading to the plain of Epidauros, centers on Mycenae.[240] Moreover, its settlement size, the size of the palace, and the "monumentality" and number of the tholos tombs cause Mycenae to stand out among the other centers in the Argolid, including Tiryns. Taking all these facts together, it appears likely that, at least from LH IIIA onward, the whole of the Argive plain was part of the kingdom of Mycenae. This explains the omission of Tiryns, Midea, and Argos, to name just the major centers in the area, in the Kom el Hetan list: only Mycenae and Nauplion, the port of arrival, were of importance to any visiting diplomat.

It is of importance to appreciate just how extensive this territory really was. None of the other Mycenaean palatial centers appears to have ruled much more than what could be considered its "natural territory," the areas roughly equivalent to modern Greece's provinces (i.e.

---

238. Cherry / Davis 2001, 154–56. The recent discovery of a tholos near the ancient city of Korinth does not negate the observation that major settlements and monuments are (with this one exception) notably absent in the Korinthia.

239. Cf. Mylonas 1966, 86; Crouwel 1981, 17.

240. Cf. Crouwel 1981.

Messenia, Boeotia, Attica). Yet Mycenae ruled a territory at least two and arguably even three times that size. Moreover, its territory would have included various major centers, such as Tiryns and Nauplion, centers that could plausibly be seen as important yet dependent sub-centers, ruled by branches of Mycenae's royal family.[241] If so, this would be paralleled by the contemporary and well-attested Hittite practice of installing members of the royal family in such centers as Carchemish and Halab, or, closer to the Mycenaean world, Mira, usually described as *Sekundogenitur*.[242] If so, the two rather unimpressive tholos tombs at Tiryns erected during the second half of the thirteenth century, at the zenith of Mycenaean power, could be interpreted as the tombs of the local vassals.

There are still more arguments in favor of Mycenae as the leading center in Late Bronze Age Greece. One of these is the scope of its contacts with the East.

Mycenae has yielded an unparalleled array of *Orientalia*, including approximately 40 objects from Egypt.[243] Apart from these *Aegyptiaca*, some 37 objects of Levantine origin and 6 objects of Cypriot origin (not counting an unspecified number of copper ingots[244]) testify to Mycenae's far-flung contacts with the East.[245] Yet, it is not only the amount of oriental artefacts at Mycenae indicating the center's extraordinary position in the Greek world, but also the quality of the finds. In this respect I note especially the faience plaques with the royal "cartouche" of Amenhotep III. Above, I noted the importance of these pieces because of their distinctly royal connotation.[246] But perhaps even more striking is the fact that one of these plaques was later used in the "cult center" of the citadel of Mycenae, i.e. in a context that is rather similar to the Egyptian practice of depositing such plaques in temples or palaces.[247] Even if one is not willing to follow Helck's proposition that

241. Kelder 2005b, 164.
242. See Bryce 2003.
243. Cf. Lambrou-Phillipson 1990; see also Cline 1994, 145 ff.; Pendlebury 1930, 55.
244. Cf. Lambrou-Phillipson 1990, 335.
245. Lambrou-Phillipson 1990; see also Cline 1994, 145 ff.
246. See above, p. 68, n. 160.
247. Cf. Phillips 2007 for extensive discussion.

the plaques at Mycenae once adorned the windowsills of an "Egyptian room" as part of an Egyptian embassy at Mycenae,[248] this indicates that the rulers of Mycenae were at least aware of the approximate "value" or appreciation of these objects in their original cultural setting (i.e. Egypt). This, in turn, argues for regular contacts between Egypt and Mycenae on a level far different, for example, from Theban connections with the Levant, where eastern status symbols such as the lapis lazuli cylinder seals were simply considered to be useful raw material.

The obvious difficulty in identifying Mycenae as Ahhiyawa is the conspicuous lack of artefacts from Anatolia. We have discussed above that the king of Ahhiyawa and the Hittite Great King exchanged messengers at least from the reign of Hattušili III onward. Considering the apparent familiarity of the Ahhiyawan court with both Hittite and Arzawan nobility, one would expect that the exchange of messengers also involved the exchange of greeting gifts, as was the practice elsewhere in the Orient. Indeed, Hattušili's complaint that the Ahhiyawan messenger did not bring him any gifts[249] suggests that this was a deviation from standard protocol. There thus is reason to assume that Hittite/Anatolian objects were sent to the Ahhiyawan court, yet Mycenae has yielded a mere three Anatolian objects, all predating the thirteenth century.[250] This problem, however, affects not only Mycenae. Cline listed a total of only twelve Anatolian objects in Aegean Late Bronze Age contexts, whereas elsewhere, including Egypt, which we know to have been in close contact with the Hittites, Hittite objects are so rare that when one is found, a whole research article is devoted to it.[251] Considering this, we may assume that Anatolian/Hittite objects have either not been recognized as such (which is unlikely) or were perishable in nature. The same may apply to the Ahhiyawan ware that must have been sent to the Hittite court.

A final argument in favor of the identification of the kingdom of Mycenae with Ahhiyawa is the relative stability of the kingdom of Mycenae. Although archaeology has demonstrated that parts of the habitation around the citadel, including some of the "houses" that

248. Helck 1995, 80. See also Haider 1996.

249. KUB XIV 3 (*supra*).

250. Cline 1994, 271.

251. As for example the single(!) Hittite pendant found in the remains of Akhetaten.

probably served some kind of administrative purpose, suffered destruction by fire sometime during the late LH IIIB2 period, there is very little to suggest that the lords of Mycenae experienced troubles or perceived any serious threat until the very end of the thirteenth century.[252] Quite the contrary; Mycenae and the other centers in the Argolid seem to have reached their peak of prosperity and population size during the mid-thirteenth century. The same applies to Korinthia, where the Nemea valley was drained so as to provide for more agricultural land.[253] Nowhere in the Argolid or in Korinthia is there any trace of severe unrest; there are no major destructions, no apparent changes in population. If there was any kingdom on mainland Greece that would fit the profile of a powerful, stable, and prosperous kingdom during the thirteenth century, it is that of the lords of Mycenae.

ARCHAEOLOGY OF EMPIRE

If we are thus arguing for a unified kingdom that controlled the larger part of the Greek mainland and centered upon Mycenae, we should investigate whether there is any direct archaeological evidence of Mycenaean unity.

This immediately raises a methodological problem. To look for a unified kingdom or "empire," as one is inclined to call it, on archaeological grounds is notoriously difficult.[254] The contemporary and near-

252. Wace (1954, 243) postulated that the so-called "House of the Oil Merchant" was destroyed during LH IIIB2 by human conduct. He suggested that the vases found inside had been used to store olive oil and were deliberately smashed to fuel the flames. Later excavations, however, yielded evidence of a destruction as a result of an earthquake, of which displaced walls are the clearest testimony (Mylonas 1983, 146). In a paper presented in 1941, Carl Blegen argued for Mycenae as a "capital" on the mainland, and that the mainland elites "deliberately adopted and absorbed a great many of refinements of Minoan civilization...the culmination of the process may be seen in the overthrow of Cretan power and the capture of the Chief Minoan centers" (Blegen 1941, 9). Though Blegen considered the rulers of Mycenae to be "arbiters" of a civilization of Minoan and mainland heritages, he appears not to have considered Mycenae to be the capital of a veritable unified state.

253. Cf. Cherry / Davis 2001, 154–56.

254. For discussions on the concept of empire, see Alcock / D'Altroy / Morrison / Sinopoli 2001 (especially Barfield 2001, 29 ff.); Turchin 2006. See for archaeological considerations Schreiber 2001; Postgate 1994; Zimansky 1995.

by example of the Hittites, whose most important sites were known decades before the Hittite script was deciphered, but whose lost empire was only pieced together after the decipherment of the latter, rings clear.[255] Moreover, "empires" may vary in territorial size, composition, ideology, and control exercised by the central authority. The Roman empire of the 2nd century AD, for example, had a totally different social organization, ideology of rule, and military structure from those of the "Holy Roman Empire" of the German Middle Ages, despite the fact that the latter was essentially built on the memory of the former.[256] Consequently, we must first address the problem of defining the concept of empire and establish the various ways in which social organization, the degree of control of the central authority on the periphery, and the ideology of imperial rule may have differed over space and time.

Roughly speaking, one can identify two different types of empire. The first could best be described as a conglomerate of peer polities, bound together by economic or military needs. The cohesion of such an empire is limited to the degree of cooperation between peer polities, with one of the member states achieving temporary hegemony over the others. Historical parallels for this type of empire are found in Early-Dynastic Sumer, Classical Greece, and the Holy Roman Empire in Germany during the Middle Ages.[257] Although the member states of such an empire could, especially when there was a clearly identifiable "common" foe, organize themselves into a military unity, such cooperation was usually limited to periods of crisis. The concept of empire in these cases was more a matter of the mind than of reality, an ideology of unity, whether through a common past (real or imagined), culture,

---

255. See for example Sayce 1910, 72 ff. on the reconstruction of the Hittite empire on the basis of Hittite glyptics, possible only after the realization that various stela found throughout the Near East (at Aleppo, Hamah, and Karabel, for example) were inscribed in Hittite hieroglyphic. Here, too, we see that the empire is still reconstructed as Syrian-based, rather than Anatolian, a result of the earliest European knowledge of the Hittites as a scattering of Syrian principalities, the Khatte in the Bible. For a brief overview of the development of Hittite scholarship, see Macqueen 1975, 22 ff.

256. Cf. Barfield 2001, 38–39; for a similar principle in the Carolingian empire, see Moreland 2001.

257. For Sumer see Postgate 1994, 1 ff.; for Classical Greece see Rhodes 2007; for the Holy Roman Empire Turchin 2006 with references.

language, or religion shared by various essentially independent and "equal" polities. On the whole, most of these polities operated more or less independently. Needless to say, empires of this sort are difficult to identify on archaeological grounds alone.[258]

By contrast, empires of a more hierarchical structure, with a Great King governing vassal states through a complex bureaucracy, with one state clearly at the head of the others, should be easier to identify in the archaeological record. The eastern Mediterranean during the Late Bronze Age was dominated by empires of this type, and examples include the Hittite empire, the Middle Assyrian empire, Babylon under the Kassites, and New Kingdom Egypt. In these cases, there was no mistaking the head of state: in official documents, proclamations, and dedications the central authority was designated as the Great King, or, in Egypt, as "Pharaoh," whereas the local vassals were referred to simply as king, chief, or mayor. To express the hierarchy of the participants in intra- and inter-state correspondence, the respective rulers adopted a family metaphor.[259] Vassals would address their overlord (and in rare cases, the peers of their overlord) as "my father," whereas they themselves were addressed as "my son." Peers would address each other as "brother." This was a totally different system from the city-state hegemonies; this was a world with a clear stratification of rulers, formalized with treaties and cemented by marriages between ruling houses. Succession, too, was secured by treaties, with vassals pledging support not only to their present overlord, but also to his rightful heir. In these power structures, the royal administration was everywhere, affecting even the lives of the common people. Taxes were collected according to a centrally organized system (which, in order to fulfil the obligations to the overlord, prompted increased centralization within the vassal kingdoms themselves), while roads were constructed to connect the various parts of the empire to the kingdom at its core.[260]

Thus contemporary texts identify two types of empire, with totally different backgrounds, organizations, ideologies, and economies. The

---

258. Note in this respect Voltaire's famous remark on the Holy Roman Empire: "Ce corps qui s'appelait et qui s'appelle encore le saint empire romain n'était en aucune manière ni saint, ni romain, ni empire"(*Essai sur l'histoire generale et sur les moeurs et l'espirit des nations*, 1756).

259. Cf. Avruch 2000, 154–57; Zaccagnini 2000.

260. Cf. Barfield 2001, 30–31.

issue is whether both types can be reconstructed on the basis of archaeological features.

In the pages below, we will propose a number of archaeologically traceable features that appear to be indicative of the existence of an empire. These features should not be considered as a *sine qua non*; if any or perhaps even all of these features are absent, we should not automatically dismiss the possibility that the area under study was, at some point, subject to one single authority. Conversely, the presence of these features does not automatically prove the existence of an empire. They should not be misunderstood as criteria, but rather as possible indices, and only become meaningful in combination with other, textual, evidence.

Listed below are various archaeological features of an empire based upon comparisons among a number of known empires, including those of Akkad, Ur III, Hammurabi's Babylon, the Hittite kingdom, Early-Dynastic Egypt, Iron Age Urartu, and a number of more "modern" parallels.

1. *Intrusive Architecture*

One of the clearest markers of an overarching authority is its architectural tradition, often markedly different from local traditions. Even in regions of general cultural uniformity, "imperial" building can normally be singled out on the basis of its standardized plans and uniformity. Good examples in this respect are Naram-Sin's fort at Tell Brak or the Assyrian governor's palace at Til-Barsip.[261] Similarly, in Proto-Dynastic Egypt, the erection of mudbrick structures replacing earlier buildings appears to have been directly related to state formation. As such, the construction of mudbrick buildings throughout Egypt, although perhaps not directly a result of the unification of Egypt, seems to have been closely related to the rise of a unified Egyptian state.[262] Likewise, the erection of a 1st-dynasty royal fortress on lands that had hitherto belonged to a local shrine at Elephantine indicates the rise of a central authority with its own agenda, sometimes conflicting with local interests.[263] Imperial structures, such as barracks, fortresses, or palaces, apart

---

261. Postgate 1994, 10; Mallowan 1947, 63–68 (*non vidi*).

262. Wilkinson 1999, 36.

263. *Ibid.*, 308, 329.

from being a monumental sign of the power of the overlord, are usually built for administrative or military purposes. Precisely because they are meant to impress the local, subjugated, population they represent a different, intrusive type of architecture.

Examples: *Mesopotamia (Akkad, Ur III, Hammurabi), Egypt, Urartu, Hittites*

2. *Uniformity of Administrative Tools*

Depending on the degree of control exercised by the central authority over the periphery, local systems of weights and measures, as well as calendars, will be changed/adjusted to a common, imperial system. An example of recent date is the use of our metric system, imposed by Napoleon Bonaparte. As such, the change to "imperial measures" can also be discernible in basic construction materials, such as the shapes and sizes of mudbricks or stones. The same applies to the sizes and shapes of clay tablets used for the administration. As a rule, in Mesopotamia at least, each political entity used its own types of clay tablets.[264] Absorption into a larger empire meant conforming to the shapes and sizes of that empire.

Examples: *Mesopotamia (Akkad, Ur III, Hammurabi), Hittites*

3. *Imperial Language*

Although the language of the imperial administration does not necessarily reflect the ethnic or cultural composition of the respective empire, imperial administration was usually recorded in a single language, the language of the triumphant entity. In Sumer, the rise of Sargon of Akkad meant that Sumerian was no longer used for the administration, whereas the collapse of the Akkadian empire and the rise of the Third Dynasty of Ur meant a return to Sumerian as the imperial language. In Urartu, the imperial language appears to have been used virtually exclusively for the empire's administration and monuments; the population, and probably a number of kings, spoke different, local, tongues.

Examples: *Mesopotamia (Akkad, Ur III, Hammurabi), Egypt, Urartu*

4. *Intrusive Uniformity in Material Culture*

Since the political order can be changed by a single historical event, it is invariably less stable than the cultural in time and space. However, if

264. Postgate (discussion), in Killen / Voutsaki 2001.

successful over time, imperial rule, almost without exception, influences and changes local customs. Cultural changes as a result of the expansion of royal power are usually most evident with local elites, as a result of the central authority's attempts to limit the elites' display of power and the local elites' desire to associate with the court and its culture. Proto-Dynastic Egypt offers a good example, where an increase in uniformity in Southern Egyptian pottery styles (Naqada I to II) as a result of mass production and increased specialization (which in turn led to the advent of a more complex pottery technology, with vessels of a new and distinctive type) appears to have been directly related to the rise of powerful elites at such centers as Hierakonpolis and This.[265] In the case of Egypt, the new style of pottery was eventually adopted in all social strata. Elsewhere, for example, in Urartu Toprakkale pottery, while closely associated with imperial fortresses, temples, and palaces, and usually considered a marker of Urartian rule, was not adopted by local potters, who continued to produce a local, grayish type of pottery. With the collapse of the Urartian state, the local pottery styles survived, whereas Toprakkale pottery vanished.[266]

Examples: *Egypt, Urartu*

5. *Religious Uniformity*

Along with the royal drive toward uniformity of material culture comes the move toward uniformity in religion. The nature of this drive is closely connected to the status of the ruler. In Early-Dynastic Egypt,

---

265. Wilkinson 1999, 34 ff. The subsequent expansion of these centers correlates with the replacement of local pottery styles in northern Egypt by these new types of southern imports. Whether the north was gradually absorbed by (one of the) southern states or not, there are clear indications for profound changes in the social organization of northern Egyptian communities, especially marked by increased hierarchy and changing burial customs, eventually leading to a socio-cultural koinè throughout Egypt by the beginning of the Naqada III period. Although the eclipse of northern culture may have been primarily the result of exchange processes, there is at least the suggestion of southern expansion toward the north, including the foundation of (trading) colonies in the eastern delta. Cf. von der Way 1991; Kemp 1995, 687.

266. Zimansky 1995, 107. A case can be made to consider Urartu as a so-called "mirror empire," emerging in direct response to imperial state formation of its neighbors (Assyria); see Barfield 2001, 34 for comparisons.

local shrines (typically of a very open nature, without enclosure walls) that apparently did not fit into the state's concept of religion were treated with notable contempt; note that in southern Elephantine the entrance to a shrine of the local deity was blocked by the erection of a royal fortress.[267] Interestingly, the state did not partake in any way of the embellishment or sustaining of local shrines. In contrast, those temples that were deemed fitting for state interest were either completely rebuilt (in stone) or adorned with stone reliefs. In those cases access to the temples became restricted (by means of an enclosure wall); state religion was in the hands of the court and did not actively involve the local population.[268] In sum, there is a clear case of the state versus local religious traditions (even if some local religious traditions may become incorporated into "state" protocol). Needless to say, Egypt, where the drive to religious uniformity went hand in hand with the erection of a number of monuments to royal power in the shape of miniature step pyramids(!) throughout the realm[269] is an extreme example of unified statehood. However, even in those cases in which an empire appears to have been a relatively "loose" construct, such as the city-state leagues of Early-Dynastic Sumer, there usually was a central shrine (whether this is conceptual or spatial is irrelevant) where the (most powerful) ruler made his offering.[270]

Examples: *Egypt, Mesopotamia (Early Dynastic, Akkad, Ur III, Hammurabi), Hittites, Urartu*

6. *Large-scale Infrastructure Projects*

In order to effectively govern even the remote parts of an empire roads were needed to provide safe passage for troops, messengers, and merchants throughout the realm.[271] In case of troublesome terrain (mountains, rivers), the construction of bridges or passes would not only further transport throughout the region, but also provide for a visible marker of royal power. In Hittite Anatolia, for instance, important mountain passes, including the Karabel Pass, were embellished with signs of royal power: a relief of the king, his patron deity, or simply the

267. Wilkinson 1999, 308, 329: see also above.

268. *Ibid.*, 272.

269. *Ibid.*, 278, pl. 8.1.

270. Postgate 1994.

271. Cf. Barfield 2001, 30; see D'Altroy 2001, 210 for Inca parallels.

name of the king. In some cases, these landmarks served also as polity boundaries, in which case (such as at Karabel) this was specified in the respective rock carving. The more centralized an empire was, the more static its territorial concepts. Roads, as a result, were not only of practical use for the transport of goods and men, but also had symbolic value, linking the various polities within the realm to the empire's heartland.

Examples: *Hittites, Mesopotamia (Akkad, Ur III, Hammurabi), Urartu, Etruscans, Roman empire, Incas.*

7. *Large-scale Agricultural/Economic Projects*

Along with a desire to link the parts of the empire to the heartland by roads is the drive toward consolidation of royal economic power. In Early-Dynastic Egypt, the installation of large "royal domains" and "royal estates" throughout the provinces producing directly for the crown (for royal cult, for palace life, for distribution amongst followers), ensured economic power over the realm and over the provincial elites.[272] This custom prevailed throughout pharaonic history, although the scale of the estates increased. During the Middle Kingdom, Amenhat III embarked on a project to drain the Fayum depression by directing superfluous water to a large canal, therewith furthering the region's agricultural potential. Part of the Fayum subsequently was allocated to the crown.[273] Centuries later, the Ptolemaic rulers of Egypt restored Amenhat's canal and embarked on a project of land reclamation in the same area, while under Roman rule, the whole of Egypt was essentially a royal estate (it did not fall under the senate's administration). Similar practice is attested in Inca Peru, where the expansion of the Inca kingdom went hand in hand with the installation of an increasing number of royal estates throughout the realm.[272]

Examples: *Egypt (all periods), Babylonia, Assyria, Roman empire, Incas.*

---

272. Wilkinson 1999, 117 ff. Domains (*pr-nswt*) were established by a particular king, above all to guarantee the maintenance of the royal mortuary cult and were substantial, though not necessarily contiguous, areas of farming land in the delta. By contrast, Estates (*ḥwt*) seem to have been a more specific institution, either a particular locality or a foundation supplying a particular commodity.

273. Especially the huge complex later known as the "Labyrinth," actually the mortuary temple of Amenhat III, was, as a royal estate, the important economic factor in the region.

274. D'Altroy 2001, 218 ff.

ARCHAEOLOGY OF THE MYCENAEAN EMPIRE

The features listed above share one characteristic: the suppression of local identity and the promotion of a state ideology. We have established previously that both the Hittite and the Egyptian textual records suggest the presence of a unified state in the Aegean and our evaluation of the archaeological evidence suggests that Mycenae is the most plausible candidate as a capital of Tanaju/Ahhiyawa. We now need to establish whether archaeological data corroborate that evaluation. Is there archaeological evidence of an "intrusive" culture on the Greek mainland in the Late Bronze Age? Can we see a conscious drive toward uniformity and can we attribute this to developments in the Mycenaean heartland?

1. *Architectural Uniformity in the Mycenaean World*

A true typology of Mycenaean domestic architecture is difficult to establish and though Pascal Darcque, in his important 2005 monograph *L'Habitat Mycénien*, distinguished between a "simple" and a "complex" type of domestic architecture, many buildings appear to have been modified rigorously over time, radically changing the character of the structures.[275] On the whole, Mycenaean houses appear to have consisted of a number of rather generic spaces without a specific purpose and used for various domestic tasks.[276] There appears to have been remarkably little development in domestic architecture throughout the Mycenaean era; shapes and building techniques are largely the same throughout the Late Helladic Period.[277] Mycenaean domestic architecture stems largely from preceding Middle Helladic traditions both in shape and location of settlement,[278] and we probably should interpret the uniformity of domestic architectural traditions throughout the Greek mainland as the result of a shared past, rather than as a product of Mycenaean (cultural) expansion.[279] Moreover, the varying sizes of

275. Darcque 2005, 353; for substantial alterations of the architecture over time (including additional rooms with a different alignment), see for example unit IV-6 at Nichoria (Darcque 2005, 350 with references, and Plan 107).

276. *Ibid.*, 353.

277. *Ibid.*, 355.

278. *Ibid.*, 354.

279. Although the use of mudbricks in Late Bronze Age Macedonia might be considered to have been the result of Mycenaean influence (Darcque 2005,

mudbricks used in the construction of (domestic?) structures at various sites strike us with a sense of "randomness"; there certainly is no evidence for a uniform measurement system.[280]

In contrast to domestic architecture, Mycenaean palatial architecture was prone to a number of innovations and developments. Although there may be some argument for continuity from Early Helladic architectural traditions (corridor houses, such as the House of Tiles at Lerna) in the construction of the Mycenaean palaces,[281] the scanty remains of a number of pre-palatial structures at various sites throughout Greece indicate that the "architectural evolution" of the Mycenaean palace was, initially at least, by no means a deliberate process, but rather a wide array of local attempts to aggrandize the focus of the settlement. Minoan aspects, local traditions, and innovations were mixed in various ways and to various degrees.[282] In a way, the early Mycenaean period can, from an architect's viewpoint, be considered a truly experimental phase with various results, some of which, such as the Menelaion at Sparta, "représenterait une sorte de prototype qui ne donnerait naissance à aucune veritable série."[283] With the wide variety of architectural traditions, innovations, and failures in mind, the sudden

---

396). Note that whereas in Thessaly and regions north of Thessaly brick was used alongside rammed earth, mudbrick appears to have been used almost exclusively in the regions south of Thessaly. Cf. Guest-Papamanoli 1978, 24.

280. Darcque 2005, 75, fig. 8; Guest-Papamanoli 1978, 14–15 (including data from Crete).

281. Darcque (2005, 376) rather unconvincingly suggests that the overall layout of the palace of Pylos (as a whole) resembles the layout of corridor houses, but fails to explain the gap in (monumental) architecture and notable change in material culture separating EH II from MH (or even EH III) and LH.

282. A large building built in LH IIIA Tiryns might, on the grounds of similarities (orientation, structure) with the later palace, be considered a veritable early Mycenaean palace (cf. Kilian 1987b, 212, fig. 7), while a number of relatively large structures at various other sites (including Mycenae [remains of wall-paintings; Immerwahr 1990, pl. XVI], the Menelaion [a well-planned megaron complex; Hope Simpson / Dickinson 1979, 108], Pylos [a large structure with Cretan palatial features? Cf. Kilian 1987b, 213–17], and Thebes [the Old Kadmeion; see above]) seem to indicate a similar drive toward increased "monumentality" of the centers of the respective local administrations, though in a different execution.

283. Darcque 2005, 374.

rise of the "true" Mycenaean palace, the structure as we know it from LH IIIB, focused upon a single large megaron, and its implementation throughout the Greek mainland—the exact layout of the palaces at Thebes and Orchomenos is unclear but Dimini in Thessaly seems to have a clear focus on a megaron—is notable and difficult to explain in terms of cultural interaction only.

It is generally acknowledged that the palaces of Pylos, Mycenae, and Tiryns, in architectural respect, essentially are the same. The newly discovered megara at Dimini may be interpreted as (part of) a palatial unit and could, perhaps, be added to the list. These palaces share a number of distinctive features, such as:

- The focus on one central megaron, alongside which relatively narrow corridors provide access to storage-rooms;
- Access to the megaron unit is provided through a court, partly surrounded by colonnades;
- The court is reached via a propylon, set on an axis different from that of the rest of the palace unit. In the case of Tiryns, there is a second propylon and a second court, whereas at Mycenae the propylon (sometimes designated with the misnomer "west porch") is built downhill, northwest of the palace and granting access to a path running uphill (which in turn, via a corridor, ends at the court).

A number of features have been attested at only some of the palaces.[284] Most notable is the presence of a second, but smaller, megaron at the palaces of Pylos, Tiryns, and Mycenae. This particular structure in all three cases appears to have been a completely integrated element in Mycenaean palatial architecture, to the point that Kilian described the typical Mycenaean palace as a "bipartite unit that consists of a main palace (megaron or great hall) and a secondary one, each with its own independent functional units."[285]

---

284. But see Younger 2005, who argues for the presence of a bathroom and a secondary megaron at Mycenae, and postulates a standardized plan, reflecting standardized concepts and functions, of the Mycenaean palaces.

285. Kilian 1988, 293; for a comparison of the various Mycenaean palaces and their reflection of typical Mycenaean political structures, see Kilian 1987a, 21–38.

In our discussion on the status of the *wanax* and the *lawagetas*, I have noted that, despite the position of both officials in Mycenaean society being quite unclear, the *wanax* is usually considered to have been the person residing in the "great" megaron,[286] whereas the smaller megaron unit is considered to have been the "office" of the *lawagetas*. In the context of a greater, unified Mycenaean kingdom, this is an interesting hypothesis, especially if one (and there seems to be space [though, it cannot be stressed enough, no conclusive evidence!] for such a concept in the Linear B texts) considers the *wanax* to have been the overlord and the *lawagetas* the local lord, in which case Kilian's "bipartite unit" may be the architectural reflection of the Mycenaean kingdom's hierarchical structure of power.

There is no point in dealing with the endless list of publications on the iconography of palace frescoes here, since essentially all these publications argue from the basic assumption that the *wanax*, as a local, autonomous monarch, resided in the central megaron, and that the iconography, therefore, was focused on his position in the local society. Proof for that assumption is, however, lacking. Suffice to note that even the iconography, for example the notable focus on marine motives (octopi, fish, and dolphins) at Pylos and Tiryns, is remarkably uniform throughout Greece.

The uniformity of palace architecture throughout Greece stands in contrast to domestic architecture, which continues to be diverse and highly "individual" throughout the palatial period and, indeed, thereafter. It is questionable, especially with the diversity in proto-palatial architecture in mind, whether this uniformity can be considered to have been the result of cultural interaction only. The Near Eastern parallels provided above would, at any rate, certainly allow for an imposition of uniform palatial architecture.

2. *Uniformity of Administrative Tools in the Mycenaean World*

It has already been noted that the uniformity of the palatial administrative system throughout Mycenaean Greece would, to a Near Eastern archaeologist at least, suggest that the various palaces were subject to a single authority. The shapes, the sizes, and the way the administration

---

286. By "residing" I mean, of course, the official duties of the *wanax* (whatever the nature), and I am not implying that the *wanax* actually lived in the megaron (though he may have lived on the first floor).

functioned (tax collection, distribution of goods etc.) are virtually identical at every palace. Similarly, the numerals and methods of measurement appear to have been the same throughout the entire Mycenaean palatial world. Whether the Mycenaean calendar was equally uniform all over Greece remains unclear, because of the limited number of relevant Linear B texts. On the whole, there is no evidence of an overlap in calendrical terms among the various palaces, although the fact that a number of month names known from Cnossos have Classical parallels might indicate a widespread terminology.[287] In sum, when it comes to uniformity of administrative tools throughout Greece, the Mycenaean palatial world conforms rather well to a highly organized empire.

3. *Imperial Language in Mycenaean Greece*

I have noted that the Linear B texts concern only administrative matters. As a result, there is little variation in the formulas or the structures of the texts. They consist mainly of simple lists of material and people. Despite the highly uniform nature of the texts, occasional mistakes, or "slips of the pen," seem to indicate that the language used for the palatial administration was not the language normally spoken by those that wrote it.[288] Underneath the layer of the administrative language there may have been a wide variety of local dialects. Assessing the various layers beneath Mycenaean Greek has proven to be a difficult exercise, and a variety of models has been proposed.[289] There is no point in

287. Vermeule 1957, 200; see also Ventris / Chadwick 1956, 199; Palmer 1955.

288. Cf. Chadwick 1976b, 103–17. Rupert Thompson (1996–97, 303–33, esp. 330) argues that there is some variety in the language used by the various palatial administrations, and that linguistic changes in the various administrations seem to differ by administration. This might be evidence that Mycenaean was not an "accounting artifice" but a veritable language, with regional differences/accents. However, as Thompson himself admits, "the level of differentiation between the language at different sites is surprisingly low" (although he suggests that this might be the result of the inadequacies of the Linear B script).

289. John Chadwick proposed that Doric, the dialect often thought to have arrived in the Greek world with the legendary invasion of the Dorians at the end of the palatial period, was already spoken by at least part of the population, possibly as a sort of lower-class dialect as opposed to the "imperial" administrative tongue. Cf. Chadwick 1976b, 103–17; see Drews 1988

dealing with those models here; suffice to state that, since Mycenaean Greek appears to have been a language used primarily for the palatial administration whereas a significant part of the population of the palatial world would have spoken different dialects of Greek, Mycenaean Greeks may very well be considered an "imperial language" or at least an elite language. As such, it may be considered as yet another argument in favor of a unified Mycenaean state.

4. *Intrusive Uniformity in Mycenaean Material Culture*

Mycenaean material culture is widely believed to derive largely from the preceding Middle Helladic culture. This is especially evident in the pottery corpus, where the adoption of Minoan shapes (and decorations) essentially marks the shift from the Middle Helladic period to the Late Helladic, Mycenaean era. The adoption of Minoan prototypes cannot be explained from a purely technological viewpoint, since late Middle Helladic pottery was, at least in a number of cases, of such a high quality that it was as good as the later Mycenaean pottery.[290] Interestingly, the "new" LH I style of pottery, including a number of shapes that are "patently of Cretan ancestry," is thought to have been developed at a single specific center, by a specific school, most likely to be situated in the northeast of the Peloponnese (i.e. the Argolid).[291] The new "Mycenaean" style developed rapidly and eclipsed local pottery traditions throughout the Greek mainland within a few generations, while

---

(with references) for critiques and, most recently, Finkelberg 2005. Regardless of such details, the point remains that the diversity of dialects throughout the palatial world strongly suggests that Mycenaean Greek was an imperial veneer, a language for the administration, not for the people.

290. Dickinson (1974, 112) noted that some decorated pottery from Nichoria and Ay. Stephanos "are hard to distinguish from Mycenaean in appearance, while on a rather rare ware that seems to have been manufactured in the northeast Peloponnese, coated with red or black and decorated with dull cream-yellow or white, the paint is as lustrous as the best Mycenaean. The clay of this particular ware, as of some other Late Phase wares, such as the later bichrome types, is quite as well prepared as that of Mycenaean vases, and the vases themselves were probably wheel made; in terms of technique Blegen was fully justified in classing it with LH I."

291. Dickinson (1974, 113), although Jeremy and Sarah Rutter (1976, *non vidi*) argue for a Laconian origin under Kytheran influence (but see Coldstream 1979).

Minoan influence became increasingly prominent.[292] It is, as a result, likely that the emerging Mycenaean elites adopted Minoan shapes and decorations for considerations of style, distinguishing them from the "commoners," who continued, in part, to produce pottery in the old MH tradition.

Throughout palatial Greece, Mycenaean pottery was notably similar; pots at Pylos were essentially made and decorated in the same way as pots at Mycenae or Thebes.[293] This koinè persisted until the very end of the palatial period and it was only during LH IIIB2 that local traditions began to emerge.[294] It is notable that "Mycenaean" pottery shapes, such as the stirrup jar and the kylix, did not survive the collapse of the palatial system for long; they became increasingly rare throughout LH IIIC and disappear from the record in the Sub-Mycenaean period. In contrast, shapes following the Middle Helladic tradition that had

292. For example, LH I pottery was found together with Late MH pottery in the shaft graves at Mycenae (see Dickinson 1974), whereas at Aegina, the earliest Mycenaean phase (Ceramic Phase K) is characterized by the introduction of a few pieces of imported mainland pottery, mainly Vapheio cups and teacups (Gauß / Smetana 2007, 66; see also Wohlmayr 2007 [although to me, his fragment 6, I think correctly identified as an alabastron, appears to be LH I, i.e. Mycenaean, rather than Late Middle Helladic]). LH II saw a significant increase in Minoan influence with the adoption of Minoan palatial-style pottery. The LH IIA corpus of shapes was mostly of Cretan derivation, though Mycenaean potters continued to adapt the shapes to their own changing tastes/needs. After LH IIB, new shapes are mainly the result of these "Mycenaean" innovations (cf. Mountjoy 1993, 31), although the introduction of the stirrup jar, probably in LH IIIA2, should probably be ascribed to Cretan influence (although Crete itself by this time was under Mycenaean control: the earliest [inscribed] stirrup jars on the mainland appear to have been imports from Ghania, followed by a few vases from Mycenae; Mountjoy 1993, 74; Catling/Cherry/Jones/Killen 1980, 100).

293. Although preferences in pottery shapes appear to have varied somewhat according to region (although the shapes themselves are perfectly koinè Mycenaean) during the LH IIIA period. One may, perhaps, ascribe these differences to varying needs by region. During LH IIIB1 even these local preferences appear to have been minimal. Cf. Mountjoy 1999, 27–34.

294. The most notable example is the above-mentioned "East Aegean, West Anatolian Interface" pottery, which emerged in LH IIIB, but only flourished during the post-palatial (LH IIIC) period. For regional differences on the mainland, see Mountjoy 1999, 36 ff.

enjoyed only minimal interest during the palatial era survived the collapse of the Mycenaean world and became, in a number of cases (such as the kantharos), increasingly popular over the course of the Iron Age.

In effect, the change from Middle Helladic pottery traditions to Mycenaean pottery during the first two centuries of the Late Helladic period appears to have been so distinct and so widespread, while the ensuing two centuries saw such an extraordinarily homogeneity in pottery production throughout the Aegean, that this is difficult to explain as a result of cultural exchange. Moreover, the prominence of Argive workshops, both in the early phases of the Late Helladic period and in the palatial period, as the "leaders in style," is, perhaps, best understood as a result of Argive political dominance over the Greek mainland and a drive toward "cultural unification," much like the principles we have observed in early Egypt or, especially, Urartu. With the collapse of royal authority, this cultural unity gradually disintegrated.

5. *Religious Uniformity in Mycenaean Greece*

Archaeologically speaking, the Mycenaeans would appear to have been a remarkably secular society. Shrines and temples are virtually absent in the archaeological record,[295] whereas Mycenaean figurines are mostly small and unremarkable. However, the Linear B texts inform us that, at least in the kingdoms of Pylos and Knossos, there must have been a variety of sanctuaries dedicated to a range of deities. Moreover, they indicate that there were religious festivities, with offerings to one or several gods. The offerings differed, but usually included libations (of wine), the offering of meat, and, most of all, the donation of quantities of olive oil. Indeed, the overall quantities of oil dedicated to the gods are such that any practical use appears unlikely. In contemporary Egypt,

---

295. On the mainland, the only clear archaeological evidence of cult activity during the palatial period is from the cult center at Mycenae, although a case may be made for cult activity at one of the megara found at Dimini (Thessaly). The shrines found at Tiryns all appear to belong to the post-palatial (LH IIIC) period. Excavations by W-D. Niemeier at Kalopodi in Boeotia may suggest that there may have been a late-Mycenaean sanctuary there (lectures at the Archaeological Service, Athens, February 2008), while shrines are known at Ayia Irini on Kea, and at Philakopi on Melos.

texts indicate that (olive) oil was used "to keep the lamps of the temples burning"[296] and we may, perhaps, think of similar principles in Greece.

The recurrence of a number of deities in texts from various palatial palaces indicates that the same gods were worshipped throughout the entire Mycenaean palatial world, although the Cretan pantheon appears to have known a number of distinctly local divinities. Similarly, there may be some indications for local deities at various mainland sites. At Tiryns there is a notable preference for bovine figurines, whereas these hardly appear at Mycenae. At the same time, the snake figurines found at Mycenae appear to have been "site specific" and have not been found elsewhere.[297] There thus is the suggestion that, much like in the Classical world, the Hittite empire, or Egypt, each center had its own patron god or goddess. On the whole, however, religion seems to have been rather uniform, although this, of course, does not mean that there were no regional differences or variations in the pantheon. This sense of general uniformity is reflected also in the archaeological record: at all palatial sites, the typical Mycenaean phi- and psi-figurines have been found.

It has been noted above that temples and shrines are conspicuously rare in the Mycenaean archaeological record. Monumental cultic buildings have not been found at any of the palatial centers, with the exception of the cult center at Mycenae. The construction of that complex seems to have been a rather late development (of the thirteenth century) and is difficult to interpret. We might speculate and view its construction, within the newly built cyclopean walls of the Mycenaean citadel, in the light of increased royal control over hitherto relatively "public" religious practice or as a central sanctuary for the worship of all the gods in the realm. However, evidence in support of either interpretation is lacking.

The problem is to establish whether the sense of religious homogeneity throughout Greece was the result of an "imperial drive" or rather the outcome of cultural interaction within the Mycenaean world. The presence of "local" gods at Knossos, as well as a number of Knossos-specific epithets for the goddess *potnia*, while the majority of attested

296. Great Harris (I) papyrus; cf. Breasted 1906 (A.R. III §239, 241; A.R. IV §236).

297. Unpublished lecture ("Was dem Volke frommt…") by Melissa Vetters at the DAI Athens, 15th May 2007.

deities in the Linear B texts are "Greek," might indicate an overlay of new (Greek) deities over the native, Cretan set of beliefs. However, without clear insight into the religious beliefs of the Middle Bronze Age society on the Greek mainland, it appears difficult to state anything with certainty about the development of Mycenaean religion on the mainland.

6. *Large-scale Infrastructure and Agricultural Works in Mycenaean Greece*

One of the most remarkable features of Mycenaean society was its ability to muster the resources and manpower to undertake large-scale infrastructure and agricultural projects. The sheer magnitude of a number of these projects makes one wonder whether any or even two or three of the "provincial centers" could be held accountable for their undertaking. Most notable in this respect are the drainage, colonization (to put it like that), and administration of the Kopaïs basin in Boeotia, the construction of a large dam near Tiryns (to prevent the flooding of the Tirynthian lower town), the drainage of the Nemea valley (originally a swamp), and, perhaps most notable, the construction of a harbor at Pylos. In case of the construction, probably sometime in LH III, of the port of Pylos, it has been stated that "the kingdom at that time had sufficient economic incentive, manpower, know-how and political authority to justify and realize such a project."[298] But the calculations behind this observation are nowhere explained. Indeed, the size of the Pylian workforce as recorded in the Linear B texts seems rather small for such an undertaking. On the other hand, such a project would be more manageable if organized by a higher authority, able to draw manpower and resources from all of Greece.[299]

Apart from furthering trade with the construction of ports capable of accommodating ships such as the one excavated at Ulu Burun (which needed a quay for loading and off-loading), and projects meant to increase agricultural capacity (such as the drainage of the Nemea valley and the Kopaïs basin), arguably the most famous infrastructure work from the Mycenaean era is the system of roads. Although it has been

298. Zangger / Timpson / Yazvenko / Kuhnke / Knauss 1997, 623.

299. And potentially add the numbers of the workforce with imported laborers from Anatolia. See the Tawagalawa Letter, and comments in Bryce 2003b, 203.

proposed that the Mycenaean roads were constructed to facilitate the transportation of bulk goods, loaded onto heavy vehicles, the general perception is that transport of large quantities of bulk goods, such as grain or olives, was rare.[300] Rather, roads served to facilitate the speedy passage of chariots. Linear B texts, especially from Pylos, indicate that the palaces had a significant number of chariots at their disposal, and it appears likely that a number of these were used by the *e-qe-ta*, the "followers" often referred to in the same texts. These and other officials may have served as liaison officers, reporting to the king, conveying orders to local commanders, or, in the case of emergencies, acting as heavy infantry brought to the battlefield by chariot.[301] Indeed, it appears likely that the Mycenaean system of roads served (perhaps not primarily, but at least prominently) a military role, facilitating the speedy deployment of troops and the monitoring of troublesome border regions.[302] To this impression add the remains of a Mycenaean road in combination with what is thought to have been a Mycenaean fortification wall, spanning the isthmus near Corinth.[303]

I have already noted above that the Mycenaean road connecting Mycenae with the isthmus is one of the reasons to consider the Korinthia as part of the Mycenaean heartland. As such, this road was part of a larger system of roads that connected the various centers in the Argolid and focussed on Mycenae.[304] Although only part of this system has survived, it seems clear that, in terms of infrastructure, the Mycenaean era saw the zenith of Greek engineering. This appears not to have been restricted to the Argive plain. Remains of Mycenaean roads have been found in Korinthia (where a highway linked Mycenae to the isthmus), Arcadia,[305] Messenia (where there is the suggestion of a road connecting Pylos to Kalamata),[306] and Boeotia (especially in the Kopaïs

300. Lavery 1990, 165; Hope Simpson / Hagel 2006, 170.

301. Cf. Crouwel 1981; Chadwick 1976a, 177; Kelder 2005a.

302. Hope Simpson / Hagel 2006, 175.

303. Broneer 1968; Hope Simpson / Hagel 2006, 124, esp. 137–40.

304. Cf. Hope Simpson / Hagel 2006, 148 ff.; Crouwel 1981, 17; Mylonas 1966, 86.

305. Cf. Krigas 1987.

306. Fant / Loy 1972, 27; Hope Simpson / Hagel 2006, 161.

basin).[307] As McDonald argued: "there are several considerations, political, economic, military, which indicate that traffic overland was much better developed in the later second millennium BC than in the Classical period,"[308] and although no remains of Mycenaean roads have (yet) been found that are unequivocally crossing the borders of the respective provincial principalities, there thus seems to be the suggestion of an overarching authority, asserting and consolidating its influence over even remote regions in a very practical (yet visible) way.

7. *Archaeological Evidence for a Unified Mycenaean State*

If we compare a number of archaeologically attested features for empires to the archaeological evidence from Mycenaean Greece, we must conclude the following:

Archaeologically speaking, the Greek mainland in the Late Bronze is remarkably uniform. To some extent, this appears to have been the natural result of developments of the rather uniform material culture of the Greek Middle Bronze Age. At the same time, various local traditions (i.e. traditions that were not the same all over Greece during the Middle Bronze Age and the early phase of the Late Bronze Age), most notably monumental architecture and pottery traditions, dwindle in significance or die out, eclipsed by a new pan-Mycenaean tradition. In case of palace architecture, it is difficult to establish the source of this "Mycenaean palatial" style, but in the case of pottery production, the Argolid appears to have provided the model for the rest of the mainland.

As has been noted above, throughout the fourteenth and thirteenth centuries BC, Mycenaean pottery was made in essentially the same way throughout palatial Greece, in the Argive way. This immediately demonstrates the weakness of archaeology as a tool for establishing the territorial extent of a prehistoric state. The Mycenaean pottery koinè extends beyond the borders of the reconstructed territory of Ahhiyawa, Tanaju, Mycenae. Iolkos (Dimini), and Crete (Knossos and Ghania) are, archaeologically speaking, virtually indistinguishable from those centers and regions within the reconstructed Ahhiyawan realm. As a result, one can either include these regions in that reconstruction, but additional

307. Cf. Knauss 1987; 1990; Hope Simpson / Hagel 2006, 162–64.

308. Mc Donald 1964, 218.

evidence for that is lacking, or reject archaeology as a reliable means to reconstruct ancient states.

Rejecting archaeology as a reliable tool appears to be most prudent. The important observation is, in sum, that the archaeological data are compatible with the Hittite and Egyptian texts, but do not prove the existence of a larger territorial state in Late Bronze Age Greece.

SYNTHESIS: THE RECONSTRUCTION OF A GREAT KINGDOM

We have seen that the "traditional" view of the Mycenaean palatial world, a world of several similar yet independent kingdoms, can no longer be upheld. There are too many inconsistencies with contemporary texts and a general lack of conclusive evidence for that remarkably "Classical" view on the Mycenaean world, with competing kingdoms bound together only by language and culture, as was the case with the later Greek *poleis* of the sixth to third centuries BC.

The Linear B texts, which have long been the "fuel" for this view, are unreliable when it comes to reconstructing any political entity, if only because of their extremely limited scope in time (last years of the palatial administration) and ambition (meant only to record the flow of men and goods in each respective territory).

It has been demonstrated that the archaeological data in no way provide any evidence for the popular scenario of a Mycenaean Greece consisting of various independent polities. By contrast, a number of archaeological features, especially the cultural uniformity, the uniformity of the palatial administrations, and the ability to embark on large-scale projects, would allow for some sort of an overarching authority. However, conclusive archaeological evidence for such a scenario is lacking.

Contemporary Hittite texts indicate the presence of an Aegean kingdom called Ahhiyawa, which strengthens its hold on western Anatolia from *ca.* 1400 till 1220 BC. During this period, the kings of Ahhiyawa are clearly able to deal with the Hittite kings both in a military and diplomatic way and are of such stature that they are called "Great King" from the mid-thirteenth century on. The major Ahhiyawan foothold in Anatolia was Miletus, a sizable, prosperous Mycenaean settlement for most of the Late Bronze Age. Yet it was only a foothold. Ahhiyawa's political center was situated elsewhere. It has been demonstrated that Mycenae is the most plausible candidate in this respect.

On the other hand, Egyptian texts indicate that from the reign of Thutmoses III till at least the reign of Amenhotep III, the Egyptians were aware of an Aegean kingdom called Tanaju, which centered upon Mycenae (and its harbor Nauplion). Other parts of this kingdom are only named as regions and include Kythera, Messenia, the Thebaid, and possibly Elis (see Map 2, above).

Because of the Kom el Hetan list, the geographical extent of Tanaju is roughly known, although some of the identifications are open to debate. With Tanaju covering most of the Peloponnese and probably the Thebaid, there is very little room left for independent entities in the Aegean. As Ahhiyawa was an important state, capable of pursuing its aims in Anatolia both politically and militarily, it is very doubtful that this entity was located in the area left in the Aegean. It also implies an unlikely gap in both Hittite and Egyptian intelligence, as both of these kingdoms apparently were unaware of an important entity in the Aegean. Pondering these matters, it is compelling to consider Ahhiyawa to be the same as the Tanaju land known from the Kom el Hetan list. In other words: Tanaju = Ahhiyawa = the (larger part of the) Peloponnese, the Thebaid, various islands in the Aegean and Miletus on the Anatolian west coast, with Mycenae as its capital.

— APPENDIX —

SITES IN WESTERN ANATOLIA

The following sites are listed in approximate north to south order (see Map 7).

Troy - Hissarlık

The site of Troy has yielded a large number of Mycenaean artefacts, predominantly pottery. Mycenaean pottery is first attested in Troy VId, which appears to be contemporary with the stylistic period LH IIA.[309] LH IIB and LH IIB late pottery has been found in the layers of Troy VIe and VIf, respectively.[310] While some LH IIIA1 pottery has been found in the layers corresponding to Troy VIg, it was only during the occupation phase Troy VIh that Mycenaean pottery of LH IIIA2 style appeared in great numbers.[311]

---

309. The site of Troy appears to have been inhabited from late Neolithic times onward. The different periods of occupation have been labelled from the first occupation onward (i.e. starting with Troy I), but later modifications and specifications have resulted in a rather complicated array of sub-divisions. The habitation layers corresponding to the Late Bronze Age all fall under the generic phase of Troy VI, with a last phase extending to Troy VIIa (which, confusingly, is culturally identical to the preceding phases). See Table 2 for further explication. Cf. Stronk 2002–3 for a recent assessment of the ongoing excavations at the site of Troy.

310. Mountjoy 1997c, 292.

311. LH IIIA2 seems to have been the period of most intensive contact as 40 percent of the Mycenaean pottery then found was dated to this period. Cf.

It has been suggested that most of the Mycenaean-style pottery found at Troy was of local production,[312] but at least part of the corpus appears to have been imported. Chemical analysis suggests that most of the imported pottery came from Boeotia, although pottery coming from Attica, the region around Dimini and Aegina, may be present as well.[313] A similar analysis suggested that at least one group came from the Argolid.[314] It appears that the corpus of imported Mycenaean vessels at Troy was of a rather mixed nature.

While exact numbers are not provided, it is now beyond doubt that the corpus of Mycenaean-style pottery numerically exceeds any other corpus in Anatolia, with the exception of that from Miletus. Already at the time of Blegen's excavations over a 1000 sherds were known, representing an estimated 700 to 800 pots from the layers of Troy VIf to VIh alone.[315] Even Troy VII was found to yield Mycenaean pottery, of which, at that time at least, less than 20 percent was considered imported. Most of the Mycenaean pottery at Troy has a linear or patterned decoration; undecorated or pictorial material has scarcely been found.[316] The corpus comprises a wide range of shapes, open and closed, including goblets, kylikes, and bowls.

Mee 1978, 147; compare to LH IIA: 14%, LH IIB: 10%, LHIIIA1: 9%, LH IIIA2: 40%, LH IIIB: 20%, LH IIIC: 7%.

312. Mountjoy 1997a, 259–67.

313. Mommsen / Hertel / Mountjoy 2001, 173.

314. A group found by Schliemann. At least 120 samples taken, in contrast to the three taken from the "Boeotian" group. Certain elements in the same article remarked upon as being irrelevant or difficult to measure appear to be taken into account only to discard the earlier Argive assignment of this group (A), with unspecified archaeological considerations apparently pointing to the same direction. Cf. Mommsen / Hertel / Mountjoy 2001, 173 ff. A discussion with Dr. Tomlinson, assistant-director of the Canadian Institute at Athens, brought up many objections against the methods used by Mommsen. Being unqualified in this matter myself, I prefer to consider the corpus at Troy of a very diverse nature, including imports from both Boeotia and the Argolid, but comprising mainly local material, without attaching too much weight to it all.

315. Cf. Blegen / Caskey / Rawson 1953.

316. A notable exception appears to be an LH IIIC krater with a lion and a bird as painted decoration. Cf. Mountjoy 1997b, 296–74.

Bęsik Tepe

Beşik Tepe is the site of what was the harbor of Troy, and includes a nearby cemetery dating to the Late Bronze Age. It has yielded a small amount of Mycenaean-style pots.[317] However, with the sea nearby, it should be taken into consideration that at least part of the site has suffered because of the waves. Testimonies to this are the reported rolled and washed sherds from this site. The cemetery certainly was very rich and knew a great diversity in burial types, including pithos graves, clay-lined structures, and stone circles designating the graves. The pottery found is comparable to the material from the "Pillar House" in Troy, i.e. representing LH IIIB2, with shapes ranging from kraters and bowls to alabastra and kylikes.[318]

Pitane - Çandarlı / Kocabağlar

Though Pitane did yield some Mycenaean pottery, the material is poorly documented and appears to be of post-palatial, i.e. LH IIIC, date. The finds include a LH IIIC stirrup jar with octopus decoration and possibly an attic stirrup jar, previously thought to have been found by Schliemann at Troy.[319] The material appears to have been found in pit graves, in association with locally made monochrome pottery.

Elaia - Karzikbağlari

Mellaart mentioned one Mycenaean sherd from this site, but did not provide further data on its stylistic phase or context.[320] Because of its proximity to Lesbos, the occurrence of Mycenaean imports in this region is hardly surprising.

317. According to the catalogue in van Wijngaarden (1999), the amount ranges from anywhere between ten to fifty pieces. I have not been able to specify the exact amount of Mycenaean sherds found at the site, but I gather that the total number does not exceed fifty.

318. Korfmann 1986, 21.

319. Mee 1978, 143; Mountjoy 1998, 60.

320. Mellaart 1968, 188.

Panaztepe - Menemen

The cemetery at Panaztepe displays a wide variety of burial types, including tholos tombs,[321] cist graves, and chamber tombs. Those that were buried at the site appear to have been relatively wealthy, with a good number of foreign contacts, judging by the amount of imports. Grave gifts include a Palestinian cylinder seal with Egyptian hieroglyphs (from a tholos tomb), faience spindle whorls, gold beads, bronze figurines, and Mycenaean pottery.[322] Nearby, at least one ashlar building was found, with LH IIIA-B pottery in association with a gray Minyan fenestrated fruit-stand and a stone mold. Material originally thought to have been found at Çiğli appears to have come from this site instead and includes a variety of Mycenaean LH IIIA2 pottery and weapons.[323]

Phocaea - Eski Foça

Despite several early but false reports of Mycenaean pottery at this site,[324] Phocaea may have yielded some Mycenaean pottery from a stratum below the archaic level.[325] As this was found in association with Protogeometric ware, I assume this to be mainly of Late Mycenaean date. In the pre-Archaic stratum two megaron structures were identified, possibly indicating Mycenaean settlement in Mycenaean times. It is, at any rate, unlikely that more than a few pieces have been found.[326]

Egriköy

Two doubtful pieces of Mycenaean pottery have been reported from this site,[327] but similar material found at Sardis is no longer considered to be Mycenaean. It has been suggested that the nearby site of Çerkes Sultaniye was the burial ground for Egriköy.

---

321. See below (Kolophon) for a brief discussion of this burial type.
322. Gates 1996, 304.
323. Mellink 1982, 565; 1984, 451; 1983b, 435; Ersoy 1988, 55–82; Mountjoy 1998, 35.
324. Cook 1960, 40 against Hanfmann 1948, 145; Bittel 1934, 92 n.2; Mee 1978, 143.
325. Mitchell 1999, 144.
326. Cf. van Wijngaarden 1999, 490.
327. French 1969, 73.

Çerkes Sultaniye

Though this site was never systematically excavated, a pithos grave was found by a local inhabitant. In it, one Mycenaean piriform jar (LH IIIB) was found, together with a local vase and a local monochrome jar.[328]

Buruncuk - Larisa

This site has not yielded any Mycenaean pottery from the palatial period. One LH IIIC1 sherd, with a decoration of spirals, from the shoulder of a jug or jar was however found, in association with local, Anatolian ware.

Çiğli

Although partially robbed, five tholos tombs at the site of Çiğli yielded a variety of local and Mycenaean artefacts, including goblets, piriform jars, three-handled pyxides, a large local pilgrim flask, as well as a socketed spearhead, a sword, a knife, a razor, and arrowheads. A sixth tholos was found during the 1985 excavations, as well as several cists and ten pithos graves. LH IIIA stirrup jars, pyxides, lentoid flasks, and three-handled jars were found then and in later years. A total of 52 vases could be restored.[329] Also, local ware (jars for cremations) and two scarabs, at least one of which dating to Amenophis III, were found.[330]

Bayraklı - Old Smyrna and Izmir

Several sherds were found during the 1951 excavation at Old Smyrna, though in unstratified conditions,[331] as strays in Protogeometric and latest prehistoric levels.[332] Cook published a picture of five of these sherds, two of which may belong to the same pot. The decoration of lines and spirals indicates a LH IIIA2 date, though the shape of the vessel remains uncertain. Furthermore, the stem of a LH IIIA2-B kylix

328. Hanfmann / Waldbaum 1968, 52, n.13; compare to Desborough 1964, pl. 1b.

329. Mellink 1988, 114.

330. Mellink 1987, 13; Jaeger / Krauss, 1990, 13.

331. Mee 1978, 142–43.

332. Cook 1952, 104–5, fig. 10.

and the false neck and the shoulder of a LH IIIB stirrup jar decorated with a flower motive(?) have been published.[333] These two sherds may belong together. An earlier report by Akurgal (1967, *non vidi*) is said to mention another LH IIIA2-B sherd.

At Izmir a Mycenaean sword was found that, albeit from unstratified circumstances, is thought to have come from a tomb.[334] A LH I date has been proposed, linking the sword to the rapiers found at the shaft graves at Mycenae. In general, Bronze Age levels at Smyrna seem scarcely touched upon, and one gains the impression that more Mycenaean material awaits the future archaeologist.

Clazomenae - Urla Iskelesi

Some 25 sherds on display in the National Museum at Athens are reported to have come from this site, although the excavation reports do not refer to any Mycenaean find.[335] Except for two sherds, the sherds have a patterned decoration and, as a consequence, cannot be considered representative of the original corpus (as one would expect linear decoration to be prevalent). The sherds are mostly of closed shape, although a cup, a krater, a mug, and a stemmed bowl have been identified as well. The majority of the material is dated LH IIIA2-B, except for one LH IIIC krater. The context is unknown, possibly of a domestic nature (housing). Later excavations yielded more LH IIIA pottery,[336] in association with gray "Minyan" and in a clearly domestic context.[337]

Liman Tepe

Late Bronze Age strata at Liman Tepe were heavily disturbed; only a well and part of the fill remained undisturbed. The site yielded "Minyan," as well as Mycenaean pottery, dated LH IIIA1 to LH IIIB. Shapes range from open to closed, including cups, jugs, and an alabastron.[338] Painted and unpainted pottery was found, including one lid with a linear sign,[339] which may be a potter's mark.[340]

---

333. Mee 1978, 143.
334. *Ibid.*, 130; Bittel 1967, 175.
335. Mee 1978, 125.
336. Mellink 1980, 507.
337. Private houses of the megaron type; Cf. Mellink 1981, 467.
338. Günel 1999, 80–81, no. 52–57.

Bakla Tepe

At nearby Bakla Tepe, a LH IIIB cup from the thirteenth century was found in a grave cut into a mound. In association, twenty pots of local origin and an ivory appliqué rosette ornament were found.[341]

Reisdere - Erythrae

An unknown number of Mycenaean sherds were found on a small peninsula about 8 km from Erythrae, between the villages of Şifne and Reisdere. Shapes,[342] context, and date are unknown. In addition, Akurgal is reported to have identified a Mycenaean settlement closer to Erythrae.[343]

Torbalı - Bademgediği Höyüğü

Rescue excavations at the site of Torbalı resulted in the discovery of a sizable settlement encircled by a LH IIIC cyclopean wall, of which 750 meters were uncovered.[344] Many sherds of local Mycenaean pottery were found, ranging from the fourteenth to twelfth centuries BC. LH IIIC early and middle pottery, such as a stirrup jar and two straight-sided alabastra, was found in the latest Bronze Age level.[345]

Ephesus - Selçuk - Kušadası

That Ephesus was an important center in the Bronze Age is unquestionable. The exact location of the Late Bronze Age center is, however, debated. The presence of what may be the remains of a Hittite(-style) fortification wall on the Medieval citadel has been taken as evidence that the Late Bronze Age acropolis lies beneath the Medieval one,[346]

339. Mitchell 1999, 147.
340. Günel 1999, 59, 97, ill. 51.
341. Mitchell 1999, 147.
342. Mellink 1968, 134; Akurgal 1967, 461.
343. Cook / Blackman 1971, 41; Akurgal 1967, 461.
344. Greaves / Helwing 2001, 506.
345. Meriç / Mountjoy 2001, 137.
346. Büyükkolanci 2000, 39; Brein 1976/1977, 65–76; Mellink 1993, 120; Erdemgil 1991 (*non vidi*).

but it has been sought also at nearby Ilicatepe.[347] Whatever the exact location of the Late Bronze Age center, it is clear that it must be sought in or around the modern city of Ephesus. To this testifies the abundance of finds from that era, including several Mycenaean artefacts. As a result, the wider region of modern Ephesus will be presented below. Only sites where Mycenaean artefacts have been found are listed; contemporary sites without (reported) Mycenaean objects are not dealt with.

A disturbed tomb on the Medieval citadel found during excavations in 1963 yielded a total of six Mycenaean vases: a LH IIIA1 piriform jar, a LH IIIA1 handleless flask, a LH IIIA2 krater decorated with Argonauts, a LH IIIA2 pilgrim flask, a LH IIIA2 rhyton, and an undiagnosed jug.[348] Apart from the pots, a number of linear decorated sherds were found.

At Kušadasi a stirrup jar dated to LH IIIA2 was found; this object is now on display with the artefacts listed above in the Museum at Ephesus.[349]

At the site of the later Artemision a variety of Mycenaean objects has been found, including Mycenaean pottery, a bronze double axe, two pieces of figurines of which one (a head) shows a distinct resemblance to the so-called "Lord of Asine."[350] This variety of objects led to the suggestion that the site of the Artemision may have been a Mycenaean cult center, a concept that is all the more attractive because of Late Bronze Age walls of Mycenaean character at that same site.[351]

In the village of Halkapinar, east of Belevi, a Mycenaean oinochoe was found in pithos.[352]

All in all, Mycenaean artefacts have been found in significant, if unspecified, quantities in the wider region of Ephesus. Of interest in this matter is not so much the presence of Mycenaean pottery, which really was to be expected at and around a center of the magnitude of Bronze Age Apaša, but the variety of the material. Though there are difficulties

347. Bammer 1994, 142.

348. Mellink 1964, 157; Mee 1978, 127.

349. Erdemgil e.a. 1989, 97–100.

350. Bammer 1990, 142; 1994, 38.

351. Gates 1996, 319; Bammer 1994.

352. On the grounds of the character of the foliate band (compare to FM 64:20) I suggest a LH IIIA2 date for this vessel.

in assigning any Mycenaean origins to the various cyclopean-style walls in the area,[353] the wide range of artefacts, such as figurines, votive offerings (the bronze axe), and pottery argues for at least strong Mycenaean cultural influence.

Kolophon

A tholos tomb at Kolophon yielded pottery that might be considered Submycenaean ware.[354] Though the tholos was dated LH IIIB-C, it did not yield any material from the palatial period. Architectural peculiarities of the tholos itself suggest that the tomb was built outside the mainstream of the tholos-building tradition[355] and a Mycenaean connection thus appears improvable, if not unlikely.[356] That those buried at Kolophon had at least some contact with the Mycenaean world is, on the other hand, not wholly hypothetical: in a grave nearby the tholos, a Mycenaean knife was found alongside an Aegean glass paste bead.[357]

Sardis

Only a few vessels have been found at Sardis that might be Mycenaean. In a sounding in the area of the "House of Bronzes," spanning the period from the thirteenth century to the early seventh century, a LH IIIB krater and a LH IIIC deep bowl were found.[358] Some 250 sherds have been reported, some of which were Late Mycenaean, others

353. See Loader 1998 for a discussion on the various types of Cyclopean masonry.

354. Pottery is not reported in Huxley 1960 ("Fehlzitat" Mee 1978, 125?).

355. Bridges 1974, 266.

356. Arguably, the tholos tomb is not an exclusively Aegean phenomenon, as tholoi occur elsewhere on the Anatolian west coast, i.e. at Panaztepe, but they occur only at very few sites and are not attested at inland sites, nor are there clear Anatolian predecessors (as opposed to the Aegean; Belli 1997, 251; the derivation of the tholos from the Cretan circular tombs, thought to be fraught with difficulties by scholars such as Branigan [1970], now is regarded as a plausible option. Cf. Rutter, Dartmouth website). As a consequence, there are some grounds to consider this at least as an Aegean-oriented feature.

357. Mee 1978, 125; Ersoy 1988, 67, n.57.

358. Mee 1978, 144.

Submycenaean, and a number of Protogeometric date.[359] The Mycenaean ware is dated LH IIIB to C2, ranging from the thirteenth to the eleventh centuries BC. Apart from the previously mentioned krater, a few sherds already had been published in 1967,[360] a few of which, to my judgment, should be LH IIIB (late?), with a few others labelled Submycenaean that might be Mycenaean too. Both closed and open shapes are present. Decoration generally is simple: bands and semicircles. Despite the occurrence of some Mycenaean pottery, the majority of the material at Sardis is firmly Anatolian. Only 2 to 5 percent of the total amount of pottery is Mycenaean.[361] It appears that at least part of the Mycenaean material at Sardis was locally produced, rather than imported.[362]

Gavurtepe - Alaşehir

A Late Bronze Age settlement has yielded a variety of Mycenaean sherds, ranging from LH IIIA2 to LH IIIB.[363] Although the material remains unpublished, a sherd from what probably was a LH IIIA2 flask, decorated with linear bands and a wavy line, and what was either an askos or a rhyton, decorated with dots and wavy lines, have been known for some time.[364] The village was deserted around 1200 BC, after at least part of the settlement, including a megaron structure, had suffered destruction by fire.[365]

Beyesultan

Seven sherds from the 1954 excavations were believed to be Anatolian copies of Mycenaean pottery, of which six proved to be from a painted pilgrim flask of central Anatolian origin. The seventh, a body sherd of a pyxis, has Trojan rather than Mycenaean affinities and is of local fabric. One sherd of truly Mycenaean origin has been found in a

---

359. Cf. Hanfmann / Waldbaum 1970.

360. Cf. Hanfmann 1967.

361. Hanfmann 1983, 22–23.

362. *Ibid.*, 23.

363. Mellink 1988, 115.

364. Mee 1978, 128.

365. Mellink 1991, 138 notes a Mycenaean handle coming from the megaron, but does not specify shape or size.

late Beyesultan III (1450–1325 BC) pavement and should be the shoulder of a LH IIIA2 or B imported stirrup jar, decorated with bands of red paint. The pavement was situated within a house (room 1) in area J.[366]

Saraköy

A possible Mycenaean sherd has been reported from Saraköy in the Meander valley.[367] No further data are provided.

Miletus

The size and variety of the corpus of Mycenaean pottery at Miletus is such that it is impossible, and unnecessary for the current research, to list each and every single specimen here. For that reason I allow myself to generalize here. Mycenaean pottery at Miletus ranges from LH IIB to LH IIIC. LH IIIB appears to have been the period of greatest diversity of shapes and decoration. Already from the size and variety of the corpus of the pottery alone, one could argue that Miletus must have been a Mycenaean settlement at that time with both open- and closed-shaped vessels appearing in virtually the same measures.

Although it has been argued that Mycenaean pottery presents only a glimpse of the total corpus of ceramics at the site, this, in fact, has been demonstrated to be inaccurate.[368] Mycenaean pottery overshadows the amount of Anatolian pottery by far, although the need for a thorough analysis of the Mycenaean pottery at Miletus still exists. This does not mean that there is no Anatolian influence at Miletus whatsoever. Indeed, especially from the transition LH IIIA2 to B1 onward, there seems to have been Hittite influence at Miletus. This may be reflected even in a, admittedly rather exceptional, piece of Mycenaean pottery with the possible depiction of a Hittite royal tiara,[369] but is especially evident in some architectural peculiarities of a defensive circuit that was built around the settlement about 1300. The wall appears to finds its closest parallels in Hittite "Kastenmauer," such as the defenses at Hattuša.[370] Whereas Anatolian or, rather, Hittite influence at Miletus

366. Mellaart 1970, 66.

367. Birmingham 1964, 30.

368. Ünal (1991, 24 *non vidi*) stated that perhaps only 5 percent of the pottery is Mycenaean. This has now been refuted by Niemeier (1998, 33).

369. Niemeier / Niemeier 1997, 204.

cannot wholly be excluded, the point remains that Hittite imports so far have not been found (or recognized as such).[371]

Apart from the pottery, a wide range of other artefacts have been found at Miletus, including Mycenaean phi- and psi-type figurines and animal figurines, dated to LH IIIB and LH IIIC.[372] Chamber tombs around the settlement and (scanty) domestic architecture point toward the Mycenaean world, too.[373] The wide range of Mycenaean artefacts, in effect, covers virtually every aspect of life: religion, funerary customs, housing, day-to-day pottery, and related food customs; it all appears to be fully Mycenaean.

As a consequence, on archaeological grounds alone, Miletus could safely be regarded as a Mycenaean settlement from LH IIB onward. Before that period, there may have been Mycenaean presence, but then in a predominantly Minoan setting.[374]

Akbük - Teichiussa

On a peninsula 4 km. north of Akbük prehistoric levels were uncovered. Apart from LM I ware and light "Minoanizing" sherds, LH IIIB and IIIC1 stray sherds were found.[375] Nearby tombs yielded more Aegean pottery, including some Minoan pottery (with Levantine affinities?), ranging from MM III to LM IB.[376] Both open and closed shapes are present.

---

370. Cf. Schiering 1975, 14–15, 80–82; Mee 1978, 135.

371. Niemeier 1998, 38.

372. Niemeier / Niemeier 1997, 217, ill. 31b; Niemeier 1984, 214; Niemeier 1998, 33; Gödecken 1988, pl.19f.

373. Niemeier 1998, 30; Mee 1978, 133.

374. Niemeier (2002, 295) suggests a gradual takeover of the Aegean isles (especially the Dodecanese) and thereafter Minoan settlements on the Anatolian mainland in an effort to secure trade routes by Mycenaean settlers. At least the second wave of migrants, dated to the first half of the fourteenth century BC, is thought to have been initiated by the palaces on the Greek mainland. For further discussion see below.

375. Mellink 1985, 552, 558.

376. Voigtländer 1988, 603–9.

Domuztepe

This site has yielded some Mycenaean pottery from the post-palatial period (LH IIIC).[377] No Mycenaean pottery predating LH IIIC has been found.

Iasos

During the Late Bronze Age, Iasos must have been an important Mycenaean center. Mycenaeans must have settled there at least as early as LH IIIA2.[378] Anatolian wares are not mentioned in the excavation reports. Although only a limited area of the LBA site has been excavated, a considerable amount of Mycenaean pottery has been found. "Frammenti Micenei," dating LH IIIA2 or IIIB (one piece may even date to LH II), were found in the area of the Protogeometric cemetery, below the Agora, and below the Basilica and the sanctuary of Artemis Astias.[379] Scanty remains of Mycenaean walls were found, heavily disturbed by later (Archaic) building activity. Some of the sherds found there may very well have been produced locally or elsewhere in the East Aegean-West Anatolian interface,[380] but certainly there also was imported ware, probably from the Argolid.[381] Moreover, during the 1979 excavations, an Argive psi-idol was uncovered while clearing a large pavement of the Mycenaean period, and the striped base of another Mycenaean idol was found in 1987.[382] Minoan (LM I–II) pottery was found too, imported as well as local fabric, giving the impression that, as has been suggested for Miletus, Iasos initially was a Minoan settlement, later taken over by the Mycenaeans.

The corpus displays a wide variety of shapes. Kylikes, deep bowls, kraters, a mug, and a stemmed bowl were found in the area of the Protogeometric cemetery, kylikes being most numerous. From the area below the basilica come a LH IIIC krater and a LH IIIC flask. Judging from the shapes, it seems that the pottery was used in daily life rather than for storage or ritual use. Remarkable is the abundance of patterned

377. Mee 1978, 126; Seton-Williams 1954, 154; Mellaart 1955, 82.

378. Mellink 1983a, 139.

379. Levi 1969/1970, 474, 480, figs. 25, 26.

380. Cf. Mountjoy 1998, 36, 53.

381. Mee 1979, 130; compare to French 1965, 200–2.

382. Mellink 1980, 507; 1989, 117.

and pictorial decoration. Spirals, zigzags, wavy lines, whorl shells, flowers, and an octopus occur, while purely linear decoration is not attested.

Of the architecture little is known. The few remains in the cemetery area represent at least one rather large building with walls of worked stone and paved floors, which was found below the Agora and seems to have functioned from MM III to LH III.[383]

Mylasa - Milas

Mee reports a LH IIIA2 jug from Mylasa, decorated with stemmed spirals, and Mellink mentions a LH pyxis from the vicinity of Mylasa.[384] More Mycenaean material from the site is reported, but no further information on shape, decoration, or context is provided. I assume that these finds consisted of pottery. The material was reported to be LH II and LH III.[385]

Stratonicaea

A carinated bowl and a stirrup jar now on display in the museum of Eskihisar are said to have come from a tomb or tombs near the theater of Stratonicaea.[386] The material is supposedly Submycenaean, though a LH IIIB-C date cannot be ruled out.[387]

Müsgebi

Situated on the Halikarnassos peninsula, Müsgebi is one of the few sites thought to have been a Mycenaean site on Anatolian soil. The cemetery was studied during the years 1963 to 1966 and yielded a total of 48 chamber tombs. Both inhumation and cremation occurred, though the number of cremations has not been specified. Pottery was found in abundance, although Mee notes that "most of the tombs are ceramically rather poor."[388] Boysal published 162 vessels from Müsgebi; while Mee provides a full account of the corpus' typological diver-

383. Levi 1969/1970, 471, 474; Lavisiosa 1972, 44.
384. Mee 1978, 142; Mellink 1978, 142.
385. Hanfmann 1948, 140–45.
386. Hanfmann / Waldbaum, 1986, 51–52.
387. Hope Simpson 1965, 193.
388. Mee 1978, 137.

sity.[389] Shapes range from piriform jars, stirrup jars, amphoriskoi, flasks, braziers, kylikes, and bowls to cups and mugs. An alabastron, an askos, and a basket vase have also been found. A considerable, if not quantified, amount of pottery is thought to have been imported from the Argolid and the Dodecanese, most notably from Ialysos on Rhodes.[390] On the other hand, local production should not be ruled out and is likely to have continued until LH IIIC times. The pottery at Müsgebi ranges from LH IIIA2 till LH IIIC. A peak seems to be the LH IIIB (early?) period. Note that the shapes represent a rather complete corpus; pottery seems to have been a common good and used for various activities, hence the occurrence of both open and closed shapes.[391]

Knidos

Love reports some sherds from the 1968 excavations at Knidos, but provides no additional data.[392]

Düver

An unspecified number of Mycenaean pots from this site are in the possession of the Burdur Museum. The pots, an imported pyxis, a jug, and three local pyxides are dated LH IIIA2-B.[393] Mellink reports squat alabastra from the cemetery at Düver, dated LH IIIB.[394]

Dereköy (II)

This site yielded a LH IIIA2 pyxis and a LH IIIB1 piriform jar. These pots were found in a cemetery close to the site, in association with local, gold-washed pottery.[395]

---

389. Boysal 1969; Mee 1978.

390. Cf. Mee 1978, 138 ff. Assignment to any specific place of origin is based on stylistic analysis only. It appears that a good deal of the material came from the Argolid and the Dodecanese; based on Mee's report this would amount to *ca.* 70 to 80 percent of the corpus of Mycenaean pots. Notably, some shapes, especially the jugs, appear to have been made locally.

391. Bass 1963, 353.

392. Love 1969, 18.

393. Mee 1978, 126.

394. Mellink 1969, 212.

395. Birmingham 1964, 30–31, ill. 2/3; corrected in Mee 1978, 126.

Telmessos - Fethiye

This site yielded a LH IIIA2-B globular stirrup jar from an unknown context.[396]

Beylerbey

A LH IIIA2 or B1 kylix sherd from unknown context is reported to come from this site.[397]

This list should not be without a reference to the Ulu Burun wreck, which provided a wealth of information on (trade and exchange) contacts in the Late Bronze Age between the Mycenaean world and various regions in the Near East. The possible presence of Mycenaean nobility onboard will be referred to on a later occasion, but on the whole, the wreck appears to be of little direct importance to the current research about the level of military and diplomatic influence of the kingdom of Ahhiyawa in western Anatolia.[398]

---

396. Walters / Forsdyke, 1930, Pl.10:24; Mee 1978, 145.
397. French, 1969, 73, n.17; Mee 1978, 124.
398. Cf. Bachhuber 2006 for the most recent evaluation of the Ulu Burun Wreck.

TABLE 1: CHRONOLOGICAL OVERVIEW

Egypt New Kingdom		*Late Helladic*		*Hittite New Kingdom*		*Events*
Ahmose	1550–1525	LH I				Egypt liberated from the Hyksos.
Amenhotep I	1525–1504	LH II				Rise of palatial society in Greece
Thutmoses I	1504–1492					
Thutmoses II	1492–1479					
Thutmoses III	1479–1425					Egyptian Empire reaches largest extent; Tanaju messengers at the Egyptian court
Hatshepsut	1473–1458					
Amenhotep II	1427–1400					
Thutmoses IV	1400–1390	LH III A1	1400–1375	Tudhaliya I / II, Arnuwanda I,		Attariššija in Anatolia
Amenhotep III	1390–1352	LH III A2	1375–1330	Hattušili II Tudhaliya III	1360–1344	Egyptian mission to the Aegean
Akhenaten	1352–1336			Suppiluliuma I	1344–1322	olives and Mycenaean pottery at Amarna
Smenkhare	1338–1336					
Tutankhamen	1336–1327	LH III B1	1330–1230			Mycenaean pottery at Deir el-Medina
Aye	1327–1323					Mycenaean pottery at Saqqarah
Horemheb	1323–1295			Arnuwanda II	1322–1321	
				Muršili II	1321–1295	collapse of Arzawa
Ramesses I	1295–1294					
Seti I	1294–1279			Muwatalli II	1295–1272	Queen Nefertari wears Aegean jewelry

Egypt New Kingdom		*Late Helladic*		*Hittite New Kingdom*		*Events*
Ramesses II	1279-1213					the Battle of Kadesh (1274 BC)
				Urhi-Tešub	1272-1267	Mycenaean pottery at Pi-ramesse
				Hattušili III	1267-1237	the Tawagalawa letter
						peace between Egypt and Hatti (1258 BC)
						destructions in Boeotia
				Tudhaliya IV	1237-1228	Šaušgamuwa Treaty
		LH III B2	1230-1190	Kurunta	1228-1227	usurper on the throne of Hatti
				Tudhaliya IV	1227-1209	
Merenptah	1213-1203			Arnuwanda III	1209-1207	Libyan invasions with Sea Peoples
				Suppiluliuma II	1207-	destruction throughout Greece
Amenmesse	1203-1200					
Seti II	1200-1194	LH III C				
Sethnacht	1186-1184					
Ramesses III	1184-1153					Sea People invasions over land and sea. Mycenaean stirrup jars on the walls of the tomb of Ramesses III

TABLE 2: TROJAN CHRONOLOGY
(after Korfmann/Mannsperger 1998)

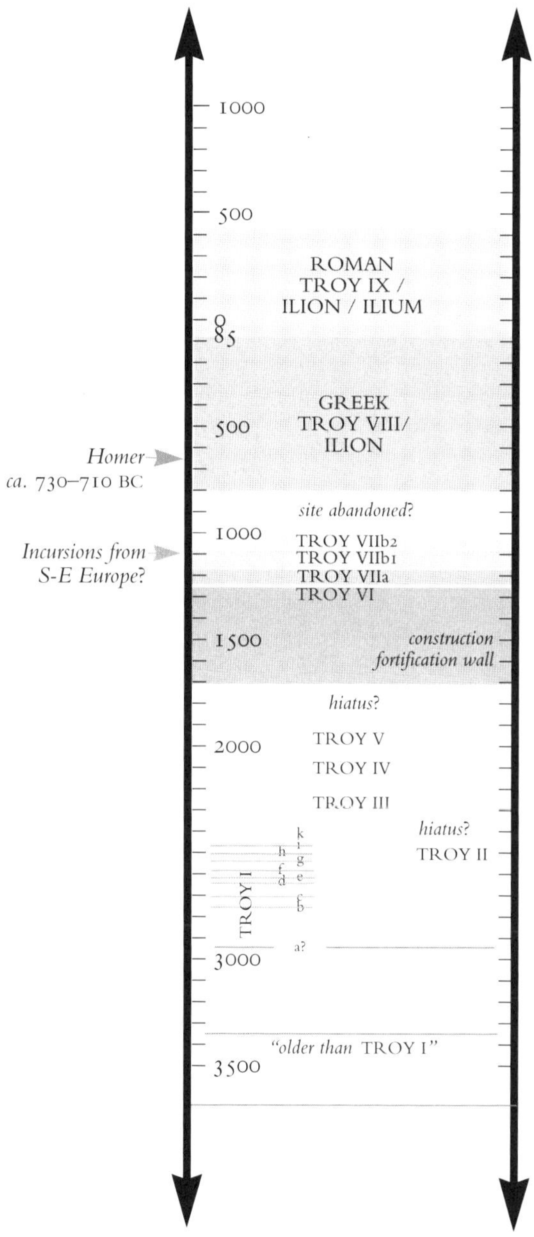

TABLE 3: SITES IN WESTERN ANATOLIA WITH MYCENAEAN POTTERY

The total numbers of finds have been divided into groups; 1=1–10; 2=10–50; 3=50–100; 4=100–500; 5=500 or more. The sites are (following the text) listed from north to south. Note that the earliest concentrations of Mycenaean pottery appear in the same regions known to have been subject to Ahhiyawan activity (i.e. the Troad, the area around Miletus and Ephesus).

	Late Helladic						
	II	IIIA1	IIIA2	IIIB1	IIIB2	IIIC	Group
Troy - Hissarlik	✓	✓	✓	✓	✓	✓	5
Besik Tepe			✓	✓	✓	✓	2
Pitane						✓	2?
Elaia							1
Panaztepe			✓	✓			3
Phocaea					✓		2?
Çerkes				✓			1
Egriköy							?
Larisa						✓	1
Bayrakli			✓	✓			2
Clazomenae			✓	✓	✓	✓	3
Reisdere							1
Torbali		✓	✓	✓	✓	✓	3?
Ephesus		✓	✓			✓	3
Sardis					✓	✓	2
Gavurtepe			✓				2
Beyesultan			✓	✓			1
Saraköy							1
Miletus	✓	✓	✓	✓	✓	✓	5
Akbük					✓	✓	1
Iasos	✓	✓	✓	✓	✓	✓	3
Mylasa	✓	✓	✓				1
Stratonicaea						✓	1
Müsgebi			✓	✓	✓	✓	4
Knidos							1
Düver				✓	✓		1
Telmessos				✓	✓		1
Dereköy				✓	✓		1
Beylerbey				✓			1

TABLE 4: MYCENAEAN POTTERY AT THE SITE OF EL AMARNA / AKHETATEN, EGYPT

(after Kelder 2002–3)

No.	*Date*	*Object*	*Function*	*Context*	*Literature*
			Mycenaean ware in the north suburb of Akhetaten *Central -western Quarter*		
1	LH IIIa	pilgrim flask	storage	residential (house of the Mycenaean Greek)	Pendlebury, 1933, 46
2	LH IIIa	stem of a goblet	eating / drinking	residential (house of the Mycenaean Greek)	Pendlebury, 1933, 46
3	LH IIIa	fragments		residential, 26: 30/207;225	Pendlebury, 1933, 48
4	LH IIIa	fragments		residential, 61: 30/257	Pendlebury, 1933, 48
			South - Western Quarter		
1	LH IIIa	fragments, 4		residential, T.36.64: 30/279	Pendlebury, 1933, 53
2	LH IIIa	fragment		residential, T.36.69: 30/296	Pendlebury, 1933, 53
3	LH IIIa	fragment of a stirrup jar	storage	residential, T.36.78: 30/379	Pendlebury, 1933, 53
4	LH IIIa	fragment of a pilgrim flask of Rhodian fabric	storage	residential, T.36.58: 30/196	Pendlebury, 1933, 55
5	LH IIIa	fragment		residential, T.36.84: 30/420	Pendlebury, 1933, 56
6	LH IIIa	handle of a stirrup jar	storage	residential, T.36.44: 30/46	Pendlebury, 1933, 57
7	LH IIIa	fragment of a pilgrim flask	storage	residential, T.36.54: 30/152	Pendlebury, 1933, 57
8	LH IIIa	fragment		residential, T.36.62: 30/345	Pendlebury, 1933, 57
9	LH IIIa	fragments		residential, T.36.76: 30/371, 372	Pendlebury, 1933, 58
10	LH IIIa	fragment		residential, T.36.79: 30/391	Pendlebury, 1933, 58
11	LH IIIa	fragments, 2		residential, T.36.57: 30/232	Pendlebury, 1933, 59
12	LH IIIa	bead-spacer of white paste		residential, T.36.74: 30/330 (public well)	Pendlebury, 1933, 61
13	LH IIIa	fragments, 2		residential, T.36.75: 30/364	Pendlebury, 1933, 62
14	LH IIIa	fragment		residential, T.34.3: 30/480	Pendlebury, 1933, 67

No.	Date	Object	Function	Context	Literature
15	LH IIIa	base of an amphora	storage	residential, S.33.1: 30/464	Pendlebury, 1933, 68

Northern Quarter

0		no fragments			

Northwestern Quarter

1	LH IIIa	fragment		(top of a shaft) burial?, T.35.6: 29/353	Pendlebury, 1933, 43
2		pair of small pottery birds, Aegean?		residential, T.35.6: 29/352	Pendlebury, 1933, 43

Southwestern Quarter

1	LH IIIa	fragment		residential, V.37.8: 26/216	Pendlebury, 1933, 8

South-central Quarter

1	LH IIIa	fragment of a globular vase, 11 cm	storage	residential, U.36.29: 29/36 (slums)	Pendlebury, 1933, 18
2	LH IIIa	fragment		residential, T.36.2 (larger estates)	Pendlebury, 1933, 24

Eastern Quarter

0		no fragments			

Mycenaean ware in the South Suburb of Akhetaten

1	LH IIIa	fragment of a stirrup jar	storage	residential, N.49.18: 21/284	Peet, 1923, 15, XXIX/1010b
2	LH IIIa	neck of a stirrup jar	storage	residential, N.49.10: 21/33	Peet, 1923, 20, XIII, fig.5, t, l.
3	LH IIIa	fragment		residential, N.49.12: 21/163	Peet, 1923, 21
4	LH IIIa	fragment		residential, N.49.35: 21/496	Peet, 1923, 26
5	LH IIIa	fragments, 2		residential, O.47.16: 22/517, 532	Peet, 1923, 28
6	LH IIIa	fragment		residential, P.46.7: 22/544	Peet, 1923, 30
7	LH IIIa	fragment		residential, P.46.8: 22/542	Peet, 1923, 31
8	LH IIIa	fragment		residential, P.46.10: 22/547	Peet, 1923, 32
9	LH IIIa	fragments		residential, P.46.15: 22/565	Peet, 1923, 33

No.	*Date*	*Object*	*Function*	*Context*	*Literature*
10	LH IIIa	fragment		residential, P.47.30: 22/531	Peet, 1923, 35
11	LH IIIa	mouth of a vase	storage	residential, P.47.31: no number	Peet, 1923, 35
12	LH IIIa	fragments, 3		residential, Petrie's House 11	Petrie, 1894, 17

Mycenaean ware in the Central City of Akhetaten

Mycenaean ware found by Carter, precise context within the central city unknown, now in the Allard Pierson Museum, Amsterdam

1	LH IIIa2	sherds, small piriform jar	storage	APM 3226/D en /4	
2	LH IIIa2	sherds, vertical flask	storage	APM 3226/B, F, H, 1,3,5,6,7	
3	LH IIIa2	sherd	storage	APM 3226/8	
4	LH IIIa2	sherd, alabastron	storage	APM 3226/G	
5	LH IIIa2	sherd, stirrup jar?	storage	APM 3226/A	
6	LH IIIa2	sherds	storage	APM 3226/2,9	

The Great Temple

0		no fragments			

Dependencies of the great temple

0		no fragments			

The Great Palace: magazines

1	LH IIIa	fragment and handle of a pilgrim flask	storage	official, 34/41	Pendlebury, 1951, 38
2	LH IIIa	fragments of stirrup jar, 2	storage	official, 34/45	Pendlebury, 1951, 38
3	LH IIIa	fragment of vase, 8.5 cm	storage	official, 35/137	Pendlebury, 1951, 49
4	LH IIIa	fragment of pilgrim flask, 5.8 cm	storage	official, 35/150	Pendlebury, 1951, 49
5	LH IIIa	fragments of pilgrim flask, 4	storage	official, 35/190	Pendlebury, 1951, 49

No.	*Date*	*Object*	*Function*	*Context*	*Literature*
6	LH IIIa	base and part of the side of pilgrim flask	storage	official, 35/180	Pendlebury, 1951, 49
7	LH IIIa	fragment of vase, 5.5 cm	storage	official, 35/196	Pendlebury, 1951, 49
8	LH IIIa	fragment of pilgrim flask, 4 cm	storage	official, 35/221	Pendlebury, 1951, 49
9	LH IIIa	fragment (rough ware)		official, 35/222	Pendlebury, 1951, 49
10	LH IIIa	fragments of vases, 4	storage	official, 35/239	Pendlebury, 1951, 50
11	LH IIIa	fragments, 4		official, 35/273	Pendlebury, 1951, 50

The Great Palace: State Apartments

1	LH IIIa	fragment of a pilgrim flask	storage	official, 34/182	Pendlebury, 1951, 65
2	LH IIIa	fragment		official, 35/382	Pendlebury, 1951, 68,CIX.3
3	LH IIIa	fragments of 2 small amphoras	storage	official, 35/373	Pendlebury, 1951, 69,CIX.5
4	LH IIIa	fragment, 7.6 cm		official, 35/492	Pendlebury, 1951, 70,CIX.3
5	LH IIIa	fragment		official, 35/415	Pendlebury, 1951, 72,CIX.3
6	LH IIIa	fragments of stirrup jars, 2	storage	official, 35/289	Pendlebury, 1951, 73
7	LH IIIa	fragments, 7		official, 35/305	Pendlebury, 1951, 73
8	LH IIIa	fragments, 2		official, 35/315	Pendlebury, 1951, 73
9	LH IIIa	fragments, 6 (3 from pilgrim flasks)	storage	official, 35/310	Pendlebury, 1951, 73
10	LH IIIa	fragments, 6		official, 35/324	Pendlebury, 1951, 73
11	LH IIIa	fragments, 3		official, 35/349	Pendlebury, 1951, 74
12	LH IIIa	fragments, 2		official, 35/359	Pendlebury, 1951, 74
13	LH IIIa	fragments, 9		official, no specification	Petrie, 1894, 17

The Royal Estate

No.	*Date*	*Object*	*Function*	*Context*	*Literature*
1	LH IIIa	fragment of an amphora, 5.6 cm	storage	official, 31/622	Pendlebury, 1951, 88
2	LH IIIa	fragment, 4.8 cm		official, 31/532	Pendlebury, 1951, 91,CIX.2
3	LH IIIa	fragments, 2		official, 31/547	Pendlebury, 1951, 91,CIX.2
4	LH IIIa	fragments of pilgrim flask, 3	storage	official, 31/553	Pendlebury, 1951, 91,CIX.2
5	LH IIIa	fragment of bowl	eating / drinking	official, 31/560	Pendlebury, 1951, 91,CIX.2
6	LH IIIa	fragment		official, 31/564	Pendlebury, 1951, 91,CIX.2

Magazines between the Royal Estate and the Temple

No.	*Date*	*Object*	*Function*	*Context*	*Literature*
1	LH IIIa	fragment		official, P.41.1&3: 31/609	Pendlebury, 1951, 107,CIX.2
2	LH IIIa	top of a stirrup jar	storage	official, Q.41.7: 31/605	Pendlebury, 1951, 107,CIX.2
3	LH IIIa	fragments of stirrup jar, 2	storage	official, Q.41.7: 31/606	Pendlebury, 1951, 107,CIX.2
4	LH IIIa	base of a stirrup jar	storage	official, Q.41.7: 31/607	Pendlebury, 1951, 107,CIX.2
5	LH IIIa	fragments, 2		official, Q.41.2: 32/260	Pendlebury, 1951, 108
6	LH IIIa	fragment of an amphora	storage	official, Q.41.4: 32/248	Pendlebury, 1951, 109
7	LH IIIa	fragment		official, Q.41.10: 32/283	Pendlebury, 1951, 109,CIX.1
8	LH IIIa	fragment		residential, R.41.1: 32.263	Pendlebury, 1951, 210,CIX.1

Record Office and its Surroundings

No.	*Date*	*Object*	*Function*	*Context*	*Literature*
1	LH IIIa	fragment		official, Q.42.1: 33/39	Pendlebury, 1951, 118
2	LH IIIa	fragment		residential, Q.42.15: 33/96	Pendlebury, 1951, 119
3	LH IIIa	fragment		official, Q.42.21: 33/142	Pendlebury, 1951, 120
4	LH IIIa	fragment		residential, Q.42.28: 33/200	Pendlebury, 1951, 121
5	LH IIIa	fragments, 5		official, Q.42.30: 33/211	Pendlebury, 1951, 121

No.	Date	Object	Function	Context	Literature
6	LH IIIa	fragment		official, Q.42.31: 33/215	Pendlebury, 1951, 121
7	LH IIIa	fragments, 2		residential, no.1:33/223	Pendlebury, 1951, 123
8	LH IIIa	top of stirrup jar	storage	residential, no.2&3:33/199	Pendlebury, 1951, 123
9	LH IIIa	top of stirrup jar	storage	residential, no.2&3:33/190	Pendlebury, 1951, 123
10	LH IIIa	fragments of pilgrim flasks, 4	storage	residential, no.15&16:33/243	Pendlebury, 1951, 123,CIX.7
11	LH IIIa	fragment		residential, no.36:33/255	Pendlebury, 1951, 124,CIX.7
12	LH IIIa	fragment		residential, no.43:33/252	Pendlebury, 1951, 124,CIX.7
13	LH IIIa	fragment		residential, no.58:33/263	Pendlebury, 1951, 125,CIX.7
14	LH IIIa	fragment		residential, no.69:33/284	Pendlebury, 1951, 125,CIX.7
15	LH IIIa	fragments, 1329		official, waste heaps	Petrie, 1894, 17
16	LH IIIa	fragment		official, waste heaps	Kemp, 1987, 119

Military and Police Quarters

1	LH IIIa	base of pilgrim flask, 7.3 cm	storage	official, R.42.9.B: 36/112	Pendlebury, 1951, 135,CIX.6
2	LH IIIa	fragments		official, R.42.9.C: 36/121,127	Pendlebury, 1951, 135,CIX.6
3	LH IIIa	fragment		official, R.42.9.D: 36/134	Pendlebury, 1951, 136,CIX.6

Southeastern Quarter

1	LH IIIa	fragment		residential, R.43.1.A: 36/181	Pendlebury, 1951, 140,CIX.6
2	LH IIIa	fragments of an amphora, 2	storage	residential, R.43.1.B: 36/151	Pendlebury, 1951, 140,CIX.6
3	LH IIIa	stirrup jar, 12 cm	storage	residential, R.43.2: 36/164	Pendlebury, 1951, 141,LXXVIII.9

— REFERENCES —

Adrados, F.R. 1969: "*Te-re-ta wa-na-ka-te-ro*," in *Minos* 10, 138–50.

Anthes, R. 1959: *Mit Rahineh 1955*, Philadelphia.

Akurgal, E. 1967: "Ildırı kazısı (Haberler)," *Belleten* 123, 460–61.

Alcock, S., D'Altroy, T.N., Morrison, K.D., Sinopoli, C.M. (eds.) 2001: *Empires. Perspectives from Archaeology and History*, Cambridge.

Andrikou, E. 1999: "Appendix: The Pottery from the Destruction Layer of the Linear B Archiv at Pelopidou Street," in Deger-Jalkotzy *et al.*, 1999, 79–102.

Aravantinos, V.L., Godart, L., Sacconi, A. 2001 : *Thèbes, Fouilles de la Cadmée I: les tablettes en Linéaire B de la Odos Pelopidou*, Pisa.

Aston, D. 1986: "The Pottery," in Aston, D., Raven, M., Martin, G. *The Tomb-chambers of Iurudef*, *JEA* 72, 15–21.

——— 1999: Section D: "The Pottery," in Martin, G.T. (ed.), *The Tomb of Tia and Tia*, London, 83–102.

———2001: "The Pottery from H/VI Süd Strata a and b: Preliminary Report," *Ä&L* XI, 167–96.

———, Aston, B. 2001: Section H: "The Pottery," in Martin, G.T. (ed.), *The Tombs of Three Memphite Officials; Ramose, Khay and Pabes*, London, 50–60.

Aura Jorro, F. 1993: *Diccionario Griego - Espanol (anejo II): Diccionario Micén (Vol. II)*, Madrid.

Avruch, K. 2000: "Reciprocity, Equality, and Status-Anxiety in the Amarna Letters," in Cohen and Westbrook 2000, 154–64.

Ayrton, E.R., C.T. Currelly, and A.E.P. Weigall, 1904: *Abydos* III, London.

Bachhuber, C. 2003: "Aspects of Late Helladic Sea Trade" (MA Thesis), College Station.

———2006: "Aegean Interest on the Uluburun Ship," *AJA* 110, 345–64.

Baer, K. 1962: "The Low Price of Land in Ancient Egypt," *JARCE* 1, 25–45.

Baines, J., Malék, J. 1981: *Atlas van het Oude Egypte*, Amsterdam.

Bammer, A. 1986–87: "Ephesos in der Bronzezeit," *Jahreshefte des Österreichischen Archäologischen Institutes in Wien* 57, Beiblatt, 1–38.

——— 1990: "A Peripteros of the Geometric Period in the Artemision of Ephesus," *Anatolian Studies* 40, 137–60.

——— 1994: "Mykene im Artemision von Ephesos," *Jahreshefte des Österreichischen Archäologischen Institutes in Wien* 63, 28–39.

Barfield, T. J. 2001: "Imperial State Formation along the Chinese-Nomad Frontier," in Alcock *et al.*, 10–41.

Basch, L. 1987 : *Le Musée imaginaire de la marine antique*, Athens.

Bass, G. 1963: "Mycenaean and Protogeometric Tombs in the Halicarnassus Peninsula," *AJA* 67, 353–61.

——— 1967: *Cape Gelidonya: A Bronze Age Shipwreck*, Transactions of the American Philological Society 57, part 8.

Beckman, G. 1996: *Hittite Diplomatic Texts*, Atlanta.

Bell, M.R. 1982: "Preliminary Report on the Mycenaean Pottery from Deir el-Medina (1979–1980)," *Annales du Service des Antiquités de l' Égypte* 68, 143–63.

Belli, P. 1997: "Architecture as Craftsmanship: LM III Tholoi and Their Builders," in Laffineur and Betancourt 1997, 251–55.

Bennet, J. 1992: "Collectors or Owners?" in J-P. Olivier (ed.), *Mykenaïka, BCH supplément* 25, 65–101.

——— 1988: "Outside in the Distance: Problems in Understanding the Economic Geography of Mycenaean Palatial Territories," in Olivier, J-P., Palaima, Th.G. (eds.), *Texts, Tablets and Scribes, Studies in Mycenaean Epigraphy and Economy*, Minos, suppl. 10, 19–41.

——— 1995: "Space through Time: Diachronic Perspectives on the Spatial Organization of the Pylian State," in Niemeier, W-D., Laffineur, R. (eds.), *Politeia*, Aegeum 12, Liège, 587–602.

——— 1998: "The Linear B Archives and the Kingdom of Nestor," in Davis, J. L. (ed.), *Sandy Pylos*, Austin, 111–13.

——— 1998–1999: "Leuktron as a Secondary Capital in the Pylos Kingdom?" *Minos* 33–34, 11–30.

——— 1999: "Pylos: The Expansion of a Mycenaean Palatial Center," in Galaty and Parkinson 1999b, 9–18.

———, Shelmerdine, C.W. 2001: "Not the Palace of Nestor: The Development of the 'Lower Town' and Other Non-Palatial Settlements in LBA Messenia," in Branigan, K (ed.), *Urbanism in the Bronze Age*, Sheffield, 135–40.

Bennett, E.L. 1956: "The Landholders of Pylos," *AJA* 60, 103–33.

Benzi, M. 2002: "Anatolia and the Eastern Aegean at the Time of the Trojan War," in Montanari and Ascheri 2002, 343–406.

Betancourt, P. P. 1976: "The End of the Greek Bronze Age," *Antiquity* 50, 40–47.

Bietak, M. 1996a: "Le début de la XVIIIe dynastie et les Minoens à Avaris," *Bulletin de la Société française d'Égyptologie* 135, 5–29.

——— 1996b, *Avaris*, London.

——— 2005, "The Thutmose Stronghold of Perunefer," *Egyptian Archaeology* 26, 13–17.

Bintliff, J. (ed.) 1977: *Mycenaean Geography. Proceedings of the Cambridge Colloquium*, Cambridge.

Birmingham, J. 1964: "Surface Finds from Various Sites I," *Anatolian Studies* 14, 29–33.

Bittel, K. 1934: *Prähistorische Forschung in Kleinasien*, Istanbul.

——— 1967: *Kleinasiatische Studien*, Amsterdam.

——— 1976: "Tonschale mit Ritzzeichnung von Boğazköy," *Revue Archéologique*, 9–14.

Blegen, C.W. 1941: *Preclassical Greece*, in *Studies in the Arts and Architecture*, Philadelphia, 1–14.

Blegen, C.W., Caskey, J., Rawson, M. 1953: *Troy III*, Princeton.

Blegen, C.W., Rawson, W. 1966: *The Palace of Nestor in Western Messenia I*, Cambridge.

Bocher, S. 2007 (forthcoming): *Oliven im Altertum*, Berlin.

Boehlau, J., Schefold, K. 1942: *Larisa am Hermos III – die Kleinfunde*, Berlin.

Borchardt, L.1907: "Ausgrabungen in Tell el Amarna," *MDOG* 34, 14–31.

——— 1913: "Ausgrabungen in Tell el Amarna 1912/13," *MDOG* 40, 1–55.

Bourriau, J. 2001: "The Second Intermediate Period," in I. Shaw (ed.), *The Oxford History of Ancient Egypt*, Oxford, 184–217.

Boysal, Y. 1967: "Müskebi kazisi 1963 kisa raporu," *Belleten* 121–22, 67–76.

——— 1969: *Katalog der Vasen im Museum in Bodrum*, Ankara.

Brandau, B., Schickert, H., Jablonka, P. 2004: *Troja wie es wirklich aussah*, Munich.

Branigan, K. 1970: *The Tombs of Mesara*, London.

——— (ed.) 2001: *Urbanism in the Aegean Bronze Age*, Sheffield.

Breasted, J.H. 1906: *Ancient Record of Egypt* (5 vols.), Chicago.

Brein, F. 1976/1977: "Zur ephesischen Topographie," *Jahreshefte des österreichischen archäologischen Instituts in Wien* 51, 65–76.

Bridges, Jr., R.A. 1974: "The Mycenaean Tholos Tomb at Kolophon," *Hesperia* 43, 264–66.

Brink, E. van den. 1987: *A Geo-archaeological Survey in the Eastern Delta*, MDAIK 43.

Broneer, O. 1968: "Cyclopean Wall on the Isthmus of Corinth," *Hesperia* 37, 25–35.

Bryan, B.M. 2000: "The Egyptian Perspective on Mitanni," in Cohen and Westbrook 2000, 71–84.

Bryce, T. 1989a: "The Nature of Mycenaean Involvement in Western Anatolia," *Historia* 38, 1–21.

——— 1989b: "Ahhiyawans and Mycenaeans – An Anatolian Viewpoint," *OJA* 8, 297–310.

———1998: *The Kingdom of the Hittites*, Oxford.

——— 2003a: "Relations between Hatti and Ahhiyawa in the Last Decades of the Bronze Age," in Beckman, G., Beal, R., McMahon, G. (eds.), *Hittite Studies in Honor of Harry A. Hoffner Jr.*, Winona Lake, Ind., 59–72.

———2003b: *Letters of the Great Kings of the Ancient Near East*, London.

Buchholz, H-G. 1987a: "Schlußbemerkungen," Buchholz H-G (ed.), *Ägäische Bronzezeit*, Darmstadt, 499–534.

———(ed.) 1987b: *Ägäische Bronzezeit*, Darmstadt.

Bulle, H. 1907: *Orchomenos I, die älteren Ansiedelungsschichten*, Munich.

Büyükkolanci, M. 2000: "Excavations on Ayasuluk Hill in Selçuk, Turkey. A Contribution to the Early History of Ephesus," in Krinzinger 2000, 39–43.

Cancik-Kirschbaum, E. 2003: *Die Assyrer*, Munich.

Carlier, P. 1987: "Palais et sanctuaire dans le monde mycénien," in Lévy 1987, 255–73.

——— 1992: "Les Collecteurs sont-il fermiers?" in Oliver, J-P. (ed.), *Mykenaïka, BCH supplement 25*, 65–101.

Carter, J.B., Morris, S.P. (ed.) 1995: *The Ages of Homer: A Tribute to Emily Townsend Vermeule*, Austin.

Catling, H. 1984–1985: *Archaeology in Greece*, Archaeological Reports.

———, Cherry, J.F., Jones, R.E., Killen, J.T. 1980: "The Linear B inscribed Stirrup Jars and West Crete," *BSA* 75, 49–113.

———, Millett, A. 1965: "A Study of the Inscribed Stirrup-Jars from Thebes," *Archaeometry* 8, 3–85.

Chadwick, J. 1972: "The Mycenaean Documents," in McDonald and Rapp 1972, 100–16.

———1976a: *The Mycenaean World*, Cambridge.

———1976b: "Who Were the Dorians?" *Parola del Passato* 31, 103–17.

———1977: "The Interpretation of Mycenaean Documents and Pylian Geography," in Bintliff, J. (ed.), *Mycenaean Geography*, Cambridge, 36–39.

Cherry, J., Davis, J. 2001: "Under the Sceptre of Agamemnon," in Branigan, K (ed.) 2001, Sheffield, 141–59.
Cline, E. 1987: "Amenhotep III and the Aegean," *Orientalia* 56, 1–36.
——— 1994: *Sailing the Wine Dark Sea*, Oxford.
——— 1995a: "Egyptian and Near Eastern Imports at Late Bronze Age Mycenae," in Davies and Schofield 1995, 91–115.
——— 1995b: "Tinker, Tailor, Soldier: Minoans and Mycenaeans Abroad," in Laffineur and Niemeier 1995, 265–87.
——— 1995c: "'My Brother, My Son': Rulership and Trade between the Late Bronze Age Aegean, Egypt and the Near East," in Rehak 1995, 143–50.
——— 1996: "Assuwa and the Achaeans," *BSA* 91, 137–51.
——— 1997: "Achilles in Anatolia," in Young, G., Chavalas, M.W., Averbeck, R.E. (eds.), *Crossing Boundaries and Linking Horizons*, Bethesda, Md., 189–207.
——— 1998: "Amenhotep III, the Aegean, and Anatolia," in O'Connor and Cline 1998.
Cohen, R., Westbrook, R. (ed.) 2000: *Amarna Diplomacy*, Baltimore.
Coldstream, N. 1979: Review of Rutter, Rutter 1976, *AJA* 83, 354–55.
Cook, J.M. 1951: "Archaeology in Greece," *JHS* 72, 92–112.
Cook, J.M. 1960: "Greek Archaeology in Western Asia Minor," *Archaeological Reports*, 27–57.
Cook, J.M., Blackman, D.J. 1971: "Archaeology in Western Asia Minor 1965–1970," *Archaeological Reports*, 33–62.
Crielaard, J.P. 2000: "Homeric and Mycenaean Long-distance: Discrepancies in the Evidence," *Babesch* 75, 51–63.
— —, Stissi, V., van Wijngaarden, G-J. (ed.) 1999: *The Complex Past of Pottery*, Amsterdam.
Crouwel, J.H. 1981: *Chariots and Other Means of Land Transportation in Bronze Age Greece*, Amsterdam.
Cullen, T. (ed.) 2001: *Aegean Prehistory, a Review,* AJA suppl. 1.
D'Altroy, T.N. 2001: "Politics, Resources and Blood in the Inca Empire," in Alcock *et al.* 2001, 201–26.
Dakouri-Hild, A. 2001: "The House of Kadmos in Mycenaean Thebes," *BSA* 96, 81–122.
———, Sherratt, S. (ed.) 2005: *Autochton*, BAR international series 1432.
Darque, P. 2005: *L'habitat Mycénien*, Athens.
Deger-Jalkotzy, S. 1978: *E-QE-TAI*, Vienna.
——— 1998: "The Aegean Islands and the Breakdown of Mycenaean Palaces around 1200 BC," in Karageorghis and Stampolidis 1998, 105–20.

——— 2006: "Theben und Pylos: Terminologische und onomastische Korrespondenzen?" in Deger-Jalkotzy, S., Panagl, O. (eds.). *Die neuen Linear B-Texte aus Theben*, Vienna, 19–36.

———, Hiller, S., Panagl, O. (eds.) 1999: *Floreant Studia Mycenaea I*, Vienna.

———, Panagl, O. (eds.). 2006: *Die neuen Linear B-Texte aus Theben*, Vienna.

Demakopoulou, K., Konsola, D. 1981: *Archäologisches Museum Theben*, Athens.

De Ridder, A. 1894: "Fouilles de Gha," *BCH* 18, 271–310.

Desborough, V.R.d'A. 1964: *The Last Mycenaeans and Their Successors*, Oxford.

Dickinson, O. 1974: "The Definition of Late Helladic I," *BSA* 69, 109–20.

——— 1994: *The Aegean Bronze Age*, Cambridge.

——— 2006: *The Aegean from Bronze Age to Iron Age*, London.

Dietz, S., Papachristodoulou, I. (ed.) 1988: *Archaeology in the Dodecanese*, Copenhagen.

Dostert, A. (ed.) 2004: *Zwischen Kulturen und Kontinenten*, Berlin.

Dothan, T. 1998: "Initial Philistine Settlement: From Migration to Coexistence," in Gitin *et al.* 1998, 148–61.

Drews, R. 1993: *The End of the Bronze Age*, Princeton.

Easton, D.F. 1985: "Has the Trojan War Been Found?" *Antiquity* 59, 188–96.

Easton, D.F., J.D. Hawkins, A.G. Sherratt, E.S. Sherratt 2002: "Troy in Recent Perspective," *Anatolian Studies* 52, 75–109.

Edel, E, 1966: *Die Ortsnamenlisten aus dem Totentempel Amenophis III*, Bonn.

——— 1975: "Neue Identifikationen topografischer Namen in den konventionellen Namenzusammenstellungen des Neuen Reiches," *Studien zur Altägyptischen Kultur* 3, 49–73.

——— 1980: "Die Ortsnamenlisten in den Tempeln von Aksha, Amarah und Soleb," *Biblische Notizen* 11, 63–73.

——— 1988: "Der Name di-qj-j-s in der minoisch-mykenischen Liste En li 8 gleich Θηβαίς?" *Zeitschrift für ägyptische Sprache und Altertumskunde* 115, 30.

Eder, B. 2003: "Noch einmal: der homerische Schiffskatalog," in Ulf 2003, 287–308.

Edwards, R.B. 1979: *Kadmos the Phoenician*, Amsterdam.

Effenterre, H. van, 1968: "Un lawagétas oublié," in Incunabula Graeca XXV, 3, *Atti e memorie del 1 congresso internazionale di micenologia*, Rome, 559–73.

Erdemgil, S. *et al.* 1989: *Katalog des Ephesos Museum*, Istanbul.

Ergan, G. 2007 (forthcoming): *Anatolian Women in Linear B Texts: A General Review of the Evidence*, Istanbul.
Erkanal, A. 1989: "Panaztepe, 1987/88," *Anatolian Studies* 39, 179.
Ersoy, Y.E. 1988: "Finds from Menemen/Panaztepe in the Manisa Museum," *BSA* 83, 55–82.
Fant, J. E., Loy, W.G. 1972: "Surveying and Mapping," in McDonald and Rapp 1972.
Feldman, M.H. 2006: *Diplomacy by Design,* Chicago.
Feltsen, F., Gauß W., Smetana R. (eds.) 2007: *Middle Helladic Pottery and Synchronisms*, Vienna.
Finkelberg, M. 1988: "From Ahhiyawa to 'Αχαιοί," *Glotta* 66, 127–34.
———2005: *Greeks and Pre-Greeks*, Cambridge.
Fossey, J.M. 1980: "Mycenaean Fortifications of the North East Kopaïs," *Op.Ath.* 13.10, 155–62.
Foxhall, L., Davies, J.K. (eds.) 1981: *The Trojan War*, Liverpool.
Frankel, R. 1999: *Wine and Olive Production in Antiquity in Israel and Other Mediterranean Countries*, Sheffield.
French, D.H. 1969: "Prehistoric Sites in Northwest Anatolia II. The Balikesir and Akhisar/Manisa Areas," *Anatolian Studies* 19, 41–98.
French, E. B. 1965: "Late Helladic IIIA2 Pottery from Mycenae," *BSA* 60, 159–202.
——— 2005: "The Role of Mycenae," in Laffineur, R., Greco, E. (eds.), *Emporia* (Aegeum 25), Liège, 125–27.
French, E.B., Wardle, K.A. (eds.) 1988: *Problems in Greek Prehistory: Papers presented at the Centenary Conference of the British School of Archaeology at Athens, Manchester, April 1986*, Bristol.
Frödin, O., Persson, A.W. 1938: *Asine 1.*
Gates, C. 1995: "The Mycenaeans and Their Anatolian Frontier," in Laffineur and Niemeier 1995, 289–98.
Galaty, M.L., Parkinson, W.A. 1999a: "Putting Mycenaean Palaces in their Place," in Galaty and Parkinson 1999b, 1–8.
Galaty, M.L., Parkinson, W.A. (eds.) 1999b: *Rethinking Mycenaean Palaces*, Los Angeles.
Gates, M-H. 1994: "Archaeology in Turkey," *AJA* 98, 249–78.
———1996: "Archaeology in Turkey," *AJA* 100, 277–335.
Gauß, W., Smetana, R. 2007: "Aegina Kolonna, The Ceramic Sequence of the SCIEM 2000 Project," in Feltsen *et al.* 2007, 57–80.
Gebhard, E.R., Hemans, F.P. 1992: "Chicago Excavations at Isthmia, 1989: I," *Hesperia* 61, 1–77.
Germer, R. 1989: "Die Bluthalskragen aus RT 54," *Miscellanea Aegyptologica,* W. Helck zum 75. Geburtstag, Hamburg, 89–96.

Geschnitzer, F. 1999: "Zum Heerwesen der Mykenische Königreiche," in Deger-Jalkotzy *et al.*, 1999, 259–60.

Gitin, S., Mazar, A., Stern, E. (eds.) 1998: *Mediterranean Peoples in Transition*, Jerusalem.

Godart, L. and J-P. Olivier, 1975: "Nouveaux textes en Linéaire B de Tirynthe," in *Tiryns* VIII, Mainz, 38–45.

Gödecken, K.B. 1988: "A Contribution to the Early History of Miletus: The Settlement in Mycenaean Times and its Connections Overseas," in French and Wardle 1998, 307–18.

Goedicke, H. 1969: "Ägäische Namen in ägyptischen Inschriften," *Wiener Zeitschrift zur Kunde des Morgenlandes* 62, 7–10.

Goren, Y., Bunimovitz, S., Finkelstein, I., N'aman, N. 2003: "The Location of Alashiya: New Evidence from Petrographic Investigation of Alashiyan Tablets from El-Amarna and Ugarit," *AJA* 107, 233–55.

Gorney, R. 1995: "Hittite Imperialism and Anti-Imperial Resistance as Viewed from Alişar Höyük," *BASOR* 299/300, 65–121.

Götze, A. 1968: *Madduwattas*, Darmstadt.

Greaves, A.M., Helwing, B. 2001: "Archaeology in Turkey," *AJA* 105, 463–511.

Guest-Papamanoli, A. 1978: "La brique crue en Égée néolithique et à l'age du bronze," *BCH* 102, 3–24.

Günel, S. 1999: "Vorbericht über die mittel- und spätbronzezeitliche Keramik vom Liman Tepe," *Istanbuler Mitteilungen* 49, 41–82.

Gurney, O.R. 1992: "Hittite Geography: Thirty Years On," in Otten 1992, 213–21.

———2002: "The Authorship of the Tawagalawas Letter," in Taracha, P. (ed.), *Silva Anatolica*, Warsaw, 133–41.

Güterbock, H.G. 1983: "The Hittites and the Aegean World: Part 1. The Ahhiyawa Problem Reconsidered," *AJA* 87, 133–43.

——— 1984: "Hittites and Akhaeans: A New Look," *Proceedings of the American Philosophical Society* 128, 114–22.

———1990: "Wer war Tawagalawa?" *Orientalia*, NS 59, 157–65.

——— 1992: "A New Look at one Ahhiyawa Text," in Otten 1992, 235–43.

Hägg, R., Marinatos, N. (eds.) 1984: *The Minoan Thalassocracy, Myth and Reality*, Stockholm, 205–15.

Haider, P.W. 1988a: "Zu den ägyptisch-ägäischen Handelsbeziehungen zwischen 1370 und 1200 v.Chr.: I: Das Handelssystem," *Münsterische Beiträge zur Antiken Handelsgeschichte* 7, 12–26.

———1988b: *Griechenland-Nordafrika*, Darmstadt.

——— 1990: "Ägäer in ägyptischen Diensten zwischen ca. 1550 und 1200 v. Chr.," *Laverna* 1, 18–49.

———1996: "Menschenhandel zwischen dem ägyptischen Hof und der minoisch-mykenischen Welt?" *Ä&L* 6, 137–56.

Hallager, E. 1987: "The inscribed stirrup jars: implications for Late Minoan Crete," in *AJA* 91, 171–90.

Hanfmann, G.M.A. 1948: "Archaeology in Homeric Asia Minor," *AJA* 52, 135–55.

———1967: "The Ninth Campaign at Sardis," *AJA* 86, 17–52.

———1983: *Sardis from Prehistoric to Roman Times*, Harvard.

Hanfmann, G.M.A., Waldbaum, J.C. 1968: "Two Submycenaean Vases and a Tablet," *AJA* 72, 51–56.

———, ———1970: "New Excavations at Sardis and Some Problems of Western Anatolian Archaeology," in Sanders 1970, 307–20.

Hankey, V. 1980: "The Memphite Tomb of Horemheb: The Mycenaean Pottery," paper at Sheffield.

———1981: "The Aegean Interest in El Amarna," *Journal of Mediterranean Anthropology and Archaeology* 1, 38–49.

———1993: "Pottery as Evidence for Trade: Egypt," in Zerner, C., Zerner, P., Winder, J. (eds.), *Wace and Blegen, Pottery as Evidence for Trade in the Aegean Bronze Age*, Amsterdam, 109–15.

———, Aston, D. 1995: "Mycenaean Pottery at Saqqara," in Carter and Morris 1995, 67–92.

———, Kelder, J.M., Leonard Jr., A., van Wijngaarden, G-J. (in preparation): *Vrowny Hankey and the Mycenaean Pottery at El Amarna.*

Haskell, H.W. 1985: "The Origin of the Aegean Stirrup Jar and its Earliest Evolution and Distribution (MB III-LB I)," *AJA* 89, 221–29.

Hawkins, J.D. 1998: "'Tarkondemos,' Boğazköy Sealings and Karabel," *Anatolian Studies* 48, 1–31.

Hayes, W. 1953: *The Scepter of Egypt II*, New York.

Heinhold-Krahmer, S. 1977: *Arzawa*, Heidelberg.

———2003a: "Ahhijawa – Land der homerischen Achäer im Krieg mit Wiluša?" in Ulf, 193–214.

———2003b: "Zur Gleichsetzung der Namen Ilios – Wilusa und Troia –Taruisa," in Ulf, 146–68.

Helck, W. 1992: "Amnisos in einem ägyptischen Text Amenophis' III," in Schäfer, J. (ed.), *Amnisos*, Berlin, 13–18.

———1995: *Die Beziehungen Ägyptens und Vorderasiens zur Ägäis bis ins, 7. Jahrhundert v. Chr.* (second edition rev. by Drenkhahn, R.), Darmstadt.

Hepper, F.N. 1990: *Pharaoh's Flowers: The Botanical Treasures of Tutankhamun*, London.

Hertel, D., F. Kolb 2003: "Troy in Clearer Perspective," *Anatolian Studies* 53, 71–88.

Heubeck, A. 1966: "Myk. wo-ro-ki-jo-ne-jo ka-ma," *ZAnt* 15, 267–70.

Hiller, S. 1989: "Die Stellung Böotiens im mykenischen Staatenverband," in Beister, H., Buckler, J. (eds.), *Boiotika, Vorträge vom 5. Internationalen Böotien-Kolloquium zu Ehren von Prof. Dr. Siegfried Lauffer*, Munich, 51–64.

Hoch, J.E. 1994: *Semitic Words in Egyptian Texts of the New Kingdom and the Third Intermediate Period*, Princeton.

Hoffner, H.A. 1997: "Deeds of Suppiluliuma," in W.W. Hallo / K.L. Younger, Jr. (eds.) *The Context of Scripture. Volume I: Canonical Compositions from the Biblical World*, Leiden, 185–92.

Hood, S. 1978: Review of Pelon 1976, *AJA* 82, 556–58.

Hooker, J.T. 1979: "The Wanax in Linear B Texts," *Kadmos* 18, 100–11.

——— 1982: "The End of Pylos and the Linear B Evidence," *SMEA* 23, 209–18.

Hope Simpson, R. 1965: *A Gazetteer and Atlas of Mycenaean Sites*, London.

———, Dickinson, O. 1079: *A Gazetteer of Aegean Civilization in the Bronze Age, I, The Mainland and the Islands*, SIMA, Göteborg.

———2003: "The Dodecanese and the Ahhiyawa Question," *BSA* 98, 203–37.

———, Hagel, D.K. 2006: *Mycenaean Fortifications, Highways, Dams and Canals*, Sävedalen.

Houwink ten Cate, P.H.J. 1983: "Sidelights on the Ahhiyawa Question from Hittite Vassal and Royal Correspondence," *JEOL* 28, 33–79.

——— 1984: "The History of Warfare according to Hittite Sources: The Annals of Hattusilis I (Part II)," *Anatolica* 11, 91–109.

Hurwitt, J.M. 1999: *The Athenian Acropolis: History, Mythology, and Archaeology from the Neolithic Era to the Present*. Cambridge.

Huxley, G.L. 1960: *Achaeans and Hittites*, Oxford.

Iakovidis, S. 1983: *Late Helladic Citadels on Mainland Greece*, Leiden.

———1999: "Late Helladic Fortifications," in Laffineur 1999, 199–203.

———2001: *Gla and the Kopaïs in the 13th Century B.C.*, Athens.

Immerwahr, S. 1990: *Aegean Painting in the Bronze Age*, University Park, Pa.

Jaeger, B., Krauss, R. 1990: "Zwei Skarabäen aus der mykenischen Fundstelle Panaztepe," *MDOG* 122, 153–56.

Kantor, H. 1947: *The Aegean and the Orient in the Second Millennium*, AJA Monograph 1.

Karadimas, N., Momigliano, N. 2004: "The Term 'Minoan' before Evans's Work in Crete (1894)," *Studi Micenei ed Ege-Anatolici* XLVI/2, 243–58.

Karageorghis, V., Stampolidis N. Chr. (eds.) 1998: *Eastern Mediterranean, Cyprus– Dodecanese - Crete 16th – 6th cent. BC*, Athens.

Karetsou, A. *et al.* 2000: Κρήτη - Αίγυπτος, Heraklion.

Katz, J. 2005: Review of Joachim Latacz' *Troy and Homer*, *Journal of the American Oriental Society* 125, 422–25.

Kelder, J.M. 2002–3: "Mycenaean Pottery in Egypt," *Talanta*, 9–18.

———2004: *Mykene, Griekenland, Ahhijawa en de Oriënt*, Phoenix, Az.

———2005a: "The Chariots of Ahhiyawa," *Dacia*, 151–60.

———2005b: "Greece during the Late Bronze Age," *JEOL* 39, 131–79.

———2007: Review of Joachim Latacz's *Troy and Homer*, BiOr.

———2008: "A Great King at Mycenae. An Argument for the Wanax as Great King and the Lawagetas as Vassal Ruler," *Palamedes, A Journal of Ancient History* 3, 49–74.

——— 2009: "Royal Gift Exchange between Egypt and Mycenae," *AJA* 113.3, 339–52.

Kemp, B. 1987: *Amarna Reports IV*, London.

———1989: *Ancient Egypt, Anatomy of a Civilization*, London.

———1995: "Unification and Urbanization of Ancient Egypt," in Sasson, J.M. (ed.), *Civilizations of the Ancient Near East, vol. II*, New York, 679–90.

ΚΕΡΑΜΟΠΟΥΔΟΣ, Α. 1909: Η Οικία τοῦ Κάδμου, Αρχαιολογική Ἐφημερίς, 57–122.

Kilian, K. 1987a: "Zur Funktion der Mykenische Residenzen," in Hägg, R., Marinatos, N. (eds.), *The Function of the Minoan Palaces. Proceedings of the 4th International Symposium at the Swedish Institute in Athens, 10–16 June 1984*, Stockholm, 21–38.

——— 1987b: "L'architecture des residences mycéniennes: origine et extension d'une structure de pouvoir politique pendant l'Age du Bronze recent," in Lévy 1987, 203–17.

——— 1988a: "The Emergence of the Wanax Ideology in the Mycenaean Palaces," *OJA* 7(3), 291–302.

———1988b: "Mycenaeans up to Date, Trends and Changes in Recent Research," in French and Wardle 1998, 115ff.

Killen, J.T. 1979: "The Cnossos Ld (1) Tablets," in Risch, E., Mühlstein, H. (eds.), *International Colloquium on Mycenaean Studies*, Neuchâtel, 151–81.

———1985: "The Linear B Tablets and the Mycenaean Economy," in Mopurgo Davies, A., Duhoux, Y. (eds.), *Linear B, a 1984 Survey*, Louvain la Neuve, 241–98.

———1998: "The Pylos Ta Tablets Revisited," *BCH* 122, 421–22.

——— 1999: "Critique: A View from the Tablets," in Galaty and Parkinson 1999b, 87–90.

———, Voutsaki, S. (eds.) 2001: *Economy and Politics in the Mycenaean Palace States*, Cambridge.

Kitchen, K.A. 1982: *Pharaoh Triumphant*, Warminster.

Klengel, H. 2002: *Hattuschili und Ramses*, Mainz am Rhein.

Knauss, J., Heinrich, B., Kalcyk, H. 1984: *Die Wasserbauten der Minyer in der Kopais – die älteste Flussregulierung Europas (Kopais 1)*, Munich.

——— 1987: *Die Melioration des Kopaisbeckens durch die Minyer im 2. Jt. V.Chr.(Kopais 2)*, Munich.

——— 1990: *Wasserbau und Geschichte Minysche Epoche – Bayerische Zeit (Kopais 3)*, Munich.

Koehl, R.B. 1999: "The Creto-Mycenaean Earrings of Queen Nofretari," in Betancourt, P.P., Karageorghis, V., Laffineur, R., Niemeier, W-D. (eds.), *Meletemata, Aegeum* 20, 421–25.

Koenig,Y. 1979 : "Catalogue des etiquettes de jarres hiératiques de Deir el-Médineh," Doc. FIFAO XXI/1, Cairo, 1–16.

Korfmann, M. 1986: "Trojan Sixth and Seventh Settlements," in Mellink, M.J. (ed.), *Troy and the Trojan War*, Bryn Mawr, 17–28.

——— 2001a: "Wilusa, (W) Ilios ca. 1200 v. Chr. – Ilion ca. 700 v. Chr.," in Theune-Grosskopf 2001, 64–76.

——— 2001b: "Die Prähistorische Siedlungshügel Hisarlık," in Theune-Grosskopf 2001, 347–54.

——— 2001c: "Troia als Drehscheibe des Handels im 2.und 3. vorchristlichen Jahrtausend," in Theune-Grosskopf 2001, 255–368.

———, Mannsperger, D. 1998: *Troia, Ein historischer Überblick und Rundgang*, Darmstadt.

Kozloff, A.P. 1977: "A New Interpretation of an Old Amarna Enigma," in *AJA* 81, 101–3.

Krigas, E.J. 1987: "Road Transport in Mycenaean Arcadia," *Kadmos* 26, 74–83.

Krinzinger, F. (ed.) 2000: *Die Ägäis und das westliche Mittelmeer*, Vienna.

Laffineur, R. (ed.) 1999: *Polemos, le contexte guerrier en Égée à l'âge du bronze*, Liège.

———, Basch, L. (ed.) 1991 : *Thalassa, l'Egée Préhistorique et la Mèr*, Liège.

———, Niemeier, W-D. (ed.) 1995: *Politeia; Society and State in the Aegean Bronze Age*, Liège.

———, Betancourt, P. P. (ed.) 1997: *Techne, Craftsmen, Craftswomen and Craftmanship in the Aegean Bronze Age*, Liège.

Lambrou-Phillipson, C. 1990: *Hellenorientalia*, Göteborg.

———1991: "Seafaring in the Bronze Age Mediterranean: The Parameters involved in Maritime Travel," in Laffineur and Basch 1991, 11–20.

Latacz, J. 2001a: "Der große Nachbar im Westen: die Griechen," in Theune-Grosskopf 2001, 54–57.

———2001b: *Troia und Homer*, München.

———2004: *Troy and Homer*, Oxford.

Lavery, J. 1990: "Some Aspects of Mycenaean Topography," *BICS* 37, 165–71.

Leekley, d., Efstratiou, N. 1980: *Archaeological Investigations in Central and Northern Greece*, New Jersey.

Leonard Jr., A. 1994: *An Index to the Late Bronze Age Aegean Pottery from Syria-Palestine*, Gotheburg.

Levi, D. 1969–1970: "Iasos, le campagne di scavo 1969–70," *Annuario* 31–32 (new series), 461–532.

Lévy, E. (ed.), 1987: *Système Palatial en Orient, en Grèce et à Rome*, Strasbourg.

Lindgren, M. 1973: *The Pylos People II, Acta Universitatis Upsaliensis, Boreas 3:1*, Uppsala.

Liverani, M. 2000: "The Great Powers' Club," in Cohen and Westbrook 2000, 15–27.

Lloyd, S., Mellaart, J. 1955: "Beyesultan Excavations," *Anatolian Studies* 5, 39–92.

Loader, N. 1998: *Building in Cyclopean Masonry: With Special Reference to the Mycenaean Fortifications on Mainland Greece*, Jonsered.

Lolos, Y.G. 1998: *The Capital of Nestor and its Environs*, Athens.

Love, I.C. 1969: "Recent Archaeological Research in Turkey: Knidos, 1968," *Anatolian Studies* 19, 16–18.

Mallowan, M.E.L. 1947: "Excavations at Brak and Chagar Bazar," *Iraq* 9, 63–68.

Macqueen, J.G. 1975: *The Hittites and their Contemporaries in Asia Minor*, London.

Maran, J. 2003: "Tiryns after the Fall of the Palace: Some New Insights," *BICS* 46, 223–24.

Marketou, T. 1988: "New Evidence on the Topography of Prehistoric Ialysos," in Dietz and Papachristodoulou 1998, 27–33.

Martin, G. 1996: "The EES-Leiden Saqqara Expedition, 1996," in *JEA* 82, 6–7.

Mataix, J., Barbancho, F.J. 2006: "Olive Oil in Mediterranean Food," in Quiles, J.L., Carmen-Ramirez-Tortosa, M., Yaqoob, P. (eds.), *Olive Oil and Health*, Trowbridge, 1–44.

McDonald, W.A. 1964: "Overland Communications in Greece during LH III, with Specil Reference to Southwest Peloponnese," in Bennet, E. L. (ed.), *Mycenaean Studies, Proceedings of the*

Third International Colloquium for Mycenaean Studies, Madison, Wisc., 217–40.
———, Rapp Jr., G. R. (eds.) 1972: *The Minnesota Messenia Expedition*, Minneapolis.
Mee, C. 1978: "Aegean Trade and Settlement in Anatolia," *Anatolian Studies* 28, 121–56.
———1981: "The Mycenaeans and Troy," in Foxhall and Davies 1981, 45–56.
———1982: *Rhodes in the Bronze Age*, Warminster.
——— 1998: "Anatolia and the Aegean in the Late Bronze Age," in Cline, E., Harris-Cline, D. (eds.), *The Aegean and the Orient in the Second Millennium* (Aegeum 18), Liège, 137–48.
Meeks, D. 1993: "La production de l'huile et du vin dans l'Égypte pharaonique," in Amoretti, M.C., Brun, J.P. (eds.), *La production du vin et de l'huile en Méditerranée*, Athens, 3–38.
Meier, S.A. 2000: "Diplomacy and International Marriages," in Cohen and Westbrook 2000, 165–73.
Melchert, H.C. 1978: "The Acts of Ḫattusili I," *Journal of Near Eastern Studies* 37, 1–22.
Mellaart, J. 1968: "Anatolian Trade with Europe and Anatolian Geography and Culture Provinces in the Late Bronze Age," *Anatolian Studies* 18, 187–202.
——— 1970: "The Second Millennium Chronology of Beyesultan," *Anatolian Studies* 20, 55–67.
Mellink, M.J. 1962: "Archaeology in Asia Minor," *AJA* 66, 71–85.
———1963: "Archaeology in Asia Minor," *AJA* 67, 1963, 173–90.
———1964: "Archaeology in Asia Minor," *AJA* 68, 1964, 149–66.
———1967: "Archaeology in Asia Minor," *AJA* 71, 1967, 155–74.
———1968: "Archaeology in Asia Minor," *AJA* 72, 1968, 125–47.
———1969: "Archaeology in Asia Minor," *AJA* 73, 1969, 203–27.
———1980: "Archaeology in Asia Minor," *AJA* 84, 1980, 501–18.
———1981: "Archaeology in Asia Minor," *AJA* 85, 1981, 463–79.
———1982: "Archaeology in Asia Minor," *AJA* 86, 1982, 557–76.
——— 1983a: "The Hittites and the Aegean World," *AJA* 87, 1983a, 138–43.
———1983b: "Archaeology in Asia Minor," *AJA* 87, 427–42.
———1984: "Archaeology in Asia Minor," *AJA* 88, 441–59.
———1985: "Archaeology in Asia Minor," *AJA* 89, 547–67.
——— (ed.) 1986: *Troy and the Trojan War*, Bryn Mawr.
———1987: "Archaeology in Asia Minor," *AJA* 91, 1–30.
———1988: "Archaeology in Asia Minor," *AJA* 92, 101–31.
———1989: "Archaeology in Asia Minor," *AJA* 93, 105–33.
———1991: "Archaeology in Asia Minor," *AJA* 95, 123–53.

———1992: "Archaeology in Asia Minor," *AJA* 96, 119–50.

———1993: "Archaeology in Asia Minor," *AJA* 97, 105–33.

Meriç, R., Mountjoy, P.A. 2001: "Three Mycenaean Vases from Ionia," *Istanbuler Mitteilungen* 51, 137–41.

Merrillees, R.S. 1972: "Mycenaean Pottery from the Time of Akhneten in Egypt," in Karageorghis, V. (ed.), *The Mycenaeans in the Eastern Mediterranean*, Nicosia, 175–86.

———2003: "Egyptian Foreign Relations," in Stampolidis and Karageorghis 2003.

Mitchell, S. 1999: "Archaeology in Asia Minor 1990–98," *Archaeological Reports* 45, 125–91.

Moeller, G. 1918: "Bemalte Tongefässe," *Amtliche Berichte aus den königlichen Kunstsammlungen Berlin* 39, Berlin, 217–27.

Mommsen, H., Lewandowski, E., Weber, J., Podzuweit, C. 1988: "Neutron Activation Analysis of Mycenaean Pottery from the Argolid: The Search for Reference Groups," in Farquhar, R.M., Hancock, R.G.V., Pavlish, L.A. (eds.), *Proceedings of the 26th international Archaeometry Symposium at Toronto*, Toronto, 165–71.

Mommsen, H., Beier, T., Diehl, U., Podzuweit, Chr. 1992: "Provenance Determination of Mycenaean Sherds found in Tell El Amarna by Neutron Activation Analysis," *Journal of Archaeological Science* 19, 295–302.

Mommsen, H., Hertel, D., Mountjoy, P.A. 2001: "Neuron Activation Analysis of the Pottery from Troy," *AA*, 169–211.

Montanari, P., Ascheri, P. (eds.) 2002: *Omero Tremila Anni Dopo*, Rome.

Moran, W.L. 1987 : *Les Lettres d' El - Amarna*, Paris.

Moreland, J. 2001: "The Carolingian Empire: Rome Reborn ?" in Alcock *et al.* 2001, 392–418.

Mountjoy, P.A. 1983: *Orchomenos V*, Munich.

———1993: *Mycenaean Pottery, An Introduction*, Oxford.

——— 1997a: "Local Mycenaean Pottery at Troia," *Studia Troica* 7, 259–67.

———1997b: "A Trojan Mycenaean Krater," *Studia Troica* 7, 269–74.

——— 1997c: "Troia Phase VIf and Phase VIg: The Mycenaean Pottery," *Studia Troica* 7, 275–94.

——— 1998: "The East Aegean- West Anatolian Interface in the Late Bronze Age," *Anatolian Studies* 48, 33–67.

———1999: *Regional Mycenaean Decorated Pottery (I)*, Rahden.

———, Mommsen, H. 2001: "Mycenaean Pottery from Qantir-Piramesse, Egypt," *BSA* 96, 123–55.

Muhly, J.D. 1991: "Egypt, the Aegean and the Late Bronze Age Chronology in the Eastern Mediterranean: A Review Article," *Journal of Mediterranean Archaeology* 4/2, 235–47.

Murray, M.A. 2000: "Fruits, Vegetables, Pulses and Condiments," in Nicholson and Shaw 2000, 609–55.

Mylonas, G.E. 1966: *Mycenae and the Mycenaean Age*, Cambridge.

——1983: *Mycenae, Rich in Gold*, Athens.

Newton, C., Terral, J-F., Ivorra, S. 2006: "The Egyptian Olive (Olea europaea subsp. europaea) in the Later First Millennium BC: Origins and History Using the Morphometric Analysis of Olive Stones," *Antiquity* 80, 405–14.

Nicholson, P.T., Shaw, I. (eds.) 2000:, *Ancient Egyptian Materials and Technology*, Cambridge.

Niemeier, B., Niemeier, W-D. 1997: "Milet 1994–1995," *AA*, 189–248.

Niemeier, W-D. 1984: "The End of the Minoan Thalassocracy," in Hägg and Marinatos 1984, 205–15.

——1998: "The Mycenaeans in Western Anatolia and the Problem of the Origins of the Sea Peoples," in Gitin *et al.* 1998, 17–65.

—— 1999: "Mycenaeans and Hittites in War in Western Asia Minor," in Laffineur 1999, 141–56.

——2001: in Akurgal, M., Kerschner, M., Mommsen, H., Niemeier, W-D. (eds.), *Töpferzentren der Ostägäis: Archäometrische Untersuchungen zur mykenischen, geometrischen und archaischen Keramik aus Fundorten in Westkleinasien*, 3. Erganzungsheft der Österreichischen Jahreshefte, Vienna.

—— 2002: "Hattusa und Ahhijawa im Konflikt um Millawanda/ Milet," in Willinghofer and Hasekamp 2002, 294–99.

O'Connor, D., Cline, E. 1998: *Amenhotep III, Perspectives on His Reign*, Michigan.

Olivier, J-P. 1967: "Le damokoro: un fonctionaire Mycénien," *Minos* 8, 118–22.

——1984: "Administration at Knossos and Pylos: What Differences?" in Shelmerdine, C.W., Palaima, Th.G. (eds.), *Pylos Comes Alive*, New York, 19–29.

—— 2001: "Les 'Collecteurs': leur distribution spatielle et temporelle," in Killen and Voutsaki 2001, 139–59.

Otten, H. 1951: "Zu den Anfangen der hethitischen Geschichte," *MDOG* 83, 33–45.

Otten, H. *et al.* (eds.) 1992: *Hittite and other Near Eastern Studies in Honour of Sedat Alp*, Ankara.

Özgünel, Ç. 1996: *Mykenische Keramik in Anatolien*, Bonn.

Page, D. 1959: *History and the Homeric Iliad*, Berkeley.

Palaima, T. 1991: "Maritime Matters in the Linear B Tablets," in Laffineur and Basch 1991, 273–311.
———1995: "The Nature of the Mycenaean Wanax," in Rehak 1995, 119–39.
———2000: "The Pylos Ta Series: from Michael Ventris to the New Millennium," *BICS* 44, 236–37.
Palmer, L.R. 1954: "Mycenaean Greek Texts from Pylos," *Transactions of the Philological Society*, 18–53.
———1955: "A Mycenaean Calendar of Offerings (PY KN 02)," *Eranos* 53, 1–13.
———1963: *The Interpretation of the Greek Mycenaean Texts*, Oxford.
Panagl, O. 1986: "Politische und soziale Struktur," in Hiller, S., Panagl, O. (eds.), *Die frühgriechischen Texte aus mykenischer Zeit*, Darmstadt, 278–88.
Papademetriou, A. 2001: *Tiryns*, Athens.
Parker, V. 1999: "Die Aktivitäten der Mykener in der Ostägäis im Lichte der Linear B Tafeln," in Deger-Jalkotzy *et al.*, 1999, 495–502.
Parkinson, R.B., Schofield, L. 1994: "Of Helmets and Heretics," *Annual of the British School at Athens* 89, 157–70.
———,——— 1995: "Images of Mycenaeans, a Recently Acquired Papyrus from El-Amarna," in Davies and Schofield 1995, 125–26.
Parkinson, W.A. 1999: "Chipping away at a Mycenaean Economy," in Galaty and Parkinson 1999b, 73–85.
Pelon, O. 1967: *Tholoi, tumuli, et cercles funéraires. Recherches sur les monuments funéraires de plan circulaire dans l'Égée de l'âge du bronze*, Athens.
Pendlebury, J.D.S. 1930: *Aegyptiaca*, Cambridge.
———1951: *The City of Achetaten III*, London.
Pendlebury, J.D.S., Frankfort, H. 1933: *The City of Achetaten II*, London.
Petrie, W.M.F. 1894: *Tell el Amarna*, London.
Phillips, J., Cline, E. 2005: "Amenhotep III and Mycenae: New Evidence," in Dakouri-Hild and Sherratt 2005, 317–28.
Phillips, J. 2007: "The Amenhotep III 'Plaques' from Mycenae: Comparison, Contrast and a Question of Chronology," in M. Bietak, E. Czerny (eds.), *The Synchronisation of Civilisations in the Eastern Mediterranean in the Second Millennium BC*, III, Vienna, 479–94.
Podzuweit, C. 1994: "Bemerkungen zur mykenischen Keramik von Tell el-Amarna," in *Festschrift für Otto Frey zum 65. Geburtstag*, Marburg, 457–74.

Porada, E. 1981–1982: "The Cylinder Seals Found at Thebes in Boeotia," *AfO* 28, 1–70.

Postgate, J.N. 1994: "In Search of the First Empires," *BASOR* 293, 1–13.

Pusch, E.B. 1985: "Ausländisches Kulturgut in Qantir-Piramesse," in S. Schoske (ed.), *Akten des 4. Internationalen Ägyptologenkongresses II*, Munich, 254.

——— 1999: "Vorbericht über die Abschlußkampagne am Grabungsplatz QIV 1997," *Ä&L* 9, 17–37.

Quintus of Smyrna: *The Trojan Epic; Posthomerica*, translated and edited by A. James, Baltimore, Md., 2004.

Ragonieri, R. 2000: "The Amarna Age," in Cohen and Westbrook 2000, 42–53.

Randall-Maciver, D., Woolley, L. 1911: *Buhen*, Philadelphia.

Redford, D. 1992: *Egypt, Canaän and Israël in Ancient Times*, Cairo.

Reeves, N. 2001: *Akhenaten*, London.

Rehak, P. (ed.) 1995: *The Role of the Ruler in the Prehistoric Aegean*, Aegeum 11, Liège.

Renfrew, C., *The Emergence of Civilization; the Cyclades and the Aegean in the Third Millennium B.C.*, New York, 1972.

———, Bahn, P. 1991: *Archaeology*, London.

Renfrew, J. 1985: "Preliminary Report on the Botanical Remains," in Kemp, B. (ed.), *Amarna Reports II*, Occasional Publications 2, London, 175–90.

Rhodes, P.J. 2007: *The Greek City States* (2nd ed.), Cambridge.

Robinson, A. 2002: *The Man who Deciphered Linear B*, London.

Romer, J. 1984: *Ancient Lives: The Story of the Pharaoh's Tombmakers*, London.

Rose, P.J. 1987: "Report on the 1986 Amarna Pottery Survey," in B.J. Kemp (ed.), *Amarna Reports IV*. London, 115–29.

Rückert, E. 1846: *Troja's Ursprung, Blüthe, Untergang und Wiedergebut in Latium*, Hamburg, Gotha.

Rutter, J.B. 2004: http://projectsx.Dartmouth.edu/history/bronze_age/lessons/les/28.html.

———, Rutter, S. 1974: *A Stratified Middle Helladic II to Late Helladic IIA Pottery Sequence from Ayios Stephanos in Laconia*, Los Angeles.

Sacconi, A: 1974: *Corpus delle inscrizioni vascolari in Lineare B*, Rome.

Sanders, J.A. (ed.) 1970: *Essays in Honor of Nelson Glueck; Near Eastern Archaeology in the Twentieth Century*, Doubleday.

Sandars, N. K. 1978: *The Sea Peoples*, London.

Säve-Söderberg, T. 1946: *The Navy of the Eighteenth Egyptian Dynasty*, Uppsala.

Sayce, A.H. 1910: *The Hittites: The Story of a Forgotten Empire*, London.

Schachermeyr, F. 1980: *Die ägäische Frühzeit 4. Griechenland im Zeitalter der Wanderungen*, Vienna, 150–52, 338–44.

———1984: *Griechische Frühgeschichte, Öst.Akt.Wiss.Phil.Hist.Kl.Sb* 425, Vienna.

———1986: *Mykene und das Hethiterreich*, Vienna.

———1987: "Kreta und Mykene, ein Vergleich ihres Kulturkarakters," in Buchholz 1987b, 379–87.

Schiering, W. 1959–1960: "Die Ausgrabung beim Athena-Tempel in Milt 1957 –I: Südabschnitt," *Istanbuler Mitteilungen* 9–10, 4–30.

——— 1975: "Die Minoisch-Mykenische Siedlung in Milet vor dem Bau der Grossen Mauer," *Istanbuler Mitteilungen* 25, 9–15.

———1979: "Milet: eine Erweiterung der Grabung östlich des Athena-Tempels," *Istanbuler Mitteilungen* 29, 77–108.

Schnapp-Gourbeillon, A. 2003: *Aux Origines de la Grèce*, Paris.

Schreiber, K. 2001: "The Wari Empire of Middle Horizon Peru: The Epistemological Challenge of Documenting an Empire without Documentary Evidence," in Alcock *et al.* 2001, 70–92.

Seeden, H. 1980: *The Standing Armed Figurines in the Levant*, Munich.

Seeher, J. 2005: *Hattusha Guide; a day in the Hittite Capital*, Istanbul.

Sergent, B,1994: "Les Petits Nodules et la Grande Béotie," *Revue des Études Anciennes* 96; 3–4, 370.

Serpico, M., White, R. 2000 : "Oil, Fat and Wax," in Nicholson and Shaw 2000, 390–429.

Seton-Williams, M.V. 1954: "Cilician Survey," *Anatolian Studies* 4, 121–74.

Shelmerdine, C.W. 1981: "Nichoria in Context: A Major Town in the Pylos Kingdom," *AJA* 85, 319–25.

———1999a: "Administration in the Mycenaean Palaces; Where's the Chief?" in Galaty and Parkinson 1999b, 19–24.

———1999b: "A Comparative Look at Mycenaean Administration(s)," in Deger-Jalkotzy *et al.*, 1999, 555–76.

——— 2001: "The Palatial Bronze Age of the Greek Mainland," in Cullen 2001, 329–77.

Sherratt, S. 1998: "'Sea Peoples' and the Economic Structure of the Late Second Millennium in the Eastern Mediterranean," in Gitin *et al.* 1998, 292–313.

——— 2001: "Potemkin Palaces and Route-based Economies," in Killen and Voutsaki 2001, 214–38.

Singer, I. 1983: "Western Anatolia in the Thirteenth Century B.C. according to Hittite Texts," *Anatolian Studies* 33, 205–18.

——— 1985: "The Battle of Nihriya and the End of the Hittite Empire," *Zeitschrift für Assyriologie und Vorderasiatische Archäologie* 75, 100–23.

——— 2006: "Ships Bound for Lukka: A New Interpretation of the Companion Letters RS 94.2530 and RS 94.2523," in *AoF* 33, 242–62.

Small, D.B. 1999: "Mycenaean Polities: States or Estates?" in Galaty and Parkinson 1999b, 43–48.

Sommer, F. 1932: *Die Ahhijava-Urkunden*, Munich.

Spallinger, A.J. 2005: *War in Ancient Egypt*, Oxford.

Stampolidis, N. Chr., Karageorghis, V. (eds.) 2003: *Sea Routesō*, Athens.

Starke, F. 2001: "Troia im Machtgefüge des zweiten Jahrtausends vor Christus," in Theune-Grosskopf 2001, 34–45.

Steel, L. 2002: "Consuming Passions: A Contextual Study of the Local Consumption of Mycenaean Pottery at Tell el-'Ajjul," *JMA* 15.1, 25–51.

Steiner, G. 1989: "'Schiffe von Ahhiyawa' oder 'Kriegsschiffe' von Amurru im Sauskamuwa-Vertrag?" *UF* 21, 393–411.

——— 2007: "The Case of Wilusa and Ahhiyawa," *BiOr* 64 no. 5–6, 590–611.

Stronk, J. 2002–3: *The Trojan Horse; Archaeology and the Art of Fundraising*, Talanta.

Strudwick, N., Strudwick, H. 1999: *Thebes in Egypt*. London.

Symeonoglou, S. 1985: *The Topography of Thebes from the Bronze Age to Modern Times*, Princeton.

Symington, D. 1991: "Late Bronze Age Writing-boards and their Uses: Textual Evidence from Anatolia and Syria," *Anatolian Studies* 41, 111–23.

Taracha, P. (ed.), 2002: *Silva Anatolica*, Warsaw.

Theune-Grosskopf, B. (ed.) 2001: *Troia, Traum und Wirklichkeit*, Darmstadt.

Thompson, R. 1996–1997: "Dialects in Mycenaean and Mycenaean among the Dialects," *Minos* 31–32, 313–33.

ΘΕΟΧΑΡΗ, Δ. Ρ. 1979: Το νεολιθικό Διμήνι, Volos.

Tournavitou, I. 1995: *The 'Ivory Houses' at Mycenae*, London.

Turchin, P. 2006: *War and Peace and War. The Rise and Fall of Empires*, London.

Tzedakis, Y., Martlew, H. (eds.) 1999: *Minoans and Mycenaeans: Flavours of their Time*, Athens.

Ulf, C. (ed.) 2003: *Der neue Streit um Troia: eine Bilanz*, Munich.

Ünal, A. 1991: "Two Peoples on Both Sides of the Aegean Sea: Did the Aegeans and the Hittites Know Each Other?" *Bulletin of the Middle Eastern Culture Centre in Japan* 4, 16–44.

Ventris, M., Chadwick, J. 1973: *Documents in Mycenaean Greek (second. ed.)*, Cambridge.

Vermeule, E. 1957: Review of Ventris, Chadwick 1956, *AJA* 61, 196–201.

———1972: *Greece in the Bronze Age*, Chicago.

Vivian Davies, W., Schofield, L. (eds.) 1995: *Egypt, the Aegean and the Levant*, London.

Voigtländer, W. 1988: "Akbük – Teichussia, Zweiter Vorbericht – Survey 1985/86," *AA*, 567–625.

Wace, A.J.B. 1954: "Mycenae: Preliminary Report on the Excavations of 1953," *BSA* 49, 231–48.

Wachsmann, S. 1987: *Aegeans in the Theban Tombs*, Orientalia Lovaniensa 20, Leuven.

Walcot, P. 1967: "The Divinity of the Mycenaean King," *SMEA* 2, 94–103.

Walters, H., Forsdyke, J. 1930: *CVA Great Britain Fasc.7 –British Museum Fasc.5*, London.

Wardle, K.A., Wardle, D. 2000: *Cities of Legend. The Mycenaean World*, Bristol.

Warren, P.M. 1969: *Minoan Stone Vases*, Cambridge.

———2000: "Crete and Egypt: The Transmission of Relationships," in Karetsou *et al.* 2000, 24–28.

———, Hankey, V., *Aegean Bronze Age Chronology*, Bristol, 1989.

Way, T. von der. 1991: "Die Grabungen in Buto und Reichseinigung," *MDAIK* 47, 419–24.

Wecowski, M. 2002: "Homer and the Origins of the Symposion," in Montanari and Ascheri 2002, 625–37.

Welcker, F.G. 1849: *Der epische Cyclus oder die Homerischen Dichter (Zweiter Teil)*, Bonn.

Wijngaarden, G.J. van. 1999: *Use and Appreciation of Mycenaean Pottery outside Greece (PhD)*, Amsterdam.

———2001: "The Cultural Significance of Mycenaean Pictorial Kraters," *Pharos* 9, 75–96.

——— 2002: *Use and Appreciation of Mycenaean Pottery in the Levant, Cyprus and Italy*, Amsterdam.

Wilhelm, G. 1989: *The Hurrians*, Warminster.

Wilkinson, T. 1999: *Early Dynastic Egypt*, London.

Willinghofer, H., Hasekamp, U. (eds.) 2002: *Die Hethiter und ihr Reich; das Volk der 1000 Götter*, Stuttgart.

Wohlmayr, W. 2007: "Aegina MH III-LH I: Ceramic Phases of an Aegean Trade Domain," in Feltsen *et al.* 2007, 45–55.

Wood, M. 1985: *In Search of the Trojan War*, London.

Woudhuizen, F. 2004–5: "Appendix: Reflexes of Anatolian Toponyms in Linear B Texts," *Talanta* 36–37, 86–87.

———2006: *The Ethnicity of the Sea Peoples*, Rotterdam.

Wundsam, K. 1968: *Politische und soziale Struktur der mykenischen Residenzen nach den Lineair B Texten*, Vienna.

Younger, J. 2005: "Some Similarities in Mycenaean Palace Plans," in Dakouri-Hild and Sherratt 2005, 185–90.

Zaccagnini, C. 2000: "The Interdependence of the Great Powers," in Cohen and Westbrook 2000, 141–53.

Zangger, E., Timpson, M.E., Yazvenko, S.B., Kuhnke, F., Knauss, J. 1997: "The Pylos regional Archaeological Project, Part II. Landscape Evolution and Site Preservation," *Hesperia* 66, 549–641.

Zerner, C., Zerner, P., Winder, J. (eds.) 1993: *Wace and Blegen, Pottery as Evidence for Trade in the Aegean Bronze Age*, Amsterdam.

Zimanski, P. 1995: "Urartian Material Culture as State Assemblage: An Anomaly in the Archaeology of Empire," *BASOR* 299/300, 103–15.

— INDEX —